TUTORING SECOND LANGUAGE WRITERS

TUTORING SECOND LANGUAGE WRITERS

Edited by
SHANTI BRUCE
BEN RAFOTH

UTAH STATE UNIVERSITY PRESS
Logan

© 2016 by the University Press of Colorado

Published by Utah State University Press
An imprint of University Press of Colorado
5589 Arapahoe Avenue, Suite 206C
Boulder, Colorado 80303

 The University Press of Colorado is a proud member of
The Association of American University Presses.

The University Press of Colorado is a cooperative publishing enterprise supported, in part, by Adams State University, Colorado State University, Fort Lewis College, Metropolitan State University of Denver, Regis University, University of Colorado, University of Northern Colorado, Utah State University, and Western State Colorado University.

The paper used in this publication meets the minimum requirements of the American National Standard for Information Sciences—Permanence of Paper for Printed Library Materials. ANSI Z39.48-1992

ISBN: 978-1-60732-406-5 (pbk)
ISBN: 978-1-60732-414-0 (ebook)

Library of Congress Cataloging-in-Publication Data
Names: Bruce, Shanti, editor. I Rafoth, Bennett A. editor.
Title: Tutoring second language writers / edited by Shanti Bruce ; Ben Rafoth.
Description: Logan : Utah State University Press, [2015] I Includes index.
Identifiers: LCCN 2015004619 I ISBN 9781607324065 (pbk.) I ISBN 9781607324140 (ebook)
Subjects: LCSH: English language—Rhetoric—Study and teaching (Higher)—Handbooks, manuals, etc. I English language—Study and teaching (Higher)—Foreign speakers—Handbooks, manuals, etc. I Report writing—Study and teaching (Higher)—Handbooks, manuals, etc. I Tutors and tutoring—Handbooks, manuals, etc. I Writing centers—Handbooks, manuals, etc.
Classification: LCC PE1404 .T878 2015 I DDC 808/.0420711—dc23
LC record available at http://lccn.loc.gov/2015004619

Cover illustration © Rudchenko Liliia / Shutterstock.

CONTENTS

FOREWORD
BEYOND HOW-TO'S
Connecting the Word and the World

Carol Severino

Reading *Tutoring Second Language Writers*, I recognized how far writing center scholarship on second language writers has come in the last twenty-five years, even in the last decade. Second language writers are now regarded as enriching our writing center work, teaching us as much about their ideas, disciplines, languages, and cultures as they do about our own. Less and less do we regard them as a challenge to our growing cultural and linguistic competencies; less and less are we uncertain about how to approach them and their drafts; therefore, less and less do we need writing center literature composed of tips and "how to" steps in order to work with them. More importantly, we no longer assume that writing center tutors are monolingual English speakers and the only arbiters of what is and is not standard in English. We no longer assume that only writing center professionals, especially monolingual ones, are sources and makers of knowledge about second language writers. In fact, second language writers can speak powerfully and eloquently for themselves and for the benefit of other second language writers and tutors, as do Jose L. Reyes Medina, Pei-Husun Emma Liu, and Pimyupa Praphan and Guiboke Seong in this volume.

Years ago, we surely needed "how to" literature if only because we wanted to be as helpful as possible to second language writers. Trapped in the monolingual context of our courses and institutions, we were not prepared; we needed to learn new tools and techniques. We had, and in fact, still have many lingering questions addressed by the contributors to this volume: What is the best balance of global and local work in a second language writing tutorial? Does the balance always depend on the writer and the situation? Or should the global always prevail even when the writer asks for language help? To what extent do the rhetorics of students' other languages and cultures influence their writing and their perceptions of how to respond to their assignments (Cox, Craig)? And what does it mean to ask students to demonstrate their critical thinking skills (Balester)?

To address these questions, the authors in this volume do more than embrace the complexities and nuances of language and culture. To paraphrase Paulo Freire, whose influence on progressive education complements Dewey's (Rafoth), the authors also closely connect the words brought to and used in the writing center to larger worlds—concentric and intersecting circles of context—textual, disciplinary, linguistic, cultural, social, political, national, international (Amevuvor). Some authors smartly explore writing center connections to language politics: what does it mean when writers are writing and speaking about their writing in English, a language they perceive as threatening their identities? (Bruce) And then what does it mean when writers and tutors decide to use their shared native language in writing center conferences, for example, to talk about English writing in Spanish? (Dvorak)

Other authors explore writing center connections to issues of othering, racism, xenophobia, and social justice (Condon and Olson; Witherite) that confront writers on and off campus. If a campus is a microcosm of society, the writing center—the most culturally diverse unit on campus—is also. Therefore, the words spoken, read, and written in a writing center intimately relate to the world and all its injustices. And through writing center work, writers and tutors can collaborate to address them.

Perhaps most importantly for writing centers as a field, contributors to this volume also connect writing center words to the world of research. After all, writing center words—in conversation, on the page, on the screen—can be investigated and analyzed in countless ways. In order to better interact with, teach, and learn from second language writers, in order for the writing center field to grow, it is imperative that we create knowledge through research; that is why accounts of the research process here (Dvorak; Hutchinson and Gillespie; Babcock; Witherite) are among the highlights of the collection, suggesting that writing centers seem to be in transition between needing to know tutorial how-to's and needing to know research process how-to's.

By connecting writing center words to multiple relevant worlds outside the center, *Tutoring Second Language Writers* sets a new, positive direction for writing center growth, research, and scholarship.

TUTORING SECOND
LANGUAGE WRITERS

INTRODUCTION

Shanti Bruce and Ben Rafoth

Tutoring Second Language Writers is a book for tutors. It is intended to advance the conversations tutors have with one another and their directors about tutoring second language writers and writing. The aim of this book is to engage readers with current ideas and issues that highlight the excitement and challenge of working with those who speak English as a second (or additional) language. The contributors to this collection have geared their chapters toward a US context, but we believe all readers, regardless of locale or the organization of their tutoring center, will find points of entry in these pages that lead to meaningful discussions about working with culturally and linguistically diverse writers and tutors.

SUGGESTIONS FOR USING THIS BOOK

This book can be used in courses and programs for preparing tutors and teachers. The chapters can be read individually or together and may be used as a basis for discussions in staff meetings and as follow-ups to tutoring sessions. The chapters serve as references to help answer questions about theoretical and practical issues. Equally important, they raise questions about the complicated task of preparing to work with linguistically diverse populations of writers. Readers can use this book to enliven their curiosity and advance tutor-led research. At the beginning of each of the book's four parts, we offer a glimpse of the topics and questions raised in each chapter. We hope readers will be drawn into the chapters and carry the discussion forward into staff meetings and the many informal discussions tutors have among themselves and with others.

ORGANIZATION OF THE BOOK

The book opens with a chapter that frames the broad focus of the collection around philosopher John Dewey's belief in reflective thinking as

DOI: 10.7330/9781607324140.c000

a way to help build new knowledge. It continues with part 1, "Actions and Identities," which includes chapters about creating a proactive stance toward language difference, thinking critically about labels, and the mixed feelings students may have about learning English. Part 2, "Research Opportunities," includes two chapters that demonstrate writing center research projects and a third that explains research methods tutors can use to further investigate their questions about writing center work. Part 3, "Words and Passages," offers four personal stories of inquiry and discovery, and in part 4, "Academic Expectations," authors confront some of the challenges tutors face when they try to help writers meet readers' specific expectations.

All of the chapters in this book draw upon research in the fields of second language writing, composition, and applied linguistics, and they connect ideas from these areas to the contexts of one-on-one tutoring. We hope readers will make them a part of the conversations they have over coffee and in staff meetings as well those they have with multilingual students outside the writing center and in the larger community.

There is a growing need for tutors who are better prepared to work with writers who speak multiple languages, including English. We see evidence of this need in the interest and concern generated in the pages of journals and conference programs and in the talks we have had with students and tutors around the world. One collection cannot tackle every question, but readers can add to the conversations begun in these chapters and carry them forward in ways large and small.

1

SECOND LANGUAGE WRITERS, WRITING CENTERS, AND REFLECTION

Ben Rafoth

Tutoring involves multiple responsibilities. Tutors must ask the right questions and listen carefully when writers respond. They are expected to read critically, explain clearly, motivate, and empathize. As they work with writers from different backgrounds and abilities on assignments from an array of disciplines, they are also expected to know their limits and reach beyond them. Tutors are asked to do many things, but it is hard to imagine any writing center where the expectations for tutors' responsibilities do not begin with understanding the purpose of education because understanding education's purpose shapes the meaning and practice of tutoring.

Philosopher John Dewey believed that the purpose of education is to foster a love of learning and a desire for more education. For Dewey (1920), education is an end in itself because openness to learning leads to greater social cohesion, democracy, and equality. These ideals were not idle abstractions in the first half of twentieth-century America when Dewey's writings were taking shape against a backdrop of grinding automation, income inequality, and child labor. Dewey's ideas were born in an American context of swelling immigration, crowded schools, and racial and ethnic tensions that were no less severe than the ones we face today. Dewey believed education was the lever that would move the United States and the world to a better place. It still holds that promise.

For tutors reading this book—from those who have little experience to those with a lot, and from undergraduate to graduate tutors—it is worth taking a moment to understand why Dewey's vision of progressive education provides a foundation for the work of writing centers. I believe it does so for three reasons: Dewey's vision is grounded in real-world experience, it looks toward the future, and it is embedded in a robust philosophical tradition. When learning is grounded in experience, it is driven

DOI: 10.7330/9781607324140.c001

by curiosity and the desire to discover new things through research and inquiry. When it looks to the future, learning is ambitious and hopeful; it tries to make a positive difference. And when learning is embedded in a robust philosophy of life, like Dewey's pragmatism, it helps us to think about teaching and writing in the context of broad philosophical perspectives that include epistemology, politics, and aesthetics.

When L2 writers striving to develop advanced literacy step into a campus writing center in the United States, they put more on the table, figuratively speaking, than drafts of their papers. They carry with them a history of their experiences with English, when and how they learned it, the values they associate it with, and the parts of their lives it displaces. They carry with them the struggles and rewards that are part of the experience of learning English. More important, they come to the table optimistic about their future and the role that education plays in it. If they seem intensely focused on their papers, it may be because they know the stakes are high. Second language writers want for themselves and the world they inhabit many of the same things almost everyone does, and they see learning to write well, in English or some variety of it, as a way up, and perhaps out. Coming as they often do from rich traditions of literacy in their homelands, they are also familiar with the aesthetic and intellectual rewards of writing and reading. They seek tutors who can help them attain whatever goals they have for writing.

Aspirations such as these find their way to writing centers because tutoring is transformative, as a number of writing center scholars have shown: Condon (2012); Fels and Wells (2011); Greenfield and Rowan (2011); Grimm (1999); Harris (1995); Kail and Trimbur (1987); and Grutsch McKinney (2013). Each of these works has its own philosophical grounding, and it is not necessarily in Dewey's pragmatism. As a whole, however, writing center scholarship devoted to bringing about greater justice in the world through education builds, at least in part, on Dewey's legacy.

I have been a writing center director and tutor for twenty-five years, and it is still remarkable to me how much knowledge, skill, and understanding it takes to be a writing tutor. Compared to a lecturer who stands before a room full of students and imagines everyone in the room to be smart, eager, and appreciative, tutoring is personal. Each session is unique, and a tutor needs to think about a lot more than the talking points in a lecture. This is the case for all of the writers we work with, but it is particularly true for L2 students. More than twenty years ago, Harris and Silva (1993) observed, "We should recognize that along with different linguistic backgrounds, ESL students have a diversity of concerns that can only be dealt with in the one-to-one setting where the focus of attention is on that particular student and his or her questions, concerns, cultural presuppositions, writing processes, language learning experiences, and conceptions of what writing English is all about" (525). Tutors must contend with learning as it unfolds in the ways Muriel Harris and Tony Silva describe, and when they falter, they must come up with something else. They also must deal with a broad range of individual differences because each student's approach to writing and learning is different, some proceeding methodically and efficiently as they navigate their boat down the middle of the river while others push off and go wherever the current is strongest. Still others spend days on dry land before they embark, collecting supplies and pacing back and forth. Amid the various courses and disciplines, levels of study, linguistic backgrounds, types of assignments, and writing processes, tutors must work close to the ground because language is always stuck to the particulars of context. Tutors must also know that language is also a practice—a tool—and thus a means for changing contexts. Alastair Pennycook (2010), an applied linguist and author of *Language as a Local Practice*, sounds a lot like Dewey when Pennycook writes, "To think in terms of practices is to make social activity central, to ask how it is we do things as we do, how activities are established, regulated and changed. Practices are not just things we do, but rather bundles of activities that are the central organization of social life" (2).

Dewey's ideas are apparent in any discussion of language and practice, which is why they remain relevant to composition theory and pedagogy (e.g., Crick 2003; Phelps 1988) and why they have also appeared in national reports on the future of teaching (National Commision on Teaching and America's Future 1996). Given the problems Dewey saw in the world at the time he wrote, in the first half of the twentieth century, it is clear his notion of reflection is the antithesis of thinking based on prejudices, impulses, unexamined beliefs, old information, discredited theories and sources, and suppressed curiosity and imagination. These ways of thinking must be isolated because they impede individual growth and social progress. One of the challenges to today's tutors is to use reflective thinking to expand opportunities for growth for themselves and all writers they work with.

For tutors who work with multilingual writers, understanding reflective thinking is an essential requirement for the job and the title. There is a lot to know about language and how people use and experience it, especially when it comes to assisting L2 writers in the context of a writing center. To read and learn from the chapters in this volume, as well as from the many other opportunities provided in the courses, books, journals, and collaborative projects that make up writing centers, means making a commitment to reflective thinking.

There is little doubt that tutors work diligently or that their directors aim to prepare them well, but the challenge is enormous nonetheless. The expectations for advanced literacy are high, and helping students learn to meet these expectations can be a humbling experience. For this reason, however, tutors must expand their capacities for teaching and learning by thinking in systematic and discovery-oriented ways. Those who supervise tutors and direct writing centers are also implicated in this call to expand their capacities for thinking (see Bushman 1999; Farrell 2007). *Teaching Second-Language Writers* provides a step in this direction, and in the remaining pages of this chapter, I hope to elaborate on reflective thinking and how it relates to tutoring and the various chapters in this collection as I see them.

Tutors have probably heard the term *reflection* used to refer to many different things. We are now to a point at which being asked to reflect on something means we are asked to *think about it*—in other words, reflecting, musing, pondering and thinking—they all sound the same. Teachers sometimes implore students *to really reflect on* an idea, which may mean they want students to do more than merely think about it. But what is that, exactly?

In *How We Think*, Dewey (1933) tried to distinguish between reflection and conventional thinking when he defined reflection as the "active, persistent, and careful consideration of any belief or supposed form of knowledge in the light of the grounds that support it and the further conclusions toward which it tends [that] includes a conscious and voluntary effort to establish belief upon a firm basis of evidence and rationality" (9). Carol Rodgers (2002, 845) points out that Dewey's notion of reflection involves these qualities:

- continuity, or connecting experiences and ideas to achieve greater understanding and social progress;
- systematic thinking, including rigorous, disciplined, and critical thinking about practices;
- interaction with others; and
- a favorable attitude toward personal and intellectual growth.

The first of these, connecting experiences and ideas to achieve greater understanding and social progress, begins with tutors connecting with the writers they serve. Ilona Leki made this point when she wrote,

There is a tendency among humans to see their own social and cultural group as highly nuanced and differentiated but to be less able to fully grasp that all social and cultural groups are equally nuanced and differentiated. . . . But the most effective way for writing center tutors to experience these nuances firsthand is to take advantage of the visits of these multilingual, multicultural individuals to the writing center and show interest in their home language, country, or culture by engaging them in the kind of small talk that usually accompanies tutoring sessions, and so get to know them one by one. (Leki 2009, 13)

The chapters that appear in this book speak to matters of language, locality, and practice. When they are read and shared in the context of a larger program of tutor training and education, these chapters provide new information, theories, and practices essential to the four qualities of reflective thinking listed above.

Take, for example, the question of tutor education and what tutors need to know in order to work collaboratively in a writing center. Chapter 2 connects the work tutors perform with L2 writers to higher education's larger responsibilities for promoting tolerance and justice. It is sometimes easy to forget that education is about the future and the kind of world we want for ourselves and the generations that will follow. However, if tutors and teachers of literacy look forward to a time when the way people speak and write is not held against them, then there must be ways for all educators, tutors included, to help make this future. Frankie Condon and Bobbi Olson write, "We believe that by giving space for tutors to engage in a deeper and more theoretical understanding of their work—particularly their work with multi- and translingual writers—writing centers can be a locus of participatory agency for change. We can help our institutions to transform the conditions in which Othered students write and learn." The coauthors describe how they helped transform conditions as the tutors in their writing center conducted research, discussed, wrote, and produced a book for future generations of tutors at their university. Drawing inspiration from the praxis-based theories of Paulo Freire, they enacted a type of reflection more political than Dewey's but equally committed to the power of teaching, learning, and knowledge making for bringing about change and justice.

Or take a question that often arises in tutoring sessions with L2 writers: what do we do when a second language writer asks for help with a draft that contains many instances of her written accent?

One quality of reflection asks tutors to think of a tutoring session as one step along a path toward greater understanding and social progress. In other words, the question of how to handle written accents requires a level of understanding that goes deeper than the knowledge required to fix or proofread a paper. It requires knowledge of the writer and his goals and of the relationship between a person's accent and his or her identity. A second quality of reflection requires systematic, disciplined, and critical thinking about the writer and his writing. For example, what are the features that manifest as accented writing, and how are they different from those considered to be unaccented writing? What is the writer's field of study and what does the instructor expect in this piece of writing? What does the student want to achieve with his writing and how does this goal relate to preserving or losing the written accent? Questions like these speak to the need for tutors to be inquisitive and to pursue their curiosity by creating new knowledge. The chapters in this book address various ways to do that: developing and testing theories, conducting observations, examining practices, writing narratives, making interpretations, counting, and qualifying. They also illustrate different types and uses of evidence to support claims, and they show how intimately connected the links are between research, practices, and persons.

Third and fourth, reflective thinking requires interaction with others and a favorable attitude toward personal and intellectual growth. Tutoring is, by definition, collaborative, but written accents are linguistically complex and tutors need to interact with one another and the wider community of multilingual students and disciplinary experts in order to expand, personally and intellectually, their understanding of written accents.

When educators practice reflective thinking in the way Dewey intended (instead of treating reflection as merely "thinking about it"), they strive for the kinds of deeper understanding that connect the decisions and actions involved in teaching or tutoring one person with the larger effort to create a better world. They think systematically and critically about learning, they work with other educators and experts in the field, and they remain open to new ideas. When tutors practice reflective thinking, they expand the possibilities for helping students, addressing not only students' short-term needs but also who they wish to become. Thinking reflectively in this way also helps tutors understand some of the conflicts they may feel about their work, such as the tendency to identify with students who are striving to meet their instructors' expectations while at the same time wanting to maintain and even celebrate the students' accents. In this case, tutors must understand that helping writers recognize and use their accents is not simply part of the writing process; it is a step toward changing our monolingual culture and helping

L2 students participate in the culture. (In the 1980s, many tutors and other academics were involved in efforts to eliminate gender bias in writing, and today the use of inclusive forms has been widely adopted, conservative outposts notwithstanding.) These aspects of working with multilingual writers—reflection, inquiry, identity, and social justice—are examined throughout the book.

In chapter 3, for example, Michelle Cox observes that some teachers penalize students for any writing that appears to lie outside the narrow boundaries of Standard Written American English. "Editing this accent out of a client's text will, in effect, render their identity as an L2 writer invisible. And yet leaving these markers in the text may leave the student vulnerable to criticism or a lower grade. What should the tutor do in this case?" Cox's nuanced perspective helps tutors better understand the tradeoffs involved when working with students whose writing is accented.

While chapters 2 and 3 help orient tutors around questions of identity and the writer's purpose, chapter 4 looks into a Spanish-dominant context in which avoiding English is part of the writing center's reality. Ambivalence toward English is the focus of this chapter, in which Shanti Bruce takes readers on a visit to the Centro de Competencias de la Comunicación (CCC) at the Universidad de Puerto Rico en Humacao (UPRH). Bruce delves into the complicated status of English teaching and learning in Puerto Rico, an island territory of the United States in the eastern Caribbean, where Bruce recognized a prime place for multilingual writing center research. Her chapter shows that language policies in places like Puerto Rico, Quebec, California, and elsewhere can be studied on location or from a distance. Recent debates on the US mainland about English-only policies and some politicians' insistence that English be required for citizenship or legal status often fail to recognize the close relationship between language, identity, and the natural resistance people feel toward having an identity imposed on them by others, even if that identity leads to greater economic opportunity. As Bruce discusses what she heard while listening to the tutors at CCC talk about English (one tutor said, "My dad wants me to sound Merengue, and my mom wants me to be totally American like Frank Sinatra"), readers can gain a deeper understanding of the complicated nature of being a language gatekeeper. By traveling to Puerto Rico, asking questions, and listening to tutors at CCC, Bruce is able to collect important data.

Ambivalence toward English is shared by many multilingual writers, including those who live in diverse places like Miami-Dade County, located in south Florida, where almost three-fourths of all residents speak a language other than English at home. This fact is reflected in students who visited the university writing center where Kevin Dvorak (chapter 5) and his tutors worked and to a lesser extent in the backgrounds of the tutors themselves. They spoke freely about their linguistic differences, but when it came to tutoring, these tutors tended to use English only when working with student-writers. This tendency changed when Dvorak and his tutors decided to examine the assumptions underlying this practice. Eventually they settled on two questions to investigate: When and how might code-switching be used during a tutoring session? What are students' and tutors' attitudes toward code-switching in the writing center? Underlying these two questions were even more basic ones: do tutors and clients prefer using both languages since that reflects the surrounding linguistic environment, or do they prefer to stick to English since that is the target language they are usually trying to learn and master?

Questions like these lead to the rich data that lives within each writing center. Many ideas can be inferred from the data tutors themselves create in the form of video recordings of their own sessions and of their responses as they watch them replayed. In chapter 6, Glenn Hutchinson and Paula Gillespie tell how they have done this kind of recording in their own center and what tutors who try it can expect. One outcome of their research for the Digital Video Project was the beginning of conversation circles, one in English for international students in the United States for their first semester who want to practice their English informally and in a low-risk environment. They also started a Spanish conversation circle so students, many of whom are children of immigrants to the Miami, Florida, area, can practice their Spanish. In other words, by examining their conferences in a systematic way, the tutors in Hutchinson and Gillespie's center discovered a way to serve the needs of those who want to improve their L1 (because most of their schooling has been in English). Audio-only recording yields interesting data too, and it has a long history as a research tool in writing centers. For tutors who are interested, a search of dissertation abstracts using the keywords *writing center, tutor,* and *audio recording* yields many hits.

A better understanding of many concepts used in writing center research, like conversation analysis, semistructured interview, action research, and grounded theory is the focus of chapter 7. Rebecca Day Babcock, whose own research has won awards and grant funding, takes the reader on a tour through various stages of inquiry. Speaking directly to her readers, she explains what scholars have studied, what opportunities await future researchers, and the reasons anyone would want to bother to undertake the investigations she proposes. Her chapter appears in the middle of the book, often the point at which readers have gathered up ideas and may be thinking about launching a research project of their own. For these readers, there is this advice from one of the tutor-researchers Babcock interviewed for her chapter.

> My advice would be to really be open when you start analyzing your research. Go in with your question, be focused—but be ready to find connections you would never expect. I ended my project in a place I never anticipated, and that I wish I'd left myself more time to explore. Also, talk to people—the best ideas come from being able to bounce your ideas off people. Finally, the writing center literature has great breadth and is pretty easily accessible—utilize the knowledge that's already there, and then use it to branch out and bring us new ideas! (158)

Whether for a tutor who wants to explore new approaches to take with multilingual writers or for a writer trying out a new genre—lasting change requires experimentation and a disposition for learning that entails risk taking. As Neal Lerner (2009, 40–41) has shown, these qualities were present in the science and writing labs dating back to the first several decades of the 1900s. Dewey is also associated with the laboratory method of instruction (Dewey founded the first laboratory school, at the University of Chicago) and promoted "attitudes of mind" that would lead to experimentation and risk taking in learning (see also Council of Writing Program Administrators 2011). These remained central to Dewey's concept of reflective thinking and his overall vision of education, even as his concept and vision were faulted by conservative critics.

Theorizing and conducting research are the lifeblood of learning. Contemplating the many possibilities for research is a good follow-up to chapter 7 and can be done independently or with other tutors. Some of the possibilities might begin with questions like these:

1. What would you like to know about the L2 students who visit your writing center? Do you talk to them outside the center? Hang out together? If so, have you developed a relationship that could give you an entrée for interviewing them for your research?

2. In staff meetings or in a tutor preparation course, have you examined samples of accented writing? If not, make a point of noticing, in your own tutoring sessions, the features of drafts containing accented writing written by second language writers and compare these features to those of drafts written by a diverse sample of L1 writers. If you are an L2 speaker in a US writing center, consider sharing your writing with the group. Look at grammatical forms as well as features that mark the piece's style and voice. Compare the two texts and try to describe the

similarities, differences, and anything else you notice. Share these finding with other tutors and researchers and invite their input into what the similarities and differences suggest about the identities of these writers and their writing.

3. For L2 tutors: L2 writers write with an accent to *varying* degrees. Why do you think this is so? In what sense do L1 writers also write with an accent?

4. Are there examples of writing on your campus, in social media, or in the surrounding community that are meant to be rude and offensive toward certain groups of people? What impact do you think they are intended to have, and do you think they have that impact?

5. Attitudes and relationships can change dramatically during the four years of college. Have your attitudes toward using Standard American Academic English changed over time? What is responsible for this change? Have the attitudes of your family members toward Standard American Academic English also changed? Explain.

The chapters that make up part 3, "Words and Passages," provide an interlude in which tutors and former tutors write about their own journeys of discovery. Though somewhat shorter than the other pieces, these chapters remind us that the path of learning is seldom safe or smooth. In chapter 8, Elizabeth (Adelay) Witherite describes how her passion for social justice led her to design an empirical study for her master's thesis, completed in 2014, and titled *Writing Center Tutors' Perceptions of Social Justice Issues: A Multiple Method Qualitative Study*. Witherite asked the question, "How do peer tutors experience and conceptualize social justice issues within the context of tutoring sessions in the writing center?" She collected data from eight participants through interviews, concept mapping, and social-category ranking tasks. This chapter tells the story of how she settled on her research question and managed to answer it after gathering more than eight hours of audio recordings and 145 pages of transcriptions. The distinction Witherite examined between experiencing and conceptualizing social justice issues turned out to have significant implications for understanding how words create or block opportunities for personal growth and social progress.

Philosophers are fond of describing those who try to solve intellectual problems as being caught on the "horns of a dilemma"—a conflict of truths, values, or beliefs; on the one hand versus on the other hand. Tutors experience these conflicts on a regular basis, and they can get caught between defending an instructor's comments and empathizing with a writer's struggle. How is a tutor to handle, say, a situation in which an instructor, who is US born and identifies as American, comes across to the student as unfair and disrespectful, while the student, who is Ghanaian, feels shamed and defeated? In chapter 9, Jocelyn Amevuvor describes her experience of reading and later interpreting a professor's written comment from two different perspectives, one from the teacher's and the other from the student's. Situations like these are difficult for tutors to sort out because one can never be 100 percent confident about the interpretation. Tutors are sometimes the only people available to help writers deal with conflicts that arise when they receive harsh or ambiguous comments. In Condon and Olson's chapter in part 1, "Actions and Identities," we saw that tutoring is implicated in conflicts such as this, where power, race, and discourse come together and demand that we think about what is fair and just. Here again, reflective thinking is necessary to address such conflicts. While an honest dialogue between the student and his professor is usually best, such dialogues often don't occur. The instructor may be unavailable or the student unwilling to speak with him. In this case a tutor becomes one of the last people the writer can turn to. What is memorable about Amevuvor's chapter is that it doesn't pretend all tutoring sessions end happily. When tutors and writers confront hard problems, tutors seldom learn how things eventually work out for the writer. Did the student and instructor come to some sort of resolution? Was the tutor helpful? Does it matter that the tutor may never know the outcome?

What does writing look like when it balances the tension between preserving a writer's identity and meeting an instructor's expectations? In chapter 10, Pei-Hsun Emma Liu describes research she conducted for her doctoral dissertation and includes the writing of one of her participants, Angela, who spent many years learning to write Chinese while she was growing up in Taiwan. Liu tells us that when it came to writing in college in the United States, Angela felt writing in English made her thoughts seem simplistic, and this bothered her. She was torn between the part of her identity that placed a premium on being a good student and pleasing her teachers and another part that treasured the fullness and beauty of Chinese writing. Liu describes how, eventually, Angela came to write in a way that seemed to mitigate her conflicted feelings.

Angela is one of thousands, and perhaps millions of people worldwide who harbor ambivalent feelings about the need to learn and use English. On the one hand, they know learning English can create upward mobility for them and perhaps the members of their families. It can significantly increase the chances for better employment opportunities, scholarships, and access to the trove of information, literature, and scholarly journals available on the Internet. It also opens the door to the wealth of prose and poetry in the Western canon. For these reasons, parents and grandparents of young people often encourage them to learn English. On the other hand, learners and their families may also know that learning English is not always necessary or even desirable. As the economies of their own countries prosper, many people around the world see that knowing English is only one alternative for achieving mobility (Liu and Tannacito 2013). Languages like Chinese, Arabic, Hindi, and Spanish also create economic opportunity. And perhaps, they think, it is not necessary to learn an additional language formally, in school, because many people do just fine figuring out ways to communicate as they go along—on the job, in the laboratory, by using translator apps, or by watching television and playing video games. Multilingual tutors can probably think of many examples of how this figuring-out operates.

In chapter 11, Jose L. Reyes Medina writes with one of the most distinctive voices in the collection, probably because he feels so passionate about the topic of how he learned English. After coming to the United States, and while attending college, Reyes Medina tutored at Bronx Community College in New York. Since then he has set his sights on earning a doctorate in psychology. Most monolingual speakers probably never give much thought to the dedication it takes to learn a language well enough to earn a college degree with it. Americans may have studied a foreign language (typically Spanish, French, or German) in high school or college, perhaps spent a couple months studying abroad, or maybe visited a place where they tried to use the language to communicate with an indulgent waiter or souvenir dealer. But learning a language well enough to study at the college or graduate level, with native speakers and in their own country, is another thing altogether. And while becoming immersed in another language and culture provides unparalleled experiences classrooms cannot even begin to duplicate, the effect is often overwhelming and takes a heavy emotional toll, at least for a time. Learning a new language in this way involves sustained levels of self-motivation and sacrifice. There are also frequent setbacks that demand persistence and confidence. Reyes Medina's chapter gives tutors a glimpse into what he did as an L2 student to learn English outside class and away from the writing center. His message is not boastful but is inspiring because it shows how much motivation Reyes Medina has and how much learning has already occurred. It may even cause monolingual tutors to begin learning another language. Doing so is rigorous but not impossible, and as Reyes Medina demonstrates, it is the accomplishment of a lifetime. Learning English made him a better tutor and a more thoughtful individual all around.

Part 4, "Academic Expectations," narrows the focus of this collection to some of the specific demands school imposes on literacy. It describes how tutors can help writers negotiate these demands, bringing to mind two of the qualities of reflective thinking in Dewey's philosophy of education: reflection requires interaction with others in communities and a disposition that favors personal and intellectual growth. The first few chapters in this section deal with key terms like *critical thinking, disciplinary writing*, and *self-editing*, terms that show up in many of the assignments and rubrics students struggle to understand.

In chapter 12, Valerie Balester begins this section of the book by posing a question that has an elusive answer: what is *critical thinking?* This term may be one of the most taken-for-granted notions in American higher education, appearing in course descriptions, college recruiting brochures, syllabi, and policies about assessing learning outcomes. Undergraduates no doubt discover it means one thing in one discipline and something else in another. International students may not be familiar with the term at all, which is not to say they do not think critically. Rather, the notion can seem strange to them, as in, "Critical thinking—is there any other kind?" In a thoughtful and wide-ranging chapter, Balester invites tutors to look outward and see how the idea of critical thinking translates to academic settings elsewhere. Balester's exploration of this concept has important practical applications too, as it demonstrates times when tutors must explain things that can seem obvious to insiders but confounding to everyone else. In these cases, Blau and Hall (2002) say, tutors must be cultural informants. Those who are not deeply familiar with American culture are often confounded by highly specific cultural references like *cowboy mentality, KKK, yard sale,* or *subs and suds.*

These responsibilities—looking outward to other disciplines and being a cultural informant—begin with another hallmark of reflective thinking: having a disposition toward personal and intellectual growth, both for oneself and for others. When Balester stresses that certain ideas and events are difficult for international students to navigate, she does so because it can appear that students are shy, withdrawn, or "just don't get it" when in fact they have no point of entry into the topic of conversation. Stepping outside the cultural bubble requires an openness to discovering things about one's own culture that are taken for granted and a willingness to participate in the give and take of conversations about sensitive topics. Orienting one's tutoring sessions around ideas relevant to students' experiences and approaching new information in an open-minded way go hand in hand with reflective thinking.

These approaches are particularly valuable when uncovering the source of confusion and misunderstanding.

Understanding what it means to enter the conversation is an aspect of intellectual growth for tutors and writers. It is the reason instructors insist that students in upper-level and graduate classes use forms of language that track closely to their field of study and narrow their audience. As Jennifer Craig says in chapter 13, tutors may feel like strangers in an unfamiliar place when reading a paper written in a discipline different from their own—along with "some degree of being awkward, lost, vulnerable, and out of control" (217). Over time, Craig explains, tutors gain confidence as they learn about other disciplines from the papers and students they encounter. Over the years, Craig has worked with writing tutors, colleagues new to disciplinary writing, and graduate teaching assistants (GTAs). Those who tutor at MIT must respond to many proposals, reports, and presentations from science and engineering students, and a big part of her job is to help those tutors find a way into those documents (by figuring out their purpose and audience, for example). She is unflinching about the challenge these sessions can pose, but she notes that along with the challenge and uncertainty comes growth. Tutoring is hard in part because writers, as they think and talk about their work, shift rapidly between disciplinary and general knowledge, not to mention subject matter and style, words and paragraphs, and local and global concerns. As other chapters in this book show, writers increasingly move between languages, codes, and discourses. Tutors must challenge themselves to learn about other disciplines and languages as they step outside their comfort zones. Craig helps her colleagues and GTAs to do this and shares the advice she gives them with readers. She also offers three vignettes to illustrate the unavoidable complications that arise outside the comfort zone: one vignette shows a tutor who focuses on the writer's rhetorical strategies and prioritizes writing skills over language-acquisition skills; a second vignette introduces a tutor who feels unready to approach a writer's text and yet must contend with the writer's resistance; a third depicts a session that teeters between convergent and divergent thinking as the writer strives to nail down the results from his data analysis while the tutor urges more reflection.

As Craig notes, tutoring L2 writers may be primarily about writing, but those writers also bring with them language issues that challenge the skills of many English monolingual tutors, most of whom would benefit from learning not only another language but also more *about* English, particularly from an applied-linguistics perspective. For example, it takes a solid understanding of the concept of *clause* (dependent versus independent, relative versus adverbial versus noun) to explain certain uses of pronouns, conjunctions, and punctuation marks that affect the intended meaning of a text. The ability to talk about clauses is also important for explaining larger rhetorical concerns such as the arrangement of *given* and *new* information. When a monolingual tutor's explicit knowledge of grammar lags behind that of a multilingual writer's, the session may be less productive than it could be, and the tutor's credibility may suffer as well. In the final chapter, chapter 14, coauthors Pimyupa W. Praphan and Guiboke Seong express their belief that tutors who work with L2 writers first need to figure out what the writers do and do not know about English, especially for the purpose of providing corrective feedback. Praphan and Seong earned their doctorates in the United States before returning to Thailand to teach English as a foreign language. Praphan also worked as an ESL tutor. They are acutely aware of the importance of *formal accuracy* and *error gravity* in learning another language, and in chapter 12 they explain why these concepts belong in the vocabulary of tutoring. Tutors will likely conclude, as Carol Severino et al. (2013) do, that these concepts add an important dimension to the debate over higher- and lower-order concerns.

Dewey said, "Education is not preparation for life. It is life itself." For writing tutors everywhere, perhaps the takeaway from this book is to keep learning—about language, languages, writing, and writers. Keep striving to discover ideas and practices that improve tutoring. Use all of the resources at your disposal, and challenge yourself.

I once read an article, published in the *New Yorker* magazine, on what it means to strive for greater understanding, systematic and critical thinking, interaction with others, and personal and intellectual growth—in other words, Dewey's notion of reflective thinking (Gawande 2011). It's a true story that involves not a vibrant young tutor but an old mentor, and not a writer but a doctor. The two men came together already highly accomplished, secure, settled. Why mess with that?

Atul Gawande, the author of this piece, is a surgeon, and the highly specific set of skills he uses makes all the difference to his patients' recovery. For a time in their careers, young and inexperienced surgeons perform worse than their older and more experienced counterparts, but over time they get better and better—up to a point. Gawande began to wonder why so many surgeons' skills tend to plateau after reaching a certain point in their careers. Surgeons should keep getting better, but they don't. He noticed his own skills had reached a plateau and he decided to do something about it. He got a tutor.

He refers to his tutor as his *coach*, and he is someone who used to be Gawande's teacher in medical school but is now retired. Gawande's tutor followed him into the operating room, sat off to the side, and took copious notes as he observed a procedure to remove a patient's thyroid gland. Afterward, they talked in the doctors' lounge, and Gawande's tutor reviewed the operation with him.

The mentor/coach/tutor reflected back to Gawande many of the things he did in a less-than-optimal way. For example, instead of draping the patient so both he and the surgical assistant could work efficiently, Gawande draped to his own advantage, which hampered the assistant. He held his elbow too high, letting wires become tangled. He used magnifying loupes that restricted his peripheral vision, and he committed a host of other mistakes that, taken together, can significantly affect the outcome of surgical procedures.

Gawande listened and took notes as his tutor broke things down for him. He is now a fan of this type of feedback and recommends it to his colleagues.

There are many lessons writing center professionals might take from this story: don't dwell on mistakes, don't wait until the situation is over to intervene when something is going wrong, don't compare tutoring to a medical operation. But two things stand out for me that I believe are easy to overlook. First, the doctor came to recognize on his own that he needed help, and second, he took action to get it. To take these parts of the story for granted is tempting because sensing that you need help seems obvious, but it's not. Most people at the top of their game (and many who are not) don't think they need help, so when they actually do ask for it, a door opens. Dewey showed us that education is most meaningful when learning is voluntary, or what some call *self-sponsored*. Gawande is famous and well respected, and he was at least as successful as his surgeon peers. No one but he knew his skills had been leveling off. But what he experienced troubled him, creating an opening for learning that Dewey called *doubt* and we might call an *exigency*. Gawande wanted to do better, and for that he had to take a risk with a novel approach. He might have done otherwise and concluded that his sickly patients, not his skills, were the reason some of his operations fell short of the desired outcome. He could have blamed his surgical assistants, the equipment he was using, or the stress hospital administrators were inflicting on him. Instead, he risked his ego and his reputation by asking a mentor to observe and critique him so he could improve. In other words, Gawande, in his midforties, decided to become a learner by replicating the kind of observation and feedback he experienced when he trained as a young doctor.

As a result, Gawande not only improved his own skills, he learned techniques about surgery, and about observing operations and giving feedback, that he now shares with other doctors. In terms of reflective thinking, Gawande's decision to break out of his comfort zone meant he adopted an attitude toward learning that gave the highest priority to personal and intellectual growth. He reached out to others who could help him do something he was unable to do by himself—that is, view his performance from a fresh, critical perspective. And he connected what he discovered to a deeper understanding of himself and the work of surgery so he could then extend what he had learned to surgeons everywhere. This doctor's movement from doubt to investigation and interaction, and from there to connection with his broad group of peers, is the essence of reflective thinking and a model for tutors.

When tutors think reflectively, as Dewey and his followers believe, they will find doing so creates its own reward, and in the company of a supportive team, can be downright transformative.

Questions to Consider

1. Suspending judgment may be one of the most important yet challenging things for tutors to do. Make a list of ten things you think tutors are most likely to judge prematurely when they work with L2 writers. If you were to ask the L2 writers who visit your center to do the same, how much do you think the two lists would overlap? If you were to do this as a full-blown research project, what are some of the sociocultural considerations you would have to take into account before you invited people to participate in your study?

2. The qualities of reflective thinking described in this chapter make demands that are sometimes hard to follow. Which ones do you find hardest? Rank the items in the list below, with one being the easiest and four the hardest, and then compare your rankings with other tutors.

   __ continuity, or connecting experiences and ideas to achieve greater understanding and social progress
   __ systematic thinking, including rigorous, disciplined, and critical thinking about practices
   __ interacting with others
   __ maintaining a favorable attitude toward personal and intellectual growth

For Further Reading

Dewey, John. (1910) 1933. *How We Think.* Buffalo, NY: Prometheus Books.

    In this short book, John Dewey shows what pragmatism means for epistemology (what it means to think well) and for pedagogy (the study of teaching and learning). Dewey defined critical thinking as "reflective thought," by which he meant suspending judgment, maintaining a healthy skepticism, and exercising an open mind. These are qualities tutors can develop, independently and with others, as they tutor, through listening, probing, questioning, and imagining.

Hughes, Bradley, Paula Gillespie, and Harvey Kail. 2010. "What They Take with Them: Findings from the Peer Writing Tutors Alumni Research Project." *Writing Center Journal* 30 (2): 12–46.

    In this award-winning article, the coauthors surveyed 126 tutor alumni from three universities to demonstrate that being a tutor has multiple and long-lasting effects. Long after they graduate and move on, former writing center tutors remember the impact of their work in the writing center on other parts of their lives. They also remember the reflective component of their training and how they learned to think deeply and critically about their work. In bestowing the IWCA's 2010 Best Article Award on this piece, the awards committee noted that it "represents a monumental achievement for the field of writing center studies" because it shows, among other things, a useful model of research for the field.

References

Blau, Susan, and John Hall. 2002. "Guilt-Free Tutoring: Rethinking How We Tutor Non-Native-English-Speaking Students." *Writing Center Journal* 23 (1): 23–44.

Bushman, Donald. 1999. "The WPA as Pragmatist: Recasting 'Service' as a 'Human Science.'" *WPA: Writing Program Administration* 23 (1–2): 29–43.

Condon, Frankie. 2012. *I Hope I Join the Band: Narrative, Affiliation and Antiracist Rhetoric.* Logan: Utah State University Press.

Council of Writing Program Administrators. 2011. *Framework for Success in Postsecondary Writing.* http://wpacouncil.org/framework.

Crick, Nathan. 2003. "Composition as Experience: John Dewey on Creative Expression and the Origins of 'Mind.'" *College Composition and Communication* 55 (2): 254–75. http://dx.doi.org/10.2307/3594217.

Dewey, John. 1920. *Reconstruction in Philosophy.* New York: Henry Holt. http://dx.doi.org/10.1037/14162-000.

Dewey, John. (1910) 1933. *How We Think.* Buffalo, NY: Prometheus Books.

Farrell, Thomas S.C. 2007. *Reflective Language Teaching.* New York: Continuum.

Fels, Dawn, and Jennifer Wells, eds. 2011. *The Successful High School Writing Center.* New York: Teachers College Press.

Gawande, Atul. 2011. "Personal Best." *New Yorker,* Oct. 3, 44–53.

Greenfield, Laura, and Karen Rowan, eds. 2011. *Writing Centers and the New Racism.* Logan: Utah State University Press.

Grimm, Nancy. 1999. *Good Intentions: Writing Center Work for Postmodern Times.* Portsmouth, NH: Heinemann.

Grutsch McKinney, Jackie. 2013. *Peripheral Visions.* Logan: Utah State University Press.

Harris, Muriel. 1995. "Talking in the Middle: Why Writers Need Writing Tutors." *College English* 57 (1): 27–42. http://dx.doi.org/10.2307/378348.

Harris, Muriel, and Tony Silva. 1993. "Tutoring ESL Students: Issues and Options." *College Composition and Communication* 44 (4): 525–537. http://dx.doi.org/10.2307/358388.

Kail, Harvey, and John Trimbur. 1987. "The Politics of Peer Tutoring." *WPA: Writing Program Administration* 11 (1–2): 5–12.

Leki, Ilona. 2009. "Before the Conversation: A Sketch of Some Possible Backgrounds, Experiences, and Attitudes Among ESL Students Visiting a Writing Center." In *ESL Writers: A Guide for Writing Center Tutors*, edited by Shanti Bruce and Ben Rafoth, 1–17. Portsmouth, NH: Heinemann.

Lerner, Neil. 2009. *The Idea of a Writing Laboratory*. Carbondale: Southern Illinois University Press.

Liu, Pei-Hsun Emma, and Dan J. Tannacito. 2013. "Resistance by L2 Writers: The Role of Racial and Language Ideology in Imagined Community and Identity Investment." *Journal of Second Language Writing* 22 (4): 355–73. http://dx.doi.org/10.1016/j.jslw .2013.05.001.

National Commision on Teaching and America's Future. 1996. "What Matters Most: Teaching for America's Future." Arlington, VA: NCTAF. http://nctaf.org.

Pennycook, Alastair. 2010. *Language as a Local Practice*. New York: Routledge.

Phelps, Louise Wetherbee. 1988. *Composition as a Human Science: Contributions to the Self-Understanding of a Discipline*. New York: Oxford University Press.

Rodgers, Carol. 2002. "Defining Reflection: Another Look at John Dewey and Reflective Thinking." *Teachers College Record* 104 (4): 842–66. http://dx.doi.org/10.1111/1467 -9620.00181.

Severino, Carol, P. Shih-Ni, J. Cogie, and L. Vu. 2013. "Higher and Lower Order Concerns and Error Gravity: Analyzing Second Language (L2) Writing Problems and Tutors' Responses to Them." Paper presented at the Midwest Writing Centers Association conference, Chicago, IL, October 18–19.

PART ONE

Actions and Identities

As we saw in chapter 1, philosopher John Dewey believed that reflective thinking gives rise to social progress when schools promote learning that engages with real-world problems and issues and continues to build new knowledge. In this book, reflective thinking begins with tutors who engage with students' diverse cultures and languages, confront matters of justice and fairness, and remain open to learning and discovery. In the first chapter of part 1, we see how tutors became involved in their center's proactive stance toward language difference, which culminated in the writing of a book for staff education. The book they created has now been used in their education course, for faculty development workshops, and at staff meetings. Chapter 3 presents an opportunity for thinking critically about linguistic and cultural differences that accrue to the ways we refer to our clients. Labels, it turns out, say something not only about the people we apply them to; they are also statements about us, the ones who apply them. However necessary, labels begin to fall away when we develop relationships with L2 writers because getting to know one another, on a personal level, is its own education. On that point, the author of chapter 4 shares personal and professional stories, based on interviews with writing center tutors at the University of Puerto Rico in Humacao. Her conversations with tutors there reveal the mixed feelings students at this university have about learning English and how they try to deal with these feelings in the writing center.

2
BUILDING A HOUSE FOR LINGUISTIC DIVERSITY
Writing Centers, English-Language Teaching and Learning, and Social Justice

Frankie Condon and Bobbi Olson

In this chapter, we are concerned with the interconnections between institutional contexts for writing center tutoring and institutional needs for social justice activism. We are interested in the ways and degrees to which peer tutors, when given opportunity and support for theorizing their own work with student writers and the intersections of that work with social justice matters, can and do produce new knowledge, transforming what is known both within the writing center and potentially across their institutions.

We describe an institutional moment and context in which peer tutors in the writing center at the University of Nebraska-Lincoln (UNL) experienced a call to leadership as writing center theorists as well as practitioners. We also describe a sense of urgency about the relationship of that work to critical, troubling, and barely implicit conditions of linguistic and cultural intolerance, xenophobia, and racism within and beyond their university. We write both as supporters and as participant-observers in a process by which peer tutors pursued a sustained intellectual, pedagogical, and activist engagement with their own education as writing center practitioners and, in doing so, created a critical, dynamic, and fluid legacy of ongoing tutor education and knowledge production to be passed forward to their successors. We describe the research and writing engaged collectively and collaboratively by graduate and undergraduate tutors in the UNL writing center, the challenges they faced, and what we learned from them as they theorized their practice.

Frankie arrived at UNL in the fall of 2007 at an institutional moment in which the university was moving to actively recruit and retain a much

DOI: 10.7330/9781607324140.c002

greater population of international students. Bobbi arrived in the fall of 2008 as a graduate student committed to writing center scholarship and practice with an interest and experience in teaching English to speakers of other languages (TESOL). With few institutional supports in place for cultural and academic transitions to a US university, increasing numbers of international students were seeking assistance from our university's writing center. The university and, in particular, those administrators most involved in the array of initiatives to grow and sustain international student enrollment were very supportive of the role the writing center was playing in contributing to the success of new international students. Significant funding was provided to the writing center for the development of ongoing tutor education to meet the diverse needs of multilingual student-writers, to grow a writing center staff sufficient to meet those needs, and for ongoing assessment of the writing center's efforts to support multilingual student-writers.

As the population of international students at the university grew, however, so too did the overt articulations of fear, resentment, and racism from the predominantly white community, both within and beyond the university. In 2012, *Inside Higher Ed* published an article publicizing blogs created anonymously at both Ohio State University and the University of Nebraska-Lincoln to expose hostile conditions within those institutions for students of color, generally, and for international English-language learning students in particular. Among the items published on those blogs (*UNLHaters* and *OSUHaters*) were the following examples:

"My poor lab TA. No one understands her chinglish."

"Just fought my way through a pack of 30 Asians on campus. Somebody get me a ninja sword."

"If you're going to have foreign exchange students working the laptop checkout, at lease make sure they speak English."

"When math teachers can't speak English but need to ensure everyone that parenthesis are important"

"Breaking news: outside of selleck and english isnt the main language being spoken"

"I feel like by the time I graduate, I'll become the minority group on campus . . . and the Asians will take over. #AsianDomination"

"Tip: look at the names of professors before you enroll in the class. If you can't pronounce it, you won't understand them."

"UNL needs to hire more american teachers. Or at least ones that speak proper English. #wtfareyousaying"

"History teacher can't spell Europe. Gotta be shitting me. #Foreigner"

"You can't even eavesdrop on the conversations while walking to class because they're mostly foreign. #asiansgalore"

The UNL writing center tutors didn't need the haters blogs to inform them of the racist and xenophobic undercurrents shaping their own living and learning experiences and those of the international and multilingual students with whom they were working. And the tutors didn't need the blogs to understand that words like these hurt. That these words wound. The tutors didn't need the blogs to know, in some cases intimately, that the injury such words cause is suffered disproportionately by those who are already marginalized within the institutions they share with folks who use social media to promote xenophobia, ethnocentrism, and racism—with those who compose and post tweets like these. The tutors also understood and frequently discussed the reality that the silences too often following hate speech have a doubling effect: those silences sustain conditions in which it seems acceptable to feel, give voice to, and act on hate, and those silences, regardless of intent, send the message to those who are targeted by hate speech that they are alone—that they are strangers and unwelcome guests in a house that was built for and belongs to those of us who occupy dominant, normalized subject positions (see Witherite, this volume).

In 1994, Carolyn Turner noted the "alien," "stranger," and "guest" status implicitly and explicitly accorded students who are racialized Other within predominantly white colleges and universities. "Like students of color," she writes, "in the university climate, guests have no history in the house they occupy. There are no photographs on the wall that reflect their image. Their paraphernalia, painting, scents, and sounds do not appear in the house. There are many barriers for students who constantly occupy a guest status that keep them from doing their best work" (Turner 1994, 356). Within our writing center, we claimed to have created a climate of hospitality in service of a community of writers we worked to support and sustain. Yet, we noted the degree to which, regardless of our intentions, we, too, were receiving and treating/teaching many students, but particularly international multilingual students, as guests in a home we had built for ourselves.

Written by R. Roosevelt Jr. and Marjorie Woodruff, the book *Creating a House for Diversity* has been helpful to us in telling a learningful story about how our writing center seemed complicit in the forms of intolerance and injustice we saw around us and in which we felt implicated.

The book is organized around a parable of sorts that we tell here in our own words but that goes something like this:

A giraffe and an elephant were best friends who liked each other so much they agreed to live together. In service of this goal, the giraffe engaged in an extensive renovation of the home they planned to share and was eager to show off the beauty of the reconstructed home to his friend. Accordingly, on the morning the house was completed, the giraffe called out to his friend. "Elephant, our beautiful home is finished! It's so lovely, and I'm so excited to share it with you." The elephant, eager to see the fruits of the giraffe's labors and delighted at the prospect of spending every day with his friend, began to climb the porch steps to the front door. The steps cracked under his weight. "Wait!" cried the giraffe. "You are breaking my beautiful steps! They weren't made for someone like you. Come round the back where I've built an egress into the basement. You can come in that way."

Accordingly, the elephant circled the home, observing the lovely landscaping of the grounds along the way, but leaving deep footprints in the freshly watered lawn. At the basement egress, the giraffe met his friend and waved him down the concrete steps into the basement. The elephant found himself in a lovely family room, graced with a home theater and a wet bar. The giraffe invited him to sit and view a movie, but when the elephant lowered himself into one of the chairs appointed for that purpose, the seat crumbled beneath him. "Wait!" cried the giraffe. "You have broken my beautiful chair! You can watch later from the back of the theater where there's room for you to stand. Let me just show you the rest of our house first." The elephant took in the craft room lined by shelves with materials for every sort of project he and his friend might embark upon together. But he couldn't fit through the door. "Nevermind," said the giraffe. "Come upstairs and see the kitchen where we'll eat together and your new bedroom." The elephant started up the staircase, but it was much too narrow, and his girth broke the bannister. By this time, the elephant was near tears. He yearned to fit into this beautiful home and felt mortified at what he was certain was his failure. "Don't worry," said the giraffe. "I know exactly what to do. You can stay outside for now. We'll put you on a strict diet and exercise regimen. I'll help you change that body for a lovely new thin one, and in no time at all, you'll fit right in here with me."

And so the elephant began the effort to transform himself so that he might fit into the house his friend, Giraffe, had promised to share with him. But in secret, he wondered whether they might not just start over and build a house from the ground up that would actually be built for both of them, with all their differences, to share.

In his book, *Racism without Racists*, Eduardo Bonilla-Silva (2006) describes the work stories do to communicate the racial identifications and commitments of their tellers but also to actualize a world that suits those identifications and commitments. He writes, "The stories we tell are not random. They evince the social position of the narrators" (75). Bonilla-Silva goes on to explain that the ideological frameworks through which we make stories of our lives and our work are too often invisible to us. The giraffe, for example, may in fact have the best of intentions with regard to making a place for his friend, the elephant, in his house. The ways in which the giraffe has built a house that is, however, uninhabitable for his friend are invisible to him. The giraffe's redesign and renovation of his home have been animated by own his desires and needs, as well as by a narrative about what will be good for the elephant based on an assumption that the elephant's needs and wants will, of course, be the same as his own. The giraffe builds the house *for* his friend rather than *with* his friend.

As we pondered with UNL tutors the dichotomies between the public commitment of our writing center to antioppression pedagogies and the practices we actually engage in teaching writing one-with-one to multilingual writers, we worried collectively about whether or to what degree we, too, were building a house for ourselves as if the needs, desires, knowledge, and expectations with which we were familiar were universal for everyone in our writing center community. We noted the degree to which, in practice, we were engaging scripts or narratives of linguistic and rhetorical, racial, ethnic, and cultural belonging and unbelonging that seemed to reproduce the very conditions of normativity that, in principle, our pedagogical commitments should have countered.

As we talked together about what we perceived to be the disparities between our aspirations to enact a well-theorized, inclusive, one-with-one writing pedagogy in our work with all student writers and the social justice principles to which we publicly subscribed, we began to see that not only were we embedded within a giraffe-like institution, we were also enacting giraffe in the very writing center we had posited as both a counter- and a transformative agent within that institution. We may not have been "rush[ing] to monolingualist hegemony" as Harry Denny (2010), author of *Facing the Center: Towards an Identity Politics of One-to-One Mentoring*, writes, but we were enacting that hegemony in spite of our best intentions not to do so (126). When, despite our extended reading and discussions around addressing patterns of error, we worked line by line with student-writers, correcting each variation (often without regard for whether the variation was a prescriptive grammatical mistake or a stylistic preference), we were—we realized—demanding assimilation in ways that protected and preserved a house designed for the comfort and ease of those who already fit rather seamlessly within normative identifications of race and ethnicity, language, and culture. We had been unreflective and uncritical of the assimilationist stance we had taken. And we had failed to consider the fact that when such a practice does not include an examination of implicit valuations of Standard Written American English (SWAE), the results marginalize and exclude those who speak and write in World Englishes.

The UNL tutors understood that to some degree they were implicated in the force of the messages posted on the haters blogs and by the institutional silence around those blog entries, if not by virtue of their subject positions (for not all of the tutors were white or native English speakers or middle class or American), then by their institutional situatedness as tutors. They felt a critical need, however, to discern means of resisting not merely their own implication but also the conditions that seemed to them to support and sustain an institutional culture too tolerant of racism and xenophobia. The tutors wanted, in other words, to make moves at rebuilding the house rather than simply making easy, but only minimal, modifications.

To these conversations about race, xenophobia, and the ways in which their work as tutors might challenge and resist those forces, the UNL peer tutors brought their own commitments and convictions as well as the collective imprimatur of a writing center already committed to a progressive political vision of literacy education and its relation to the work of antiracism, even though we were inadequately realizing that commitment. Informed by the work of Harry Denny as well as scholars such as Elizabeth Boquet (2002), author of *Noise from the Writing Center* and coauthor of *The Everyday Writing Center: A Community of Practice*, and Sarah Nakamaru (2010), author of "Theory In/To Practice: A Tale of Two Multilingual Writers: A Case-Study Approach to Tutor Education," the writing center staff became increasingly convinced that our collective and individual change agency would begin and be sustained by a culture of inquiry. The staff wanted to extend our writing center's notion of tutor education from the writing center theory and practice classroom and the staff meeting to the everyday—from the day-to-day operations of the writing center to the consultation and subsequent critical reflection in and on practice. With Denny, we collectively agreed that "it's not the prescriptions for making this or that session effective that matter; rather, it's the processes we make possible, the conversations we reward and make time for, the faces that come to the center, margins that change the center. To them, we're indebted. For them, the writing center exists" (Denny 2010, 167). As we talked about how we might proceed in productively challenging social and institutional forms of and tolerance for racism and xenophobia, we agreed that we wanted to create and sustain conditions for learning in which tutors and writers could do their best work, together. We wanted to begin and continue to construct a different kind of house altogether. We agreed that taking on challenges and obstacles to social justice within our writing center, our institution, and beyond is critical to the creation of productive conditions for learning. And we understood that such conditions can never be constructed for others: that Bobbi and Frankie could not do this work for tutors any more than the tutors could do this work for writers. We would need to learn to cocreate, to coconstruct, to coauthor an inclusive center.

Toward this end, for three weeks following the close of the 2012 spring term, we gathered eight consultants (four graduate and four undergraduate) and paid them through an internal grant to study our center's work with multilingual writers and to compose a body of philosophy and theoretical understanding that might serve as a foundation for ongoing staff education. Together the consultants examined assessments gathered over the previous five years. Individually and in small working groups, consultants gathered articles and books that seemed to them to be relevant to our inquiry and important reading for all of us to discuss. Together we talked each day about these materials, the sense we were making of them, and the questions that seemed to us to arise from them. Together in their groups, tutors began to draft a book: not a manual of how-to's, but a text that in successive chapters would lay out key questions and core principles with which future consultants might engage in order to sustain an ongoing, critical, and reflective dialogue about their praxis. By *praxis* we mean the dynamic relationship between theory and practice. Praxis is the process by which ideas are put into practice, practices are reflected upon, and ideas are transformed or revised in an ongoing feedback loop.

Over the course of the three weeks they spent together, the tutors composed a core principle: "The UNL Writing Center takes a strengths-based multi-competency approach to our work with multi-lingual and English Language Learning student writers." They agreed that a writing center animated by a shared sense of convictions about the relationship between language learning and social justice must recognize and acknowledge through its pedagogical approaches the experiences, knowledge, ability, and skill individual writers already possess, building upon those strengths in service of learning. The tutors agreed also that such a writing center must be cognizant and respectful of student-writers' goals but also honest and realistic about the possibility of achieving those goals in the near term. They agreed that discursive and rhetorical hybridity were values they would hold both as they worked with student-writers and as they developed workshops and seminars for faculty and students beyond the bounds of the writing center. Finally, the tutors agreed that humility and compassion were richer grounds for building meaningful and learningful relationships with writers than any "mastery" of language or of writing practice that might be possessed by a tutor. They agreed that rather than privileging their own credentials and good intentions in their work with multilingual writers, in particular, our individual and collective philosophies and practices as tutors and administrators in the UNL writing center should orient around our uncertainties—the questions into which we continue to inquire and do not yet (may never) know the answers to—and our recognition that neither we nor the writers with whom we work can ever fully know ourselves, our abilities and our limitations, the discourses that shape us and the world in which we make our relations. Rather than asserting certainties we don't possess, then, the tutors agreed that our individual and collective praxis might be better shaped by sharing our culture of inquiry with the writers with whom we work.

To prompt their own and other tutors' understanding and consideration of their work in the writing center, the tutors composed a book in four chapters (or movements), the first of which centered around collaboration. They prioritized humaneness as a necessary condition for collaboration as well as for the ongoing collective practice of decentering authority within and beyond the tutorial. The tutors talked at great length about the qualities of a collaborative conversation between tutor and writer. While they recognized and honored processes of negotiating roles, goals, and directions, they also affirmed that the initial maps of these negotiations do not constitute the territory itself: that collaborative conversations are only sustained through ongoing dialogue and transparency as roles, goals, and directions shift in the changeable environs of a consultation. The second chapter took up linguistics, discourse, and rhetorical theory focusing on the complex relationships between form and meaning, on the politics of teaching SWAE in one-with-one settings, and on the array of dynamic complexities that might trouble tutors' attempts to enact political principle in easy and thus authoritarian ways. In this sense, the second chapter cycled back to principles articulated in the first chapter in order to inquire into the possibilities for collaborative dialogue during consultations with multilingual writers.

Tutors organized the third chapter around the concept of agency. To them, working with writers to create and sustain conditions for writing in which writer agency was possible and realizable was a primary value. The tutors felt that agency as writers was critical for multilingual writers facing and laboring against forms of bias, discrimination, and marginalization on the basis of language, race, and nationality. Transparency made a return appearance in this chapter as tutors talked and wrote about the necessity for honesty and clarity about the array of discursive and rhetorical choices available to writers as well as the ways in which those choices might be limited by reader expectations (and the constellation of ideological as well as intellectual and rhetorical forces shaping those expectations). Finally, the tutors discussed and wrote about the relationship between agency and difficult dialogues about difference. They agreed that agency is occluded by silence on the matter of difference—that if writers are to act as agents in their own learning as well as in the production of their own writing, tutors can neither behave as if difference doesn't exist or its effects are minimal, nor as if the institutional conditions around matters of difference are insignificant to conditions for learning and the production of new knowledge by multilingual writers.

In the final chapter of their book, tutors worked to redefine success, both in terms of individual consultations and in terms of their own praxis. They agreed that, as difficult as such a concept might be in practice, they needed to work with writers to understand the success of consultations in terms of ongoing learning rather than completion—in terms of what becomes possible for a writer to conceive and to practice after a consultation both in the revision of a current text and in the drafting of new work. They agreed also, however, that as well as being open and honest about their senses of success, they needed also to listen and attend to writers' senses, their felt and expressed needs and interests, and to navigate differences with writers rather than in spite of them. Tutors felt that in order to reconceptualize success, they needed to understand time differently and to share that understanding with the writers with whom they work. Taking up the concept of a big here/long now, or what writing center scholar Anne Ellen Geller (2005) has termed "epochal time," the tutors worked to theorize conditions within consultations in which tutors and writers might together press back against the constraints (and anxieties) associated with the right here/right now of due dates, clocks, and immediate needs. (Condon 2012, 125–26; Geller 2005, 8)

Finally, the tutors affirmed their collective valuation of learningful failure as integral to their own development as tutors. They talked and wrote about the value of narrative—of storytelling—to their own growth as tutors (and writers) (see Medina Reyes, this volume) and to the ongoing quality of staff development as a whole in our writing center. Just as they had affirmed the necessity and value of difficult dialogues between tutors and writers, the tutors also affirmed the necessity and value of difficult dialogues to inquiry-based staff development. They needed, they felt (and wrote), time to share stories with their colleagues, to be supported but also questioned and challenged in service of learning from those stories. They felt convinced, as Elizabeth Boquet (2002) has written, that "freedom of inquiry is not a one-person job; it is a many-persons job" and that the shared labor of free inquiry needed to move dynamically between theory and practice via tutor stories collected and shared as an integral part of ongoing staff education (59).

The book begun by tutors over the course of that three-week collaborative effort has been nearly continuously drafted and revised during the time since our initial gathering. It served as a required text for the writing center theory and practice course offered the following autumn. Undergraduate and graduate students enrolled in that course grappled with its philosophical orientation and pedagogical claims, read the source material that shaped the work in both theoretical and practical terms, and prepared themselves as future tutors to contribute to its ongoing revision. The book has been used by tutors to design faculty development workshops as well as seminars and workshops for student-writers. It has served as the basis for weekly staff-development meetings during which tutors have inquired into questions or problems raised by the work or unaddressed, in some sense, within it. Although the book has some qualities of a manifesto, as a continuous work in progress, subject always to question, debate, and revision, it has not become nor was it intended to be a statement of doctrine or dogma. Even the ways its key principles, arguments, and source materials enable and constrain inquiry have been available for debate—for the very sort of difficult dialogues valued by the tutors who composed the originary text.

LESSONS AND CHALLENGES: STANDARD WRITTEN AMERICAN ENGLISH (SWAE) AND THE CONFLICT BETWEEN WRITING CENTER THEORY AND PRACTICE

Although none of us on the staff of the UNL writing center were surprised by the vitriol of the tweets posted on the *UNLHaters* blog, we were deeply troubled by them. They confirmed realities with which we had long been contending in the writing center. Many of the student-writers with whom we worked frequently and, indeed, some of us—international and US multilingual tutors and writers—were regularly subjected on our campus to surveillance; they/we were observed closely and with profound suspicion by some peers and faculty and judged by them in and outside of classrooms in ways that seemed animated by racist, white-supremacist, and nationalist perspectives on language, culture, and belonging/unbelonging. The hostility articulated explicitly in those tweets on the *UNLHaters* blog and implicitly through the everyday experiences of many international and multilingual writers and tutors as they moved through classrooms, cafeterias, residence halls, and across campus made for an institutional environment that was far from hospitable. However much we might have liked to separate our writing center from the hostility of those implicit and explicit messages, and as committed as we all were to creating a writing center community that would be welcoming and supportive of all students, we felt deeply the ways and degrees to which that inhospitable climate infected our best efforts at community building regardless of our intentions.

In working together on the book project, the tutors began to recognize a relationship between the privileging of particular languages and discourses within and beyond the classrooms they moved through and the animus directed at multilingual members of the university community in the tweets published on the blog. Their research suggested to them that the forms of linguistic imperialism and its underlying logics they detected in those tweets had long attended and sustained both global and local forms of cultural, social, political, and economic domination. They became convinced that so long as tutoring practices in the UNL writing center worked within rather than challenging the logics of linguistic supremacy, in particular, the effect of our work would be to reinforce the fabric of institutional intolerance at the intersections of SWAE with normative racial, ethnic, national, and linguistic identifications and exclusions. We needed, the tutors realized, to address the most powerful underlying logics of our practice—our understanding of language difference—if we were to address the faulty structure of our writing center rather than merely repairing the roof, as it were. In this regard, the tutors argued, their study of the ways language difference is addressed extended necessarily beyond the boundaries of our university and writing center to universities and writing centers across the United States and to widely shared assumptions within many institutions and writing centers about the relationships among language, intellectual ability, individual value, and national belonging.

The tutors were familiar with claims by writing center administrators and tutors at other predominantly white institutions that their schools are free of the kind of racism and white supremacy, ethnocentrism, and nationalism evinced in the above tweets. Many of them had heard such claims at regional and international writing center and tutoring conferences over a period of years. To be honest, however, neither we nor the tutors with whom we worked in the UNL writing center ever believed those claims. We agreed that there might be local differences in institutional conditions, but all of us remain convinced that at this historical moment, pressures around racial, ethnic, national, and cultural normative identifications in the United States are ubiquitous. Collectively, we believed that within predominantly white colleges and universities across the country, including UNL, the presence of difference—the presence of Othered bodies, Othered voices, Othered languages and cultures—is still represented and treated as a "problem" for those who occupy normative subject positions. This (il)logic is taken up in the classroom and in the writing center in and over student bodies, student voices, and student texts that classroom teachers and writing center tutors alike still seem too frequently compelled to "fix."

The *Inside Higher Ed* article and wave of public discussion and debate about the haters blogs following the article's publication confirmed for all of us that our institution was not unique, nor were our writing-centered perceptions of the impacts of institutional, linguistic, cultural, and social marginalization on multilingual writers wrong. UNL and colleges and universities across the country are seeking to increase international enrollments in order to both diversify and internationalize their student bodies and to increase tuition revenues. As the numbers of international, multilingual students—particularly those students who will be perceived as students of color in the United States regardless of their experience of racialization in their home countries—increases at our nation's universities, so too do the racial, cultural, and linguistic anxieties of white, monolingual, American students.

There is, it seemed to the tutors, a plethora of evidence available that access and opportunity are in fact distributed unequally along lines of privilege and normative identity. Within a cultural, political, and economic milieu in which educational and economic opportunities are represented as being finite and distributed by virtue of individual merit alone, historically privileged students are taught that they have earned the historical benefits they possess and to feel fear or anxiety about the loss of those benefits. Within such a milieu, students of color and multilingual students, in particular, seemed to all of us to be experiencing a different yet related anxiety. The students with whom we worked felt keenly the pressure to change their languages/change themselves in order to gain access and opportunity that might otherwise be denied to them. A third form of anxiety emerged among tutors working in the writing center, including those who participated in the initial project of collaboratively researching and composing the sourcebook. Even as we acquired more and more evidence of the ways in which normative identities and the privileges that attend possession of those identities overlap with and are reinforced by the underlying logics of linguistic supremacy, many of the tutors wrestled with their belief that their job was to assist multilingual students to earn their access and opportunity by normalizing their identities—by helping multilingual writers perceive, feel and think, read, write, and speak as if they were "white," "American" (in the case of international student-writers) native speakers of American academic Englishes. Tutors who felt this way understood the impossibility of the task they set before themselves and the writers with whom they worked, and yet they believed this was the only ethical and pedagogically sound choice—a choice that was, in effect, not a choice at all (see Liu, this volume).

It wasn't just individual tutors who struggled with how and to what degree our work in the writing center should focus on SWAE. To one degree or another, in our discussions of tutoring praxis and social justice, *all* of us struggled with learned beliefs in the superiority of SWAE and/or with our sense of the power of SWAE. Convinced that students would fail academically and, later, professionally as well if they didn't compose in SWAE, within the writing center we grappled with our individual and collective propensity to represent SWAE as the "correct" English, the only English in which new knowledge might be produced and effective professional communications composed. We struggled, in other words, quite literally with the very (il)logics professed in the tweets posted on the haters blogs.

We wanted to believe our intentions were better than those of the folks who composed those tweets, but the frames of our stories about the English language and English-language learning—stories that shaped our practice—were similarly predicated on foreignness, on strangeness, and on wrongness. Oddly and discordantly, all of us clung to these (il)logics in our ideas about SWAE and the practice of tutoring, even as we understood and discussed Patricia Bizzell's (2002) claim that "at any given time [SWAE's] most standard or widely accepted features reflect the cultural preferences of the most powerful people in the community. Until relatively recently these people in the academic community have usually been male, European American, and middle or upper class" (1). In theory, we understood SWAE to be a racialized (and gendered and classed) discourse. In practice, we continued to struggle with what to do with that knowledge in the moment of the consultation. We felt, observed, and heard the conflict between our theory and our practice, for example, in tutor narratives about working through teacher feedback on student writing produced by international multilingual writers (see Amevuor, this volume). The tutors heard that conflict also as they narrated and struggled with their conviction that it was their responsibility to help multilingual writers eliminate any trace of "accent" in their texts, particularly when instructor feedback was inclined in that direction.

These conflicts and others like them magnified the anxieties we felt as we imagined our job was to manage linguistic, cultural, and racial difference in service of somehow producing sameness. We encountered similar anxieties around SWAE among the faculty who attended the regular workshops and seminars we offer across campus. We encountered this anxiety as well among aspiring tutors in the writing center theory and practice course we offer each fall semester. Tutors and classroom teachers articulated with great clarity and conviction the sense that their *job* requires them to teach SWAE, regardless of whether to do so is possible or desirable, fair, or just.

In this regard, the UNL tutors articulated an ongoing need to investigate often-unexamined ideas about language use—and how writing center tutors across institutions teach language in the writing center—for the degree to which those implicit notions of difference as deficit create not only a hierarchy of language use but also a hierarchy of language users. As Laura Greenfield (2011) notes, "Language prejudice is not a figment of the imagination" (50). Vershawn Young (2010) makes this point even more clearly: "Dont nobody's language, dialect, or style," he writes, "make them 'vulnerable to prejudice.' It's ATTITUDES. It be the way folks with some power perceive other people's language" (110). Myths about the quality and authority of SWAE, and the attitudes and anxieties those myths agitate in tutors and teachers of writing, result in everyday forms of discrimination based only ostensibly on language but more accurately on the array of meanings and value—or lack of meanings and value—attributed to speakers and writers. Since "language is also race in America," (Villanueva 1993, xii) writing center tutors and directors must pay careful attention to what their pedagogical choices signify for and about multilingual writers. All of this is to say the languages in which we speak and write, including the multiple forms and discursive registers of English we employ as teachers and tutors of writing, are always already ideologically freighted as well as materially consequential. If "language and culture are inextricably interwoven," as Jennifer Grill (2010) claims, writing centers must be particularly careful about what language (and subsequently racial, ethnic, culture, and national) identifications are privileged (361)

That old canard about writing centers making better writers not better writing took on new and troubling valences for all of us as the tutors researched and composed the book. To the extent that we were focusing on fixing students' languages and, hence, their racial, ethnic, and cultural identifications in the writing center alongside classroom teachers and, indeed, the institution as a whole, we worried about whether or how we might be treating the canary in the coal mine rather than addressing in a sustained, theorized, and activist sense the range of conditions writ large and small, global and local that sustain predominantly white culture within the US academy.

To do the important work of recognizing the teaching of language as a form of activism toward social justice, the tutors began to argue, writing center tutors and administrators must be aware of the ways in which attitudes regarding language "difference" are rooted in attitudes about the bodies within and through which these language "differences" are made material. They referenced Dees, Godbee, and Ozias (2007), who remind us of the danger of reifying "difference." "Differences," the coauthors write, "are more than just differences: they become unfair organizers of our lives, providing some of us with fewer opportunities, less insider knowledge, and limited access." The tutors came to believe that what is frequently represented as best practice in the tutoring of writing has been shaped by popular beliefs about language diversity in the United States largely informed by two dominant language ideologies. The first of these is a monolingual ideology manifested as a monolingual English ideology in the United States (Wiley and Lukes 1996, 514), and it is easily identifiable in the rhetoric of the English Only movement. The second is the ideology of standard language, or, more specifically in the context of the United States, the ideology of Standard English. Both of these linguistic ideologies are tied to other ideological assumptions related to beliefs about the relationship between language and national unity and between language and social mobility (Wiley and Lukes 1996, 512). That is, notions of linguistic Otherness and deficiency are essentialized and mapped onto social representations of those who are identified as deficient Others by virtue of their linguistic difference.

Linguistic Otherness and deficiency, in other words, are racialized, handcuffed to what people "are" or are represented as being.

Armed with insights from Terrence Wiley and Marguerite Lukes, the tutors argued that basing writing center consultations upon dominant-language "standards" had the effect of engaging them, knowingly or not, in the practice of cataloguing the bodies of those who speak and write "differently" and, given the authority of linguistic supremacy, in deciding whom those bodies and their utterances must be made or taught to be instead. As the tutors searched for alternative theory and more just practice to reconceive and refigure their work with Othered student writers, they became increasingly convinced of Denny's argument that the general attitude evinced in professional conversations in the field of writing center studies seems to be that multilingual writers "are a problem that requires solving, an irritant and frustration that resists resolution" (Denny 2010, 119). In contrast to the ongoing actualization of such attitudes in tutoring practice, a social justice orientation toward the teaching of writing one-with-one requires bringing issues of language "difference" and language privileging to the forefront. All of us, the tutors acknowledged, feel pressure to avoid naming difference. We have been taught that to notice difference of any kind aloud is to be, at least, uncivil. The proscription against naming difference, however, is predicated on the notion that difference signifies deficiency and, therefore, that to name difference—to talk about difference openly—is to name also broadly and deeply held convictions about who is normal, right, and superior and who is not. These proscriptions, we concluded, must be actively resisted both by tutors and by writing center administrators if we are to transform our writing centers and participate in the democratization of our institutions.

In search of a bridge between their emerging sense of philosophical commitment and their sense of the ways and degrees to which their practices seemed to fail that philosophy, the tutors turned to Carol Severino's (2006) essay "The Sociopolitical Implications of Response to Second-Language and Second-Dialect Writing." Severino delineates three positions on a spectrum of teacher/scholar orientations toward World Englishes. The tutors considered Severino's analysis of these positions as well as her alignment of them along a continuum when composing their book. Proponents of assimilation, Severino suggests, might teach multilingual students "to smoothly blend or melt into the desired discourse communities and avoid social stigma by controlling any features that in the eyes of audiences with power and influence might mark a writer as inadequately educated or lower class" (338). Within an assimilationist frame, Severino notes, "linguistic differences would be regarded as 'errors' or instances of Ll 'interference'—cultural or lin-guistic—to be eliminated" (338). Proponents of what Severino terms a "separatist stance," on the other hand, "believe that the society and the class of employers or educators that disparage or discriminate against ESL and SESD [Standard English as a second dialect] speakers should be challenged and changed, not the ESL and SESD speakers themselves or their discourses. Separatists want to preserve and celebrate linguis-tic diversity, not eradicate it" (339). While Severino notes that "separat-ists read ESL texts generously," at their worst, she suggests, "separatist responses, forgiving or applauding deviations from Standard English rhe-torical and grammatical patterns, inevitably set students up for a shock when the next teacher, tutor, or employer they encounter tends toward an assimilationist stance" (339). Finally, Severino explores an accommo-dationist stance or "'compromise' position (Farr 1990)" (Severino 2006, 340). Proponents of accommodation, Severino suggests, advocate that rather than "giving up their home oral and written discourse patterns in order to assimilate," multilingual students "instead acquir[e] new dis-course patterns, thus enlarging their rhetorical repertoires for different occasions" (340); "In the best of all possible accommodationist worlds," Severino suggests, "patterns are only gained, not lost" (340). She writes further that "at their best, accommodationist responses are compre-hensive and rhetorical, emphasizing that certain discourse features are appropriate or inappropriate for certain occasions. At their worst, they are longwinded, laden with conditions, and hard to process" (340). Adding a further distinction, Severino writes that "sensitive accommoda-tionists are, according to their name, accommodating of both linguistic differences and societal conventions. Insensitive accommodationists are overexplainers, whose own agenda, shared by many separatists, to rid themselves of any association with academic or linguistic assimilation or colonization, can overwhelm their teaching of writing" (340).

In many ways, the spectrum described and stances/practices along that spectrum offered by Severino became helpful frameworks for us as we worked to understand the various approaches one might take in multilingual tutoring and what the implications might be for each approach. The case studies Severino offers in her essay as examples of both particular and blended approaches were especially useful to all of us. As we talked together, about both Severino's article and the tutoring practices we had engaged or observed other tutors engaging in the UNL writing center, the tutors articulated concerns about the ways in which they and their fellow tutors seemed to be adopting one stance and using it unilaterally. Absent a theoretical framework that might enable tutors to make discerning choices about which strategies to employ under what circumstances, the tutors observed that they tended always to land on or near assimilationism by default. They worried that the term *separatism* effectively warned them away from exploring with writers productive engagement with the blending of discourses within a single text, or code-meshing (Young 2010, 114). In order to make informed and pedagogically sound decisions about tutoring strategies, the tutors felt they needed to learn or to develop means of conceptualizing the relationship between systemic inequality, language difference, and their individual work with student writers.

To create inclusive theoretical and pedagogical spaces/relations within communities of writers, writing center practitioners—especially monolingual tutors and administrators—will be well served, we concluded, by using categories like those delineated by Severino carefully and critically as starting points for reexamining attitudes about language and identity. In the UNL writing center, we hope, however, that those conversations will take up the limitations or reductiveness of complete subscription to any single approach even as more recent scholarship is examined. We believe in the importance of continuing to study the degree to which common assumptions and practices are mythologized even within the categories outlined above, underwritten within them rather than challenged by them.

As we considered the mythologizing of various approaches to the teaching of writing, we were struck by Jennifer Grill's insight that SWAE anxieties are rooted, in fact, in certain myths about the language itself. We note the degree to which such myths undergird what can seem like very ordinary, "commonsensical" sorts of conversations between tutors and writers. Jennifer Grill's work from TESOL, for instance, lays out "Assumptions about Language" (Grill 2010, 359) that need to be reconsidered:

> Myth 1: Standard English is the Best and Most Correct Form of English.
>
> Myth 2: English Dialects Are Improper and Randomly Created Forms of the Language. [We would add that perceived linguistic "divergences" regarded as improper and randomly created forms of language is also a myth]
>
> Myth 3: Dialects Interfere with Learning "Proper" English and Should Not Be Used in the Classroom. [We would add that linguistic "divergences" as interference is also a myth; in fact, these "divergences" can help enrich a text]

As they studied and talked together, the tutors began to recognize the ways and degrees to which these myths constituted our own writing

.center version of the (il)logics of the tweets published on the UNL haters blog and how buying into these myths helped perpetuate the "guest" status of multilingual writers and tutors. Collectively, we sought to continue to study the ways and degrees to which these myths may inform, albeit perhaps implicitly, our practice of working with multilingual writers. We all noted, with Severino, that "because it is impossible to separate language issues from their political contexts, and because the international and national 'macropolitics' affect the 'micropolitics' of the relationships among teacher, student, and text, it is important for L1, L2/ ESL composition, or any endeavor concerned with English language teaching to acknowledge and make explicit the sociopolitical implications of response to writing" (Severino 2006, 346–47). However difficult the dialogue may be, continuing dialogue among tutors about the ways in which the mythologies underwriting monolingual writing pedagogies tend to operate along national and racial lines seems critical to the project of ongoing and dynamic tutor education.

In short, the tutors not only noted but also developed a conceptual vocabulary with which to name the array of systemic inequalities that might trouble their work with writers. All of us began to grapple with the realization that there are critical linkages between the identification of linguistic difference as fundamental difference, the racialization of an Other, and the operations of linguistic supremacy over and against that Other. As a staff, we needed and continue to need to acknowledge the ways and degrees to which, however unintentionally, racism might continue to inflect our practice, for its logics are "deeply entrenched in our discourses about language" (Greenfield 2011, 34). A treatment of language "differences" as a deficit perpetuates and sustains processes of racialization that reproduce conditions of inequality in all of our writing centers, regardless of whether or not we claim a social justice mission. To address this array of systemic inequalities in our writing centers and to make such a mission actionable requires sustained critical inquiry that continuously and dynamically shapes the ways we conceive of collaborative tutor practice with all writers, especially with writers who have historically been Othered and marginalized within and beyond our colleges and universities (see Balester and Cox, both in this volume).

HOW TO KEEP ON KEEPING ON

As we were beginning to realize that the house we had built in our writing center was not, in fact, a house for diversity but one designed to exclude or erase difference, and beginning also to conceptualize the project of reenvisioning and revitalizing ongoing staff education in our writing center, we began traveling regularly together as a staff to conferences, listening and talking with administrators and tutors from other institutions across the country. At those conferences, we heard established writing center scholars and directors struggling to come to terms with the relationship between the framing of linguistic difference as deficit and the racialism inherent in linguistic supremacy. Absent this understanding, many "elders" in the field seemed to feel that addressing social justice issues in a writing center is too much for tutors, too difficult a labor for them (for us) to bear. As we pondered taking up and countering the kinds of hate articulated directly and indirectly across our campus, the tutors acknowledged the weight of that burden. But as we, collectively, began to understand that the very (il)logics undergirding hate speech were also manifest in our writing center work, the tutors discussed and wrote about their emerging perception that the social justice labor they felt called to do was less a burden than a pedagogical responsibility. If we accepted this responsibility and chose to act on it, we realized, we would have to think deliberately, reflectively, and collectively about how to enact our principles on the ground, as it were, as well as how to keep on keeping on, even and especially when the work gets particularly hard and when one or all of us get tired.

Below are five lessons we learned, offered provisionally because—let's face it—we're still learning.

1. We really aren't alone! Learn to recognize your allies and build new alliances across your institution, within your community, and with other writing center tutors and activists.

Much of our work together involved turning toward one another and to others for help, for support, for learning. Together, as a staff, we read the work of scholars such as Vershawn Ashanti Young, Min Zhan-Lu, Suresh Canagarajah, Bruce Horner, John Trimbur, Donna Lecourt, Victor Villanueva, Paul Kei Matsuda, and Geneva Smitherman. And as we worked to cultivate a shared pedagogical praxis rather than individual tutoring scripts and "toolkits," we realized we are not alone in our struggle to enact our commitments in performative ways, to share the labor of creating, in other words, a just and inclusive community of writers with those who, although characterized and treated as Others, also share stakes in the institution and the discourses in and through which we make ourselves and our world.

As we began to think of social justice work in our writing center as a pedagogical responsibility, we began to understand that taking up that responsibility might bring us not to overwhelmment but to a sense of alliance, of interconnectedness, and to the best kind of interdependence and mutual support with other similarly committed and laboring individuals and institutional sites across our university. We can, we learned, choose to take on the conditions that produce hate speech from where we are situated institutionally, and this work is not incidental to social justice work on our campus but critical to that work.

When we began to think in terms of actual and potential alliances, we began to recognize administrators, faculty, and staff, as well as graduate and undergraduate students across our institution, who were already similarly committed and with whom we could work. We recognized the degree of support we could both give and receive from the Antiracism Special Interest Groups (SIGs) active within the Midwest Writing Centers Association, the National Conference on Peer Tutoring in Writing, and the International Writing Centers Association. Sometimes these connections are as simply supportive as individual tutors sharing a lunch or coffee and conversation with a colleague from across campus and bringing back what they've learned to a staff-education gathering or inviting an ally to one of our staff meetings. Sometimes they involve groups of tutors working together to develop workshops rooted in our collectively conceived philosophy and practice for our allies across campus. Sometimes these alliances grow from introductions at SIG gatherings, Facebook friendships, or conference-panel proposals. However they are enacted, the alliances we build within our institution and beyond its bounds sustain our hope as well as help us to learn better how to craft our work as writing center tutors to better match our convictions and our intentions.

2. The work isn't about getting to innocence; it's about continuous learning and practice.

We believe that neither the epistemological and pedagogical processes we have engaged as a staff in writing a book for tutor education nor the ongoing revision by successive generations of tutors is sufficient to confer innocence upon the UNL writing center. Conditions of inequality, marginalization, and exclusion continue to operate beneath the surface of our institution (as they do in every predominantly white college and university at this historical moment), and we are still implicated in the reproduction of them. We do think, however, that the process of tutors engaging with tutors in critical and reflective analysis of the politics of language and language learning, and of the normalization and privileging of particular discourses and rhetorics, is an integral means by which our writing center makes actionable its commitment to social justice. We see, in other words, that the range of theoretical and pedagogical inquiries we value as scholars, teachers, and tutors of writing are not separate and distinct from our commitments to social justice writ large or to antioppression activism and pedagogy within our institution; they are contiguous with those commitments and essential to them.

Paulo Freire (1993) defines praxis as "reflection and action upon the world in order to transform it" (36). Praxis is not only the practice of making theoretical understanding actionable but also of reflecting carefully and critically upon the relationship of theory to practice in order to extend understanding. In other words, the concept of praxis, as Freire defines it, is the labor of human agents—teachers and learners—who are both public intellectuals and public activists. For a tutor to make pedagogical choices responsibly and responsively, she must be critically engaged with the underlying logics of those choices, the reasons they might be desirable or productive, and for whom. Without this critical reflection, implicit dominant ideological forces will manifest in untroubled, uninterrogated ways in and through our tutoring practice. Tutoring multilingual writers well requires theoretical or philosophical understanding that shapes and is in turn shaped by practical know-how (see Rafoth, this volume).

This kind of praxis requires reading current scholarship broadly, including research from the fields of composition and rhetoric, writing center studies, and TESOL. Tutors should join the communities of scholars inhabiting those fields and contribute to what is known within them. The production of new knowledge within those fields should become part of the work tutors are expected to engage and rewarded for engaging. We learned through the collaborative work of reconceiving tutor education at UNL that there is a critical, recursive relationship between the UNL tutors' knowledge production, their ability to tutor with flexibility and adaptability, and their willingness to bring the complexity of the tutoring moment back to the table as we collectively (re)consider whether or how our principles work in practice (see Hutchinson and Gillespie, this volume).

3. If our fear of failure leads us to inaction, we will have failed catastrophically. If we proceed with courage as well as with an ongoing commitment to learning, we may fail, but we will learn from our failures such that we can keep on and do better next time.

Tutors in the UNL writing center have discussed (and continue to work through) their fear that student-writers will suffer to the extent that tutors explore with them greater ranges of discursive and rhetorical choice. We have agreed that we want to continue these conversations, for we think these fears are understandable and frequently legitimate. With the UNL tutors, we have come to believe, though, that tutors can support writers more effectively by helping them to understand the rhetorical concepts of audience, purpose, and context and to make writerly decisions for themselves. Ultimately, we have come to the conclusion that tutors should reach for high-risk/high-yield practice and be able to recognize the differences between catastrophic pedagogical failures (which, in our experience, are rather few and far between) and learningful pedagogical failures: between failures that produce little or no learning for either writer or tutor and failures that may produce discomfort or frustration but that both tutors and writers can learn from and out of which tutors might produce new tutoring scholarship to be shared within our center during weekly staff-development meetings, at regional and international writing center and composition conferences, and at workshops and seminars for faculty, staff, and students across our university (see Babcock, this volume).

We have learned that high-risk/high-yield tutoring isn't necessarily dramatic, though we know from the stories we have shared in the UNL writing center that it can certainly *feel* quite dramatic at times. We have come to believe, though, that tutors talking openly with multilingual writers about SWAE, and the potential consequences of "fixing" texts rather than enacting rhetorical agency, is unlikely to produce catastrophic failure (see Praphan and Seong, this volume). We have learned that working with writers to find balance together between the contending imperatives for success measured by grades and success measured by learning can yield terrific learning. Silence about the forces that shape the learning experiences of Othered writers in conversations with those writers may feel safer for tutors, but isn't, in actuality, safer for Othered writers or learningful for them.

4. The point of collaborative work on the design and delivery of tutor education is not to construct a standard practice or to produce conformity but to enable, encourage, and support a wide array of approaches to tutoring one-with-one that are open to reflection and revision as we learn both individually and collectively.

None of us are interested in creating tutor education that cultivates writing center tutors who are doctrinaire in their approach to tutoring, nor are we interested in tutors as dogmatists. We recognize with Dinitz and Kiedaisch (2003) that each tutor will bring "to the writing center a unique vision of tutoring, shaped by past experiences as a writer and with other writers, by career goals, personality, values, socio-economic status, politics" (73–74). Without exposure to and critical engagement with scholarship that makes visible the (il)logics of the status quo and that critiques the hidden assumptions and imperatives of dominant perspectives on language, culture, and belonging—on racial, ethnic, and national identification—the tutors of UNL concluded, and we concur, that all of us will, wittingly or not, subject ourselves and the student-writers with whom we work to that status quo. In redesigning ongoing staff education, the UNL tutors never insist that all tutors endorse a particular array of practices or subscribe to (believe in) a particular philosophical orientation toward the work of tutoring one-with-one. The tutors working on the staff-education project did expect that their colleagues and successors would arrive at the philosophical and pedagogical stances they occupy through sustained engagement with past, current, and emerging scholarship—that they would equip themselves with understanding such that they would be able to offer a full and fair account of research that might counter their tutoring philosophies and practices before they discredit or dismiss that research (see Rafoth, this volume). And this, we still believe, is a reasonable expectation.

5. If our aim is to be finished with the problems of racism, xenophobia, and linguistic supremacy, we'll soon lose hope. These are wicked problems, and we aren't going to resolve them from our writing centers or from anywhere anytime soon. If our aim is to keep on keeping on—to learn more and contribute much—we may catch glimpses as we move together of the world we have never known but hope to inhabit one day.

We are learning, however slowly and haltingly, that *finishing* the crafting of our writing center as a house for diversity is not, in fact, our aim. Instead, our aim is to *keep on crafting.* Our aim is collective humility in the face of what we do not yet know, may never know. Our aim is compassion for ourselves and others as we teach and learn together within conditions of inequality. Our aim is continuous resistance of those conditions using those means we have most readily at hand: our understanding of the power of inquiry and our evolving practice of questioning, analyzing, critiquing, experimenting, of sharing and studying our stories together, of articulating what we think we know, recognizing what we do not know or only partly know and opening ourselves up to challenge in service of learning, growth, and transformation.

Questions to Consider

We offer these questions for the purposes of exploration rather than as if they could or should be answered definitively. We hope they will generate dialogue in your writing center as they have been generative in the writing center at UNL.

1. What do you know as a writing center staff about the experiences of multilingual writers at your school, and how could you learn more?

2. What ideas about Standard Written Academic English and linguistic difference shape the individual and collective tutoring practices in use in your writing center?

3. When you consider that your work as a writing center tutor could also be work in service of increasing access, opportunity, and support with and for historically marginalized or excluded populations of students, what do you most worry about or fear? How might you address those fears and move through them individually and/or as a writing center staff?

For Further Reading

Canagarajah, A. Suresh. 2013. *Translingual Practice: Global Englishes and Cosmopolitan Relations.* London: Routledge.

Suresh Canagarajah's book provides an overview of practices writing center tutors can adopt to support multilingual writers. In particular, the methods outlined by Canagarajah will help tutors help writers to produce texts that do not merely conform to SWAE but that also draw creatively and critically upon the multiple discourses and language varieties of the writers.

Conference on College Composition and Communication. 1974. *Students' Right to Their Own Language.* National Council of Teachers of English. http://www.ncte.org/library/NCTEFiles/Groups/CCCC/NewSRTOL.pdf.

First adopted by CCCCs in 1974, this resolution affirms students' right to speak and write in their mother tongues and home dialects. Although controversial when it was first endorsed, the resolution was, in fact, prescient; SRTOL accurately forecasts findings reported in the most current and cutting-edge scholarship on linguistic difference.

Horner, Bruce, Min-Zhan Lu, Jacqueline Jones Royster, and John Trimbur. 2011. "Opinion: Language Difference in Writing: Toward a Translingual Approach." *College English* 73 (2): 303–21. https://louisville.edu/faculty/bmhorn01/Translingual Statement.pdf.

This essay serves as a foundational piece to help tutors (re)consider teaching practices within the writing center; a "translingual" teaching approach, according to Horner et al., "sees difference in language not as a barrier to overcome or as a problem to manage, but as a resource for producing meaning in writing, speaking, reading, and listening" (303).

Norton, Bonny. 2000. *Identity and Language Learning: Gender, Ethnicity and Educational Change.* Harlow, UK: Pearson Longman.

Bonny Norton's book examines the impacts of second language learning on identity. In particular, Norton addresses relations of power between multilingual language learners and realizes the extent to which the teaching of language is never neutral and is always embedded in relationships among language, power, and identity.

Young, Vershawn Ashanti, and Aja Martinez, eds. 2001. *Code Meshing as World English: Pedagogy, Policy, Performance.* Urbana, IL: National Council of Teachers of English.
    This edited collection includes essays tutors may find helpful for understanding how teaching practices might be changed to acknowledge the legitimacy and value of texts composed in World Englishes as well as the theoretical grounding for those changes to pedagogical approaches.

References

Bizzell, Patricia. 2002. "The Intellectual Work of 'Mixed' Forms of Academic Discourses." In *ALT DIS: Alternating Discourses and the Academy,* edited by Christopher Schroeder, Helen Fox, and Patricia Bizzell, 1–10. Portsmouth, NH: Boynton/Cook.

Bonilla-Silva, Eduardo. 2006. *Racism without Racists: Color-blind Racism and the Persistence of Racial Inequality in the United States.* 2nd ed. Lanham, MD: Rowman and Littlefield.

Boquet, Elizabeth H. 2002. *Noise from the Writing Center.* Logan: Utah State University Press.

Condon, Frankie. 2012. *I Hope I Join the Band: Narrative, Affiliation, and Antiracist Rhetoric.* Logan: Utah State University Press.

Dees, Sarah, Beth Godbee, and Moira Ozias. 2007. "Navigating Conversational Turns: Grounding Difficult Discussions on Racism." *Praxis Writing Center Journal* 5 (1).

Denny, Harry C. 2010. *Facing the Center: Toward an Identity Politics of One-To-One Mentoring.* Logan: Utah State University Press.

Dinitz, Sue, and Jean Kiedaisch. 2003. "Creating Theory: Moving Tutors to the Center." *Writing Center Journal* 23 (2): 63–76.

Freire, Paulo. 1993. *Pedagogy of the Oppressed.* New York: Continuum.

Geller, Anne Ellen. 2005. "Tick-Tock, Next: Finding Epochal Time in the Writing Center." *Writing Center Journal* 25 (1): 15–24.

Greenfield, Laura. 2011. "The 'Standard English' Fairytale: A Rhetorical Analysis of Racist Pedagogies and Commonplace Assumptions about Language Diversity." In *Writing Centers and the New Racism: A Call for Sustainable Dialogue and Change,* edited by Laura Greenfield and Karen Rowan, 33–60. Logan: Utah State University Press.

Grill, Jennifer. 2010. "Whose English Counts? Native Speakers as English Language Learners." *TESOL Journal* 1 (3): 358–67. http://dx.doi.org/10.5054/tj.2010.226823.

Nakamaru, Sarah. 2010. "Theory In/To Practice: A Tale of Two Multilingual Writers: A Case-Study Approach to Tutor Education." *Writing Center Journal* 30 (2): 100–23.

Severino, Carol. 2006. "The Sociopolitical Implications of Response to Second-Language and Second-Dialect Writing." In *Second-Language Writing in the Composition Classroom: A Critical Sourcebook,* edited by Paul Kei Matsuda, Michelle Cox, Jay Jordan, and Christina Ortmeier-Hooper, 333–50. Boston: Bedford/St. Martin's.

Turner, Carolyn. 1994. "Guests in Someone Else's House: Students of Color." *Review of Higher Education* 17 (4): 355–70.

Villanueva, Victor. 1993. *Bootstraps: From an American Academic of Color.* Urbana, IL: National Council of Teachers of English.

Wiley, Terrance G., and Marguerite Lukes. 1996. "English-Only and Standard English Ideologies in the U.S." *TESOL Quarterly* 30 (3): 511–35.

Young, Vershawn Ashanti. 2010. "Should Writer's Use They Own English?" *Iowa Journal of Cultural Studies* 12: 110–117.

3
IDENTITY CONSTRUCTION, SECOND LANGUAGE WRITERS, AND THE WRITING CENTER

Michelle Cox

Identities are complex, multiple, contingent, and dynamic. We perform identities, try on identities, resist identities, mask identities, and showcase identities, identities such as student, tutor, mother, teacher, Catholic, Red Sox fan, biker, skier, cashier, bus driver. There are the identities we are born with or inherit—race, ethnicity, gender, socioeconomic class, language, religion. There are identities we create—straight-A student, athlete, musician, knitter. And there are identities that are constructed for us—the many assumptions people make based on our appearance, mannerisms, what we say, and how we say it.

In this chapter, I explore the construction of identity in relation to second language (L2) writers and the writing center. While I have chosen this focus, you should know that identity and second language writing is a broad topic that includes discussions on how L2 identity impacts participation in academic (Chiang and Schmida 1999; Ortmeier-Hooper 2008) and workplace communities (Cox 2010), the flexible and dynamic nature of L2 identities (Harklau 2000; Kanno 2003; Shuck 2010), L2 identity in relation to social context (Ortmeier-Hooper 2010; Schwartz 2010), and issues of power and access in relation to L2 identity (Ibrahim 1999; Norton 2000). While all of these topics have implications for L2 writers in the writing center, identity construction is particularly salient.

In a tutoring session, the task of identity construction begins immediately. In fact, identity construction may start even before the session begins. If the writing center website features profiles of the tutors, the student writer may enter the session with certain impressions of and expectations for the tutor based on the identities represented by and interpreted from these profiles. If the writing center keeps files on

DOI: 10.7330/9781607324140.c003

student writers that include notes from past sessions, the tutor working with an unfamiliar student writer may make assumptions about the focus and dynamics of an upcoming session. Intake forms can also serve to construct a student writer's identity for a tutor, as these forms often ask questions about a student writer's language background. Even a person's name can lead to assumptions about nationality and language. This process of identity construction continues when the tutor and student writer meet, as both will make assumptions about the other's identities based on the person's spoken accent, ethnicity, interactions, and body language.

Identities are also constructed during the session itself as the tutor and student writer learn more about each other, interact, and react. When I tutored in a writing center and asked students why they came to the session, students often answered "because I'm ESL." In these cases, the students were intentionally creating a certain identity. I also had the experience of making tutoring decisions based on my assumptions about L2 students. Some of these decisions led to more effective tutoring, while others limited my view of the student's strengths and areas of knowledge, as I will discuss later in this essay.

Students who use English as a second language (L2) have as many identities as any other student. But they are often identified only by their language status, as if they part of a monolithic group. Ilona Leki (1992) tells us that L2 students "differ so much [from each other] that it is not an exaggeration to say that sometimes the only similarity they share is that they are not native speakers of English" and lists the many identities they may embody:

> ESL students are graduate students and undergraduates; forty-five years old and eighteen years old; highly educated doctors, lawyers, and teachers in their home countries and naïve, inexperienced teenagers; newly arrived immigrants, graduates of U.S. high schools; poor writers in English but good writers in their L1, or illiterate in their L1; those hoping to remain in the United States, those eager to get back home; those extremely critical of life in the United States or U.S. foreign policy and those wholly in support of anything the Unites States does. They are also diverse in their expectations of life in the United States, their financial situations, their willingness to integrate into a new society. (39)

And yet these students are all often lumped together under the heading "ESL student" or another term that refers only to their linguistic identity. In this chapter, I explore terms that have come to be used to identify groups of L2 writers and connotations of these terms, how an understanding of student writers' linguistic histories can impact tutoring, identities tutors may take on during L2 tutoring sessions, and the implications of these identity constructions for the tutor-student writer relationship, perceptions of the student as a writer, and writing center practice. I then discuss steps writing centers can take to better understand their L2 student body and come to a clearer philosophy regarding L2 students.

STUDENT WRITERS' IDENTITIES AND WHY THEY MATTER

In order to talk about L2 students, we must use terms to discuss them, terms that distinguish them from English L1 students (while keeping in mind that the terms only refer to linguistic identity and therefore are necessarily reductionist). One of the most fraught areas for scholars of second language writing is in deciding which of the many available terms to use when writing about these students. In the writing center, too, you'll need to decide what terms to use to talk about L2 students during discussions among writing center staff. Further, if you decide to read more scholarship on L2 writers, you'll need to know that certain terms when used in search databases will call up articles only from a certain era.

You may have noticed that in the above introduction and throughout this chapter, I use the term *L2* (a choice I discuss further below). The above quotes from Leki (1992) include the terms *ESL* and *native speaker*. The other chapters in this collection may use still other terms: *multilingual writer, English-language learner, English as an additional language*. Some terms that refer to linguistic identity were developed to refer to particular groups of L2 students, and others came into use to avoid negative connotations that became associated with older terms. Terms used to identify students who use English as an L2 have implications for how the students are perceived (or, how the student perceives the user of the term) but also provide information useful for tutoring. In this section, I review these terms, discussing each term's history and connotations, and then I discuss how knowing more about a student's linguistic history can impact the work of writing centers.

International students: This term refers to students who come to the United States on a student visa for the purpose of studying in a US college or university. Some of these students are here for a short term, such as a semester or a year. Others are here for entire degree programs. The term *international student* is an appropriate term when referring to visa status but an inappropriate term when referring to linguistic identity, as not all international students use English as a second language. Some of these students come from countries where English is one of the primary languages (such as India), and some of the students from countries where English is not a primary language will have studied abroad or at educational institutions where English is the language of instruction. And not all college students who use English as an L2 are on a student visa. Until the late nineties, the overriding perception of college L2 students was that they were all international students, an identity construction that led to mistaken assumptions about students' knowledge of US culture, experiences with learning writing, and understanding of US academic conventions. In fact, most of the scholarship written on L2 students until the late nineties focused exclusively on international L2 students.

Permanent-resident L2 student. Particularly useful for tutors to know, this term distinguishes between international L2 students and L2 students who live in the United States as residents. This term includes students who were born in the United States and live in a home where a language other than English is used, students who immigrated to the United States during their childhood or adolescence and went to school in the United States, and nontraditionally aged college students who immigrated to the United States as adults (Dana Ferris distinguishes among these groups by referring to those who were born in the United States or immigrated before age eight as "early-arriving resident students" and those who arrived in the United States after age eight as "late-arriving resident students") (see Ferris 2009). This group also includes transnational students (Roberge 2002), students who split their time between the United States and their family's heritage country. These students may spend summers in their family's heritage country or even do part of their schooling in this country. Since the late 1990s, research on resident students has focused on generation 1.5 college students, students still in the process of acquiring English who graduated from US high schools (see Harklau, Losey, and Siegal 1999). This research has uncovered important differences in the ways in which international students and resident L2 students have learned English, their attitudes towards English, and their literacy histories—all important factors in writing development and identity. For instance, Joy Reid (2006) has described international students as "eye learners," as these students have learned English primarily through their eyes—through reading textbooks, doing grammar exercises, and translating texts. In contrast, she describes resident L2 students as "ear" learners, as they have learned English primarily through their ears by listening to spoken English and US media and by interacting with peers. Due to these differences in how English is learned, international L2 students often write with a more formal academic style, while permanent-resident L2 students often write with a looser style more akin to spoken English. A tutor may have difficulty identifying a resident L2 student as L2 at first. Often, these students wear Western-style clothing, are adept at idiomatic English, and are familiar with US pop culture and history. Their strengths in speaking English may mask their linguistic history and cause tutors (and faculty) to be surprised when they read resident L2 students' writing, which often contains L2 markers as well as idiomatic English.

English as a second language (ESL): This term refers to any student who uses English as a second (third, fourth, etc.) language. This is the term with the longest history on this list. Because of this longevity, it is the term that is the most recognizable but that also comes with the most baggage. This term has been challenged for several reasons. First, numbering the languages a writer uses can be problematic, as some writers will use more than one "first language," and even for those who have one first language, the writer may have learned English not second, but third, fourth, and so forth. To address this possibility, the term *English as an additional language* emerged but, perhaps due the acronym. but never really caught on in the US, though it is widely used in Canada, the UK, and Australia. Second, the term can be seen as putting undue emphasis on English, implying that this language has more status than the student's other languages. Third, the term *ESL* implies that English is not used as a primary language, when, in fact, English becomes the primary language for many L2 writers for use in certain domains. Indeed, for many resident L2 students, English becomes the primary language for civic, business, and academic purposes. For many international L2 scholars, English becomes their only language for academic reading and writing. This term has also come to be associated with English-language support programs at US secondary schools. Because many resident L2 students in college have exited ESL programs during secondary school (or earlier), they often no longer want to be identified with this term. As research by Christina Ortmeier-Hooper (2008) and others has shown, they often see themselves as no longer ESL. However, international students typically do not have negative associations with this term and have often been told to use the term *ESL* when searching for language support at US colleges and universities. Until a tutor knows whether the student is an international or resident L2 writer, they should refrain from using this term.

Second language (L2): This term was first used to broaden what was then ESL writing studies to include research in other linguistic contexts in which a language other than English is used as the L2 (3, 4, etc.). This term is also used to demarcate the field dedicated to studying writing in an L2, second language writing studies (SLW). Because I do research in this area, I often use the term *L2* in order to associate my work with this field of study. You may have also noticed that *L2* is the term of choice in this collection, as the editors asked contributors to use this term for the sake of consistency. A benefit of this term is that it doesn't carry the same baggage as the term *ESL*. In my experience as a teacher of L2 sections of first-year composition, I have found that resident L2 students tend not to take issue with the term *L2* as they seem not to associate it with *ESL*. However, *L2* retains some of the same problems associated with the term *ESL*: it asserts that English is the second language learned by the writer, implies that English has more status than other languages, and implies that English is not one of the writer's primary languages. Another problem with this term is that it is less precise than the term *ESL*. For instance, my research and teaching are entirely focused on students who use English as a second language, not students who use French or Spanish or another language as a second language. And yet I call myself an L2 writing specialist when, technically, I am an ESL writing specialist.

Native English speaker/nonnative English speaker (NES/NNES): These terms are used to avoid the problems associated with numbering languages. The term *native speaker* refers to a speaker who learned English as their first language and, implicitly, to an English user who was born in what Braj Kachru (1985) has called an "inner circle" country in his delineation of World Englishes: the United States, Anglophone Canada, the United Kingdom, Australia, New Zealand, and Ireland. Nonnative speakers include speakers of English who learned English as an additional language (and were not born in one of Kachru's inner-circle countries). These terms have fallen out of favor, largely due to Kachru's work on World Englishes. Kachru also identified two other circles: the outer circle (countries where English has a historical or governmental role, including such countries as India, Malaysia, and Pakistan) and the expanding circle (countries where English is gaining prominence but does not have a historical or governmental role, including such countries as China, South Korea, and much of Europe). So, a person from the outer circle may use English as one of their first languages, but, according to this term, would not be seen as a native speaker. In other words, the term *NES* is used to describe a person born in a Western country (i.e., the UK), but not in a country where English was brought in through colonization (i.e., India) or through language contact (i.e., China). However, you will still see these terms used in the literature, particularly *NES*, largely because there are few terms available to refer to students who use English as a first language (the only terms I know of are *English L1*, which is often shortened to *L1*, and *English monolingual*, a term that makes assumptions about the students' proficiencies with languages other than English). *NES* and *NNES* are terms often used by international students during tutoring sessions, though, who will ask tutors to tell them how a native speaker of English would express a certain idea.

Limited English proficient (LEP)/English-language learner (ELL): If you are an education major or minor, you have probably encountered these terms, as they are the terms currently used by the US Department of Education to categorize L2 students. Based on language proficiency assessment, L2 students are labeled either *LEP* or *ELL*. Students can move from *LEP* to *ELL* (by improving scores on proficiency exams), but once labeled *ELL*, the label sticks throughout their K–12 education, becoming an identity that continues to follow the students even when they no longer need English-language support. This label can be a problem for students who no longer want to be identified as such but also a problem for educators who want to best serve these students. A student who reaches ELL proficiency in elementary school has a different literacy profile than one who reaches ELL proficiency in the sophomore year of high school, and yet when they enter senior English class, they both bear the same label. It is unlikely that student writers will use these terms to identify themselves, but they are still good terms to know, as they come up in the literature on L2 writing, particularly scholarship based in K–12 contexts. Also, faculty sometimes use these terms to avoid the more problematic terms available.

Multilingual learner (MLL): This is a term that has gained favor lately; it avoids some of the problems associated with other terms on this list, as it does not number languages and seems to come with only positive connotations. One issue with this term, though, is its vagueness. It refers to anyone who uses multiple languages, so it also includes students who use English as an L1 and study other languages. It is, in other words, an umbrella term, one that could potentially be used to refer to all students at a college or university if the institution has a foreign-language requirement. However, in some of the literature, scholars use the term *multilingual* to only refer to L2 students. This term is a safe one to use with both international and resident L2 students, as it won't offend either group, but it may be unfamiliar to them. For instance, if this term is used on a writing center website, international students looking for language support may not see it as applying to them and therefore may not identify the writing center as a place that offers them support.

The truth is that all of these terms, while important vocabulary for tutors to be familiar with, can come to have negative connotations.

Suresh Canagarajah (2002) has written about the "difference-as-deficit" perspective of L2 writers, a perspective that focuses on what L2 writers cannot yet do with English and does not recognize these students' strengths with language and literacy across multiple languages, including English. Indeed, students who enter the writing center and immediately proclaim themselves ESL, as if this one designation explains all of their challenges with writing, may have internalized this deficit perspective.

Once internalized, this deficit perspective may negatively impact a student's conception of self as a writer and user of English, a student's goals for writing and using English, and how the student perceives readers of their work. For instance, in my case study of an international L2 graduate student from South Korea in a communication science and disorders master's program (Cox 2010), Min interpreted all supervisor feedback on her writing as comments on English-language issues. In my analysis of the comments, it was clear that her supervisors sometimes did comment on language issues but more often sought to share with Min discipline-specific discourse and style. While Min saw these comments as a response to her identity as an ESL student, they were, in fact, a response to her identity as a newcomer to the field. As I stated in my chapter on this study (Cox 2010), "Min's interpretation of the feedback as commenting on her ability to write correctly in English further chip[ped] away at her confidence as an English language user and negatively affect[ed] her vision of herself as a novice professional" (89). The ways in which we interpret others' constructions of our identities affect how we construct our own identities.

A deficit perspective may lead a tutor to use an approach to tutoring that Carol Severino (1993) has called the "assimilationist approach," in which the tutor attempts to reshape the student's writing so it matches that of an English L1 writer. This approach is sometimes rhetorically appropriate, such as when the student is engaged in high-stakes writing with inflexible standards, such as resume writing, but when the assimilationist approach is motivated not by the rhetorical situation but by an assumption that all differences in the student's writing are deficits, this approach can be damaging. It sends the message that only native-like English is valued, and writing in native-like English is an unattainable goal for most L2 students without the help of an English L1 writer (Silva, Leki, and Carson 1997). Further, it implies that a written accent—indicated by such markers as missing or incorrect articles, pluralization, verb endings, and prepositions—should not remain on the page, though written accent can be seen as a display of identity. Consider, for instance, this statement, made by an undergraduate international student from

Bulgaria who was part of Terry Myers Zawacki and Anna Sophia Habib's study of L2 students writing across the curriculum:

> When you ultimately succeed in writing is when you have your own accent. When I speak, my accent reflects who I am and where I come from. Well, I want my writing to reflect me in that way. (Zawacki and Habib 2010, 70)

For this student, an assimilationist approach to tutoring does not "correct" a student's writing but eradicates signs of the student's identity and heritage.

IMPLICATIONS OF STUDENT WRITERS' LINGUISTIC HISTORIES FOR TUTORING

Identifying a student as L2 can lead to more effective tutoring decisions as well as help tutors avoid problematic assumptions.

Let me start by sharing a story from my teaching, a story that has implications for tutoring. When I taught sections of first-year composition as a graduate student at the University of New Hampshire, I worked with a student I'll call Steve. I remember thinking that this student was lazy, due to the number of errors in his writing and I was perplexed by his apparent sloppiness because he otherwise came across as a dedicated student: he was always polite, came to class on time and prepared, and met every deadline. Years later, after I graduated and attained my first faculty position, I came across his essays while unpacking. By this point, I had studied SLW and had more experience working with linguistically diverse students. I was floored when I realized that the errors I had noticed were actually L2 markers: missing verb endings, missing articles, incorrect prepositions. The student was likely a resident L2 student, one who was so fluent with spoken English that I missed the fact that he wrote with an accent. Had I known Steve was an L2 student, I would have been a more effective writing teacher for him, reading, responding to, and assessing his writing with more sensitivity.

Though I do not remember noticing anything about his cultural background in Steve's writing, writers' cultural backgrounds can also impact the ways in which they make rhetorical decisions—how they organize text, make an argument, and relate to readers (an area of research called *contrastive rhetoric*, a topic more fully explored by Valerie Balester, this volume). If a reader does not know a student is writing from a non-US rhetorical tradition, the text can appear haphazard and disorganized. In fact, it can be disorienting for US academic readers to read texts that don't follow US academic rhetorical conventions. Knowing a student uses English as an L2 can help a reader suspend their expectations and read the paper on the paper's own terms, reading to understand the logic behind the organization rather than reading to impose US academic conventions (for more on this, see Matsuda and Cox 2009).

Understanding whether an L2 student is an international student or a resident student can also be helpful when making decisions about approaches to tutoring. International students often have strengths in understanding English grammar and are familiar with the language used to describe grammar. Further, they are typically not embarrassed by grammatical errors but see them as a natural part of language learning. International L2 students are often adept at comparing US educational culture with the educational systems of their home countries and may find conversations comparing how they learned to write in their L1 and in English in their home countries with US writing practices and instruction to be illuminating. However, international L2 students, particularly those who have not yet spent much time in an English-medium setting, typically haven't yet developed an intuitive sense of the language. Therefore, approaches like asking the student to read the paper aloud will typically be ineffective and may even distract the student from their writing, as their focus will turn to pronunciation (Matsuda and Cox 2009, 47). The Socratic approach often used in writing centers, where tutors ask student writers open-ended questions about their writing, may also not be effective, as these questions typically rely on an intuitive sense of the language (see Harris and Silva 1993 for alternative strategies).

Resident students' strengths lie in their proficiency with spoken English. The many techniques tutors have for using talk to support writing are often effective for these students. Asking the student to read their writing aloud is also an effective technique for these students. Not only does this approach allow the student to draw on their intuitive sense of the language, it also allows the tutor to understand the ways in which the student is drawing on spoken English when writing. For instance, by hearing the writer's spoken accent, a tutor may see that a word that appears as an odd choice or misspelling may in fact be a phonetic representation of another word. Resident students are also typically adept at thinking rhetorically, as they have had to negotiate many rhetorical situations in the United States to make it to college. Tutors can draw on this knowledge when focusing on higher-order concerns such as organization and rhetorical moves. Resident L2 writers may, though, be sensitive about errors in their writing, so the tutor may want to use care when addressing issues of grammar and usage, the same care that would be used with an English L1 student. For instance, rather than assume the writer isn't familiar with English grammar and usage, the tutor might ask questions that help the tutor see if the student has made a performance error or an error due to lack of knowledge. Further, resident L2 students may be offended if the tutor attempts to act as a cultural informant, an identity tutors may come to inhabit during sessions with L2 students (described further below). Some resident L2 students work hard to "pass" as US L1 students; any comment that implies they are seen as foreigners will likely be met with disgruntlement.

A problem related to all the terms I described above is the danger of using the term as the sole identifier of the student. Doing so elides the many strengths and areas of knowledge the student has as a member of a discipline, a college student, a writer in many languages, and a rhetorician, strengths and areas of knowledge that may be used as resources during tutoring. Identifying a student with only one term may also prevent the tutor from finding common ground with the student, an important part of creating a productive tutor-student relationship. Tutors often tell me about their anxieties related to working with L2 student writers. They fear that the tutoring approaches they have found effective with English L1 students will not work with L2 students. While it is true that tutors need to adjust their approach for each student they meet, the differences in tutoring L2 students may not be as extreme as these tutors fear if they recognize that these students are not just L2 students; they are also students trying to develop an effective writing process, express themselves in ways seen as effective in different disciplines, negotiate often opaque assignment descriptions, find out how readers will respond to a draft, and learn how to use past writing experiences when facing new ones—the same challenges all student writers face. If tutors identify L2 students by their multiple experiences as students and writers as much as they identify them by their linguistic backgrounds, anxieties will ease.

TUTOR IDENTITIES AND WHY THEY MATTER

Not only the identities constructed by and for L2 students matter during tutoring sessions; the identities of the tutors matter as well. In writing center literature on tutoring L2 writers, a number of these identities have been written about, including cultural informant, rhetorical informant, and linguistic informant (see, for instance, Harris and Silva 1993). These identities may be ones tutors choose to take on in response to their own construction of the L2 student's identity or may be ones an L2 student expects of the tutor. In this section, I discuss these three tutor identities and their implications for tutoring L2 writers.

Cultural informant: Tutors take on the identity of cultural informant when they inform a student writer about US culture, US academic culture, or the culture of a specific discipline (Blau and Hall 2002; see also Balester, this volume). They may take on this role when they perceive that lack of cultural knowledge is preventing the L2 student from writing effectively or when they seek to promote cross-cultural understanding.

Rhetorical informant: Tutors take on the identity of rhetorical informant when they inform a student writer about the rhetorical situation of a writing task, which includes the roles, characteristics, and relationships among reader(s), context, genre, and the writer. Tutors may adopt this role when they perceive the L2 student to be unfamiliar with US academic culture or writing conventions.

Linguistic informant: Tutors take on the role of linguistic informant when they describe English grammar, usage, and vocabulary to the student writer. Tutors may adopt this role when they perceive that the cause of errors in the student's writing is a lack of knowledge about English structure and vocabulary.

As discussed by Harris and Silva (1993), these roles, which tutors may take on during any session, may be more prevalent in sessions with L2 writers. Indeed, all writers need an understanding of the cultural, rhetorical, and linguistic contexts in which they are writing in order to write effectively. Further, as shown in studies by Leki (1995, 1999, 2007) on students writing across the curriculum and by Joy Reid and Barbara Kroll on their analyses of US college writing assignments, many assignments assume knowledge of US history, popular culture, and politics (Reid and Kroll 1995). In addition, many college writing assignments implicitly require knowledge of US writing culture, including ways in which writing is taught in the United States and rhetorical patterns preferred by US academic readers. For instance, how many times have college students heard professors tell them to "forget the five-paragraph essay learned in high school"? How many college professors simply expect students to use thesis-driven, deductive, and heavily cited arguments without making these expectations clear? Tutors who take on the roles of cultural, rhetorical, and linguistic informants and share their insider's perspective may be providing important information to L2 students, information that helps level the playing field for these students.

However, tutors must take care to be sure these roles are desired by the student writer. To ensure that the tutor's assumptions about a student writer's linguistic identity aren't getting in the way, the tutor may ask the student writer questions about the decisions they have made as a writer. For instance, if the tutor notices the student has written an argument organized inductively with the thesis implied towards the end of the essay, the tutor could stop and ask the student why they made this choice. If the students says, "This is the way arguments are written in my country," the tutor can proceed to take on the role of a rhetorical informant and discuss thesis-driven deductive arguments.

Further, the roles of cultural, rhetorical, and linguistic informants do not need to be reserved for the tutor. Indeed, the tutor can also encourage L2 student writers to take on these identities during a session. L2 students, who have traversed multiple cultural, educational, rhetorical, and linguistic landscapes, can often compare cultures, educational systems, rhetorical preferences, and language systems. These comparisons can help these students become more aware of differences across these areas and more aware of the reasons behind their own decisions as writers. Tutors may also help L2 students draw on these areas of knowledge to negotiate US-centric writing assignments, a move Leki (1995) observed. She noticed that L2 students, in order to succeed, often "rewrit[e] the terms" to make an assignment more manageable by drawing on knowledge of their home country or culture (243). For instance, an assignment that asks for a rhetorical analysis of a commercial may be "rewritten" to focus on a commercial in the student's L1, or may focus on a US commercial in English but be explicitly analyzed using the perspective of a person from the student's home country. Such a stance would empower L2 students, allowing them to draw on knowledge other students in the class may not have. Encouraging L2 students to draw on these areas of knowledge can help them become more confident students and more independent writers. Further, these approaches to tutoring shift the tutor's identity from informant to collaborator—a role that shifts the dynamic of the session from the unilateral provision of knowledge from the tutor to the tutee to the bilateral exchange of ideas and knowledge.

WRITTEN ACCENT: A MATTER OF IDENTITY OR WRITING THAT REQUIRES EDITING?

Written accent is one of the most fraught issues related to L2 writing and identity. Just as an L2 student is expected to speak with an accent, an L2 student writes with an accent, an accent that is made visible through such markers as missing or incorrect articles, verb endings, and prepositions. Editing this accent out of a student writer's text in effect renders their identity as an L2 writer invisible. And yet leaving these markers in the text may leave the student vulnerable to criticism or a lower grade. What should the tutor do in this case?

In my own practice as a tutor, I work with the L2 student to make this decision. There are circumstances in which a written accent can be detrimental to the student. These circumstances include high-stakes writing tasks, such as applications, resumes, and grant proposals, as well as situations the student sees as high stakes. For instance, in a recent tutoring session, I questioned a student on the reasons she wanted my assistance in editing an assigned blog entry, which to me seemed like a low-stakes activity. She explained that while the teacher would not mark down the blog entry for grammar or syntax, she knew that her classmates, who would also be reading the blog entries, were critical and judgmental of L2 students.

However, there are contexts in which written accent would either not be seen as detrimental or would be seen as positive. When writers are working on low-stakes writing activities, such as reading responses, journal entries, and first drafts of essays and papers, tutors should not assume the student will be assessed based on grammar and syntax, as these kinds of activities focus on learning and thinking as the main objectives. Creative writing, including creative nonfiction, is often enhanced by the inclusion of written accent. Asking the student writer about the rhetorical context of the writing assignment and how it will be evaluated could help the student assess the importance of editing·the piece for written accent.

There are also circumstances in which elimination of written accent in a student writer's text may have detrimental effects for the student. If an instructor is accustomed to reading texts from the student that contain L2 markers, suddenly seeing writing from the same student without these markers may make the instructor suspicious of some type of academic dishonesty. Indeed, one theory for the reasons multilingual students are more often charged with plagiarism than L1 English students is that it is easier to detect "copied" passages in L2 writing: instructors often simply identify passages that does not contain written accent. Further, Carol Severino (2009), in "Avoiding Appropriation," warns writing center tutors not to mask the linguistic proficiency of a student writer: "Intermediate ESL students should not come across as advanced on a paper after a few trips to the writing center" (59). One reason Severino gives for this advice is that writing that too closely reads as writing by an English L1 student may cause a teacher to expect the student to be more familiar with US academic culture, pop culture, and/or history than the student actually is. Also, this masking of the student's English proficiency also masks the student's growth as an English user. Comparing past writing to present writing is one way students measure their growth as writers, in any language.

One approach tutors may use is to encourage student writers to see the presence of written accent in a positive light, as did the international student from Bulgaria included in Zawacki and Habib's (2010) study (see above). This student feels pride in her ability to write in multiple languages and pride in her written accent's reflection of her identity. This feeling of pride in L2 identity is one I believe writing centers should foster. Leki (1992), in a book on L2 writers for faculty across the curriculum, encourages this same perspective.

> ESL students can become very fluent writers of English, but they may never become indistinguishable from a native speaker, and it is unclear why they should. A current movement among ESL writing teachers is to argue that, beyond a certain level of proficiency in English writing, it is not the students' texts that need to change; rather it is the native-speaking readers and evaluators (particularly in educational institutions) that need to learn to read more broadly, with a more cosmopolitan, less parochial eye. The infusion of life brought by these ESL students' different perspectives on the world can only benefit a pluralistic society which is courageous enough truly to embrace its definition of itself. (132–33)

I realize tutors are in the position of helping students meet rhetorical contexts the tutors themselves cannot control, rhetorical contexts often determined by faculty. But tutors may help L2 students resee those contexts. Research has shown that some faculty, especially those experienced with reading L2 texts, are able to read past indicators of written accent to focus on what the student is communicating through their writing (see, for example, Vann, Meyer, and Lorenz 1984; Zawacki and Habib 2014). Asking questions about how a particular instructor responded to and evaluated past writing can help both tutor and student determine the instructor's sensitivity to written accent. Discussing differences in students' writing as markers of "written accent" may also help the students resee their own writing.

NEXT STEPS FOR WRITING CENTERS

In this chapter I have discussed steps tutors can take during sessions to learn about L2 student writers' multiple identities, draw on L2 writers' cultural, educational, rhetorical, and linguistic knowledge, and explore the rhetorical context of an assignment in terms of written accent. In this concluding section, I explore what a writing center can do to learn more about L2 clients and create a climate within the center that is, to use Leki's (1992) words, "courageous enough truly to embrace its definition of [a pluralistic society]" (133).

Learn more about L2 writers. There are a few approaches writing centers can use to learn more about L2 writers. They can hire more L2 tutors so the writing center can benefit from these students' perspectives on multilingualism and L2 student identity. English L1 writing center tutors can make an effort to befriend more L2 students in their classes and on campus, to get to know L2 students more personally. The writing center can also maintain richer files on L2 student writers. These files may include information on the student's linguistic and educational background as well as the student's field of study, goals as a writer, and challenges as a writer, plus samples of the student's writing and notes on the tutor's observations during sessions. Writing centers that only identify L2 students by checking off *ESL* in a student's file are limiting a tutor's view of the student, focusing on the student's identity as an L2 writer rather than their rich experiences with multiple languages, cultures, rhetorics, educational systems, and literacies.

Gather data on the institution's population of L2 students. Gathering existing data from multiple offices can help create a picture of the L2 students on campus. All institutions maintain data on international students that include their countries of origin and their majors. Some institutions share this information through their websites while others only provide the barest of data (such as the percentage of overall international students). In these cases, the writing center director may need to request the data from the institution's office of institutional research. Few institutions collect data on residential L2 students, as this data cannot be gathered during the admissions process due to the risk of discrimination. Some first-year writing programs gather this information, so it is worth contacting the writing program administrator. You might also contact the campus diversity office and ESL office or program, if there is one, to find out whether they collect information on L2 students.

Conduct a needs assessment to learn more about how students and faculty perceive the needs of the institution's L2 students. This needs assessment may include surveys of both L2 students and faculty to learn more about L2 students' language and literacy strengths and needs, perspectives on campus-climate issues, and perspectives on the kinds of support from which L2 students would most benefit (see the appendix for a survey I developed, a needs assessment of international graduate students at Dartmouth College; while this survey was not designed for use by a writing center, the types of questions asked may serve as useful models). Conducting a needs assessment that explores the ways in which L2 students use languages in different rhetorical and literacy contexts could provide rich profiles of the students as language users.

Explore the ways in which the writing center identifies and represents L2 writers. What terms are used to identify these students during staff meetings? How are L2 writers represented in tutoring materials and on the writing center website? What information is gathered in the intake form and a student writer's file, and how would this information construct a student's identity? Transcripts of sessions can also be great sources of information. Analyses of transcripts could explore how an L2 student constructs their own identity as a language user and writer, how an L2 student constructs the tutor's identity, assumptions made by the tutor about the L2 student, identities the tutor and student writer adopted in relation to each other, tutoring practices the tutor chose when working with L2 students, and how the L2 students reacted to these practices.

Use the data you collect to develop a writing center philosophy on L2 writers. Conversations on this philosophy might address the following questions: What terms will the writing center use to identify L2 writers? What identities will tutors take in relation to L2 student writers? What position does the writing center take in relation to written accent? How do L2 writers fit into the writing center's overall mission? How does the writing center want to be identified by L2 students? What vision of L2 writing and writers does the writing center want to endorse to the larger campus community? What role does the writing center want to play in larger campus conversations about linguistic and cultural diversity?

Answers to these questions can help a writing center come to a clearer philosophy regarding L2 students, a philosophy that can then inform practice, enhance L2 students' perceptions of the writing center, and allow the writing center to become a campus leader in endorsing an inclusive and progressive vision of L2 writing and writers.

Questions to Consider:

1. In this chapter, the discussion on terminology focuses on tutees, but what terms should be used for the tutors? Would it be useful for the writing center to identify tutors who specialize in tutoring L2 writers, tutors who use English as an additional language, and tutors who have studied languages other than English? If so, what terms should be used to identify them? (For an exploration of tutoring in languages other than English, see Dvorak, this volume).

2. As discussed in this chapter, tutors often must make difficult decisions related to "written accent." How do you make decisions on handling written accent during a tutoring session?

3. Examine the ways in which L2 students' identities are constructed through writing center texts: the writing center's website, promotional materials, advertised services, and texts within the writing center itself (i.e., posters, handbooks, posted notices). Based on these materials, how might an L2 student perceive the writing center's perspective on L2 students?

4. What vision of L2 writing and writers would you want the writing center to endorse to the larger campus community? How might the writing center endorse this vision?

For Further Reading

Cox, Michelle, Jay Jordan, Christina Ortmeier-Hooper, and Gwen Gray Schwartz. 2010. Introduction to *Reinventing Identities in Second Language Writing*, edited Michelle Cox, Jay Jordan, Christina Ortmeier-Hooper, and Gwen Gray Schwartz, xv–xxviii. Urbana, IL: National Council of Teachers of English.

This introduction provides a succinct overview about the ways in which identity has been theorized and researched in composition studies and in second language writing studies.

Chiang, Yuet-Sim, and Mary Schmida. 1999. "Language Identity and Language Ownership: Linguistic Conflicts of First-Year University Writing Students." In *Generation 1.5 Meets College Composition: Issues in the Teaching of Writing to U.S.-Educated Learners of ESL*, edited Linda Harklau, Kay M. Losey, and Mary Siegal, 81–96. Mahwah, NJ: Erlbaum.

In a landmark collection that shifted attention in the field of SLW studies from international L2 students to permanent resident L2 students, Yuet-Sim Chiang and Mary Schmida explore the ways in which L2 students in first-year composition courses self-identify as ESL. As they discovered, students describe themselves as ESL to not only refer to proficiency in a language other than English but also to refer to cultural heritage, and sometimes they have little to no proficiency with what they see as their first language. This article raises important questions about what it means, to students, to "be ESL."

Ortmeier-Hooper, Christina. 2008. "English May Be My Second Language, but I'm Not 'ESL.'" *College Composition and Communication* 59 (3): 389–419.

Adding to the conversation about what it means, to students, to "be ESL," Christina Ortmeier-Hooper follows three L2 students enrolled in mainstream sections of first-year composition and analyzes the ways in which these students perform their linguistic identities in their writing and negotiate their classroom identities as ESL—sometimes intentionally constructing their identities as ESL and other times resisting the ways in which the instructor or writing program position them as ESL.

Reid, Joy. (1998) 2006. "'Eye' Learners and 'Ear' Learners: Identifying the Needs of International Students and US Resident Writers." In *Second-Language Writing in the Composition Classroom: A Critical Sourcebook*, edited by Paul Kei Matsuda, Michelle Cox, Jay Jordan, and Christina Ortmeier-Hooper, 76–89. Boston: Bedford/St. Martin's.

While the two above articles explore identity construction in relation to L2 students, this article points to the reason it's important for tutors to learn about student writers' linguistic and education histories; research has shown that the differences in the ways in which international L2 students and permanent resident L2 students have learned English have real implications for the ways they write in English in college.

Appendix
Needs Assessment of International Graduate Students

Default Question Block

Dartmouth International Graduate Students - Spring 2013

Arts & Science Graduate Studies and the Institute for Writing and Rhetoric are conducting a study to better understand the language strengths and needs of Dartmouth's international graduate students. Results from this study will be used to develop more comprehensive and effective language support programs and will contribute to our knowledge in the fields of writing studies and English Language Teaching.

Participation in the survey is voluntary; choosing not to participate will not impact your role at Dartmouth in any way. The survey should take no more than 10 minutes to complete and is completely confidential. You will not be individually identified in any way.

Survey results will be made available to survey participants later this summer.

Thank you for your participation.

Block 1

Part I: My Background

1. What language(s) are used in your home:

2. What is your educational background?

	Primary (school years 1-6)	Secondary (years 7-12)	Undergraduate (years 13-16)	Graduate (years 17+)
Location of school (name of country)				
Primary language(s) used in school				
Language(s) studied in school				

Block 2

Part II: How I Use Language

3. Please indicate your current language use below. For each language you list in the left column, indicate how well you understand and communicate in this language.

	Understanding spoken language			Understanding written language			Communicating through speaking			Communicating through writing		
	Not well	Fairly well	Very well	Not well	Fairly well	Very well	Not well	Fairly well	Very well	Not well	Fairly well	Very well
1. English	O	O	O	O	O	O	O	O	O	O	O	O
2.	O	O	O	O	O	O	O	O	O	O	O	O
3.	O	O	O	O	O	O	O	O	O	O	O	O

Figure 3.1.

4.		O	O	O	O	O	O	O	O	O	O	O	O
5.		O	O	O	O	O	O	O	O	O	O	O	O

4. To what degree do you currently use English in the following situations?

	Never	Occasionally	Often	Always	N/A
Talking about topics related to my field	O	O	O	O	O
Talking with family	O	O	O	O	O
Talking with friends	O	O	O	O	O
Reading academic texts (e.g. research articles, monographs)	O	O	O	O	O
Reading for information (e.g. research articles, news articles)	O	O	O	O	O
Reading on the web (e.g. blogs, websites)	O	O	O	O	O
Reading for pleasure (e.g. literary writing)	O	O	O	O	O
Writing formal academic texts (e.g. term papers, tests)	O	O	O	O	O
Writing informal academic texts (e.g. taking notes, brainstorming)	O	O	O	O	O
Writing for the web (e.g. blog, website)	O	O	O	O	O
Writing for pleasure (e.g. poetry, diary)	O	O	O	O	O
Writing to friends (e.g. email, letters)	O	O	O	O	O
Dreaming	O	O	O	O	O

Block 3

Part III: Campus Climate

5. To what extent do you agree with the following statements?

	Not at all	Somewhat	Strongly	N/A Do not know
I feel confident speaking during class discussions.	O	O	O	O
My professors value my contributions during class discussions as much as the contributions of students from the U.S.	O	O	O	O
When grading my papers, professors take into account my language skills and refrain from penalizing me for errors in grammar and syntax.	O	O	O	O
When grading my papers, professors take into account my cultural background and refrain from penalizing me for using ways of arguing, organizing text, and relating to the reader preferred by my culture.	O	O	O	O
I feel that professors value what I bring to my academic work as a multilingual and multicultural student.	O	O	O	O
When I participate in group projects, students from the U.S. value my written contributions as much as those of U.S. peers.	O	O	O	O
When I participate in group projects, students from the U.S. value my spoken contributions as much as those of U.S. peers.	O	O	O	O
Peers from the U.S. are welcoming to me and feel comfortable socializing with me.	O	O	O	O
Overall, I feel that perceived differences in my writing and speech as a multilingual student are valued at Dartmouth.	O	O	O	O
Overall, I feel welcomed and valued for the cultural perspectives I bring to the classroom as an international student at Dartmouth.	O	O	O	O

Block 4

Part IV: Goals as an English Language User

Figure 3.2.

6. To what extent do the following statements represent your goals as an English language user?

	Not at all	Somewhat	Closely
To communicate like students who use English as a first language, producing "error-free" English when writing and speaking	O	O	O
To communicate like students in the US, using ways of arguing, organizing text, and relating to readers preferred by US readers	O	O	O
To communicate well enough to meet the speaking and writing demands of graduate study in the U.S. (although my speaking and writing may not be "error-free")	O	O	O
To blend my cultural ways of communicating with U.S. ways of communicating (i.e. ways of arguing, organizing text, relating to readers)	O	O	O
To retain differences in my speaking and writing due to my accent and culturally-preferred ways of arguing, organizing text, and relating to readers.	O	O	O

7. What are your goals following your graduate degree? *(Check all that apply)*

☐ To pursue further study (another degree or a post-doc) in the U.S.

☐ To pursue further study in a university outside of the U.S.

☐ To be employed in a non-academic position in the U.S.

☐ To be employed in a non-academic position outside of the U.S.

☐ To be employed in an academic position (i.e. lecturer, tenure-track faculty) in the U.S.

☐ To be employed in an academic position outside of the U.S.

☐ To publish scholarship in English.

☐ To publish scholarship in a language other than English.

Block 5

Part V: Support Services for Multilingual International Graduate Students

8. To what extent would you benefit from additional support in the following areas?

	Not at all	Somewhat	Greatly
Writing papers for courses	O	O	O
Writing theses and dissertations	O	O	O
Writing conference proposals, abstracts, and papers	O	O	O
Writing for publication	O	O	O
Writing job/internship letters of application and resumes	O	O	O
Developing effective presentations (i.e. for courses and/or conferences)	O	O	O
Strategies for writing (e.g. developing a more effective writing process, analyzing sample texts from the field to learn field-specific language)	O	O	O
Strategies for reading academic texts (e.g. developing a more effective reading process, learning field-specific strategies for reading)	O	O	O
Practice with non-academic spoken English	O	O	O
Practice with non-academic written English	O	O	O

Please provide any additional comments related to support services.

9. To what extent would you benefit from the following types of support?

Figure 3.3.

	Not at all	Somewhat	Greatly
A workshop series on aspects of academic writing, reading, and presenting	O	O	O
A graduate course for international students that focuses on academic writing, reading, and presenting	O	O	O
Regular meetings with peers for peer review of academic and professional writing	O	O	O
Regular meetings with peers for practicing non-academic English (written and spoken)	O	O	O
Regular meetings with peers for discussing non-academic reading (i.e. novels, non-fiction books)	O	O	O

Please provide any additional comments related to support services.

[ ]

10. How often have you used the following kinds of English language/writing support during your graduate study at Dartmouth?

	Please indicate how often you used the support/program.				If this helped, how did it meet your goals as an English language user?
	Never (I was not aware of it.)	Never (I did not use it.)	Sometimes	Often	Please type in your answer.
I have met with					
+ the Multilingual Specialist (Michelle Cox or Judith Hertog) to work on: ++ academic writing	O	O	O	O	[ ]
++ professional writing (e.g. a conference proposal, a resume)	O	O	O	O	[ ]
++ a presentation	O	O	O	O	[ ]
+ a peer tutor at RWIT	O	O	O	O	[ ]
+ the Graduate Career Services Office to work on professional writing (e.g. resume, application letter)	O	O	O	O	[ ]
+ Cindy Tobery in DCAL for feedback on teaching-related materials	O	O	O	O	[ ]
I have participated in + the LACE (Language and Cultural Exchange) Program	O	O	O	O	[ ]
+ a peer writing group (i.e. a group that meets to give feedback on each other's writing)	O	O	O	O	[ ]
I have asked for feedback on my writing from + peers who use English as a first language	O	O	O	O	[ ]
+ peers who do not use English as a first language	O	O	O	O	[ ]
+ a professor	O	O	O	O	[ ]
I have had my writing copy-edited by + a peer	O	O	O	O	[ ]
+ a professional copy-editor	O	O	O	O	[ ]

Please list any other types of support that you have used.

[ ]

11. How likely is it that you would take advantage of support (i.e. tutoring, seminars, workshops) during the following periods?

	Not likely	Somewhat likely	Very likely

Figure 3.4.

Fall term	○	○	○
Winter break	○	○	○
Winter term	○	○	○
Spring break	○	○	○
Spring term	○	○	○
Summer break	○	○	○
Summer term	○	○	○
The period between summer term and fall term	○	○	○

12. Please indicate the days and times during the term that you are most available for tutoring/workshops. *(Check all that apply)*

	Monday	Tuesday	Wednesday	Thursday	Friday
Early morning (8-10 AM)	☐	☐	☐	☐	☐
Mid-morning (10 AM-12 PM)	☐	☐	☐	☐	☐
Lunch (12-1 PM)	☐	☐	☐	☐	☐
Early afternoon (1-3 PM)	☐	☐	☐	☐	☐
Late afternoon (3-5 PM)	☐	☐	☐	☐	☐

13. Please provide any additional comments about your experiences and needs as an English language user at Dartmouth.

Block 6

As you know, we have asked the Office of Institutional Research to collect the data to ensure confidentiality. The survey will be analyzed by OIR staff and results will be only presented in aggregate. In order to increase the usefulness of the survey, OIR may combine your survey responses with existing institutional data such as TOEFL score, program/school, and admission date.

We would also like to use the results of this survey and institutional data provided by OIR for research. OIR will remove all identifying information from the data.

Do you give us permission to use the results of this survey for research? (All identifying information will be removed from the data.)

○ Yes
○ No

Thank you!

Figure 3.5.

References

Blau, Susan, and John Hall. 2002. "Guilt-Free Tutoring: Rethinking How We Tutor Non-Native-English Speaking Students." *Writing Center Journal* 23 (1): 23–44.

Canagarajah, A. Suresh. 2002. *Critical Academic Writing and Multilingual Students.* Ann Arbor: University of Michigan Press.

Cox, Michelle. 2010. "Identity, Second Language Writers, and the Learning of Workplace Writing." In *Reinventing Identities in Second Language Writing,* edited by Michelle Cox, Jay Jordan, Christina Ortmeier-Hooper, and Gwen Gray Schwartz, 75–95. Urbana, IL: National Council of Teachers of English.

Ferris, Dana R. 2009. *Teaching College Writing to Diverse Student Populations.* Ann Arbor: University of Michigan Press.

Harklau, Linda. 2000. "From the 'Good Kids' to the 'Worst': Representations of English Language Learners across Educational Settings." *TESOL Quarterly* 34 (1): 35–67. http://dx.doi.org/10.2307/3588096.

Harklau, Linda, Kay M. Losey, and Mary Siegal, eds. 1999. *Generation 1.5 Meets College Composition: Issues in the Teaching of Writing to U.S.-Educated Learners of ESL.* Mahwah, NJ: Erlbaum.

Harris, Muriel, and Tony Silva. 1993. "Tutoring ESL Students: Issues and Options." *College Composition and Communication* 44 (4): 525–37. http://dx.doi.org/10.2307/358388.

Ibrahim, Awad el Karim M. 1999. "Becoming Black: Rap and Hip Hop, Race, Gender, Identity, and the Politics of ESL Learning." *TESOL Quarterly* 33 (3): 349–69. http://dx.doi.org/10.2307/3587669.

Kachru, Braj B. 1985. "Standards, Codification and Sociolinguistic Realism: The English Language in the Outer Circle." In *English in the World: Teaching and Learning the Language and Literatures,* edited by Randolph Quirk and Henry G. Widdowson, 11–30. Cambridge: Cambridge University Press.

Kanno, Yasuko. 2003. *Negotiating Bilingual and Bicultural Identities: Japanese Returnees Betwixt Two Worlds.* Amsterdam: John Benjamins.

Leki, Ilona. 1992. *Understanding ESL Writers: A Guide for Teachers.* Portsmouth, NH: Heinemann.

Leki, Ilona. 1995. "Coping Strategies of ESL Students in Writing Tasks across the Curriculum." *TESOL Quarterly* 29 (2): 235–60. http://dx.doi.org/10.2307/3587624.

Leki, Ilona. 1999. "'Pretty Much I Screwed Up': Ill-Served Needs of a Permanent Resident Student." In *Generation 1.5 Meets College Composition: Issues in the Teaching of Writing to U.S.-Educated Learners of ESL,* edited by Linda Harklau, Kay M. Losey, and Meryl Siegal, 17–43. Mahwah, NJ: Erlbaum.

Leki, Ilona. 2007. *Undergraduates in a Second Language: Challenges and Complexities of Academic Literacy Development.* Boston: Routledge.

Matsuda, Paul Kei, and Michelle Cox. 2009. "Reading an ESL Writer's Text." In *ESL Writers: A Guide for Writing center Tutors.* 2nd ed. Edited by Shanti Bruce and Ben Rafoth, 42–50. Portsmouth, NH: Boynton/Cook.

Norton, Bonnie. 2000. *Identity and Language Learning: Gender, Ethnicity, and Educational Change.* Harlow, UK: Longman.

Ortmeier-Hooper, Christina. 2010. "The Shifting Nature of Identity: Social Identity, L2 Writers, and High School." In *Reinventing Identities in Second Language Writing,* edited by Michelle Cox, Jay Jordan, Christina Ortmeier-Hooper, and Gwen Gray Schwartz, 5–28. Urbana, IL: National Council of Teachers of English.

Reid, Joy M., and Barbara Kroll. 1995. "Designing and Assessing Effective Classroom Writing Assignments for NES and ESL Students." *Journal of Second Language Writing* 4 (1): 17–41. http://dx.doi.org/10.1016/1060-3743(95)90021-7.

Roberge, Mark. 2002. "California's Generation 1.5 Immigrants: What Characteristics, Experiences, and Needs Do They Bring to Our English Classes?" *CATESOL Journal* 14 (1): 107–29.

Schwartz, Gwen Gray. 2010. "Subtexting Mainstream Generation 1.5 Identities: Acculturation Theories at Work." In *Reinventing Identities in Second Language Writing,* edited by Michelle Cox, Jay Jordan, Christina Ortmeier-Hooper, and Gwen Gray Schwartz, 29–50. Urbana, IL: National Council of Teachers of English.

Severino, Carol. 1993. "The Sociopolitical Implications of Response to Second Language and Second Dialect Writing." *Journal of Second Language Writing* 2 (3): 181–201. http://dx.doi.org/10.1016/1060-3743(93)90018-X.

Severino, Carol. 2009. "Avoiding Appropriation." In *ESL Writers: A Guide for Writing Center Tutors,* 2nd edition, edited by Shanti Bruce and Ben Rafoth, 51–65. Portsmouth, NH: Boynton/Cook.

Shuck, Gail. 2010. "Language Identity, Agency, and Context: The Shifting Meanings of *Multilingual.*" In *Reinventing Identities in Second Language Writing,* edited by Michelle Cox, Jay Jordan, Christina Ortmeier-Hooper, and Gwen Gray Schwartz, 117–138. Urbana, IL: National Council of Teachers of English.

Silva, Tony, Ilona Leki, and Joan Carson. 1997. "Broadening the Perspective of Mainstream Composition Studies: Some Thoughts from the Disciplinary Margins." *Written Communication* 14 (3): 398–428. http://dx.doi.org/10.1177/0741088397014003004.

Vann, Roberta, Daisy Meyer, and Frederick Lorenz. 1984. "Error Gravity: A Study of Faculty Opinion of ESL Errors." *TESOL Quarterly* 18 (3): 427–40. http://dx.doi.org /10.2307/3586713.

Zawacki, Terry Myers, and Anna Sophia Habib. 2010. "'Will Our Stories Help Teachers Understand?' Expectations across Academic Communities." In *Reinventing Identities in Second Language Writing*, edited by Michelle Cox, Jay Jordan, Christina Ortmeier-Hooper, and Gwen Gray Schwartz, 54–74. Urbana, IL: National Council of Teachers of English.

Zawacki, Terry Myers, and Anna Sophia Habib. 2014. "Negotiating 'Errors' in L2 Writing: Faculty Dispositions and Language Difference." In *WAC and Second Language Writers: Research towards Linguistically and Culturally Inclusive Programs and Practices*, edited by Terry Myers Zawacki and Michelle Cox, 183–210. Fort Collins, CO: WAC Clearinghouse and Parlor.

4

EL CENTRO DE COMPETENCIAS DE LA COMUNICACIÓN AND THE FRAUGHT STATUS OF ENGLISH

Shanti Bruce

I traveled to the Universidad de Puerto Rico en Humacao (UPRH) and spent several days visiting their Centro de Competencias de la Comunicación (CCC). Having been to numerous writing centers across the United States where English is the primary language of instruction, I wanted to learn from people working at a center where English is not the dominant language. While at the CCC, I took a case-study-method approach to learning about the way their center works. I conducted observations and talked about tutoring with students and faculty. From scheduling appointments, tracking usage, and leading APA workshops, to insisting the CCC is not a fix-it shop, taking turns with students reading papers aloud, and encouraging students to hold the pen, what I saw and heard seemed similar to what I had encountered in the States. On the surface, the center was familiar, but when people began talking with me about the English language, I learned a great deal about its fraught status in Puerto Rico and how that status plays out in the writing center. As in many places, there are language issues related to family, politics, culture, and identity. Many of the people I spoke with struggle with the impact of English and question its effects on their history and way of life. This struggle puts added stress on the writing center as it strives to serve many students who are not altogether convinced that what they are studying is both necessary and good. Whether or not a center is situated in a place where learners have a history of distrust of the English language, writing center staffs in many places encounter students who have mixed feelings toward the subjects and languages they are studying.

In her keynote address for the annual meeting of the International Writing Centers Association in 2008, Nancy Grimm challenged the field to conceptualize the twenty-first-century writing center as a place "that embraces a concept of multiliteracies, [in which] effective tutors learn

DOI: 10.7330/9781607324140.c004

to engage with difference in open-minded, flexible, and non-dogmatic ways" (Grimm 2009, 21). Writing centers that truly embrace a multitude of languages, whether in the States or in Puerto Rico, do not do so in a vacuum. They are making a political statement that may be seen as a moral triumph by some and as a tragic forsaking of culture and identity by others.

As writing centers move toward becoming more multilingual, toward embracing multiliteracies, resistance can be expected. Therefore, it is helpful to look at a center like the CCC that operates in an environment that has long experienced the potential language clashes writing centers may face. In this chapter, I provide background information on the political climate surrounding Spanish and English in Puerto Rico. I then describe my experiences traveling to the UPRH writing center and share insights about language and identity provided by the faculty, tutors, and students I met. The chapter ends with a focus on how writing centers can act as change agents and work to become places that welcome all people and all languages, contributing to a greater acceptance of difference.

SPANISH AND ENGLISH IN PUERTO RICO

Puerto Rico is a US territory where Spanish, rather than English, is the dominant language. According to the 2012 American Community Survey, administered by the United States Census Bureau, over 94 percent of the Puerto Rican population (who live in Puerto Rico) speaks a form of Spanish at home (US Census Bureau 2012). In addition to speaking Spanish at home, these speakers use Spanish in their everyday lives outside the home. Of those speakers, over 84 percent reportedly "Speak English less than 'very well.'" In his article, "The Fight for English in Puerto Rico," William Marquez (2012) said, "Most do not speak a word of English although—along with Spanish—it is the official language of the island." In an effort to produce more fluent speakers of English, in 2012, pro-statehood (Partido Nuevo Progresista) Governor Luis Fortuño pushed to mandate bilingual education. Juan Manuel Mercado, at the time a pro-independence (Partido Independentista Puertorriqueño) candidate to be resident commissioner in Washington, opposed the plan, believing "Puerto Ricans reject any kind of acculturation because they are rooted in their identity as Hispanics and not as Americans. . . . We express our 'Puerto-Ricaness' every day through our language" (Marquez 2012). Fortuño lost the 2012 election to Alejandro García Padilla, who is pro-commonwealth or pro-Estado Libre

Asociado—the current status of the island represented by the Partido Popular Democrático.

Soon after the election, Governor García Padilla was asked a question in English during a press conference. He asked for the question to be repeated and struggled to find the words to express his answer. Many took to the Internet to post clips of the event and make fun of what appeared to be a lack of English language proficiency. García Padilla, who is a proficient speaker of English, responded by saying, "I did the best I could do. I got hung up on the word flow" (*Caribbean Business*, Nov. 13, 2012). This criticism seems at odds with the widespread resistance to English. As Schweers and Vélez (1992, 13) said, "With respect to the learning of English, it's a case of being damned if you do (you're betraying your Hispanic heritage and giving in to the forces of Americanization from the North) and damned if you don't (you're severely limiting your potential for socioeconomic mobility)." In other words, "English has long been viewed on the island as both a tool of liberation and an instrument of oppression" (Pousada 1999, 33).

The status of English in Puerto Rico also gained attention from the candidates for US president in the 2012 election. During the Republican primaries, former Senator Rick Santorum and Governor Mitt Romney both visited Puerto Rico. Santorum expressed his belief that English would have to be the main language in order for Puerto Rico to be considered for statehood, and Romney differed, saying that while he supported English, "he would have 'no preconditions' on language for Puerto Rico to gain statehood" (Helton 2012). President Barack Obama endorsed the 2011 President's Task Force on Puerto Rico's Status, which included in its report "Recommendation #6: The President and Congress should ensure that Puerto Rico controls its own cultural and linguistic identity. The Task Force recognizes that, if Puerto Rico were admitted as a State, the English language would need to play—as it does today—a central role in the daily life of the Island" (Office of Intergovernmental Affairs 2011, 4). The recommendation is not totally clear, as it seems to impose the central importance of English while saying Puerto Rico should decide on its own language identity. It also seems a bit ill informed as it suggests that English is currently a part of the citizens' "daily life."

Alfonso Aguilar, executive director of the Latino Partnership for Conservative Principles, believes gaining statehood would make English more important in Puerto Rico. He said, "Obviously the majority of Puerto Ricans don't speak English because we are not a state. It will naturally happen. Part of this status conundrum is to keep us in limbo so that there is no incentive for people to say, 'I want to learn English'" (Ricardo Varela 2013). Bernard Spolsky's (2010) research has shown that "a change in political situation . . . is regularly associated with a change in the language of government and, possibly also of, education" (176). It seems, then, that Aguilar could be correct, but so far in Puerto Rico, neither becoming a territory nor gaining citizenship has resulted in a majority of the population becoming bilingual. These types of political moves have not changed the dominance of Spanish on the island.

In the States, English-language proficiency is also scrutinized. Many people in positions of power are expected to use a form of Standard American English and to speak with no accent—read: Northern Midwest American accent—and deviating from that norm often draws criticism. Many writing centers are also guilty of privileging that norm in written form: Standard Written American English. In this volume, Frankie Condon and Bobbi Olson explain that

> many of the tutors with whom [they] worked had learned to believe that their job was to assist multi- and translingual students to earn their access and opportunity by normalizing their identities—by helping multi- and translingual writers perceive, feel and think, read, write and speak as if they were "white," "American" (in the case of international student-writers), native speakers of American academic Englishes. Tutors who felt this way understood the impossibility of the task they set before themselves and the writers with whom they worked, and yet they believed this was the only ethical and pedagogically sound choice—a choice that was, in effect, not a choice at all (See Liu, this volume). (39)

While tutors work with students to help them achieve this impossible standard, tutors themselves are also often held to it. For example, tutors may be considered employable only if they speak and write with a minimal level of accent, and in some writing centers, even a minimal written accent is seen as suspect. This bias reflects a certain obsession with correctness that is hard to justify in terms of clarity or comprehensibility, so, like critics of the Puerto Rican candidate, it becomes more about the desire among some people to stigmatize forms of language they don't approve of or identify with. Thus, the insistence on particular forms of English and tutors who speak and write a certain way has political implications in writing centers and on campuses.

Puerto Rico became a colony of Spain in the sixteenth century and then an unincorporated territory of the United States in 1898 after the Spanish American War. In 1902, both Spanish and English were acknowledged as official languages. English was used at the beginning of the twentieth century consciously as an Americanization tool in the public schools. Protests led by Puerto Rican educators eradicated that practice by the 1940s, when public schools went back to teaching all subjects except English in the Spanish language. The argument was, and still is, that people learn better when they are taught in their mother tongue (Sylvia M. Casillas-Olivieri, personal communication).

In 1991, as the English-only movement in the States gained support, Puerto Rico removed English as an official language to try to protect itself, but English was reinstated as a co-official language in 1993. As Luis Muñiz-Argüelles (1989) of the University of Puerto Rico explains, to some, the English-only movement in the States "means nothing less than cultural genocide," but others believe such eradication of culture would never happen because new laws would be created to protect Puerto Rico's Spanish language (464). Spolsky (2010) studies the connections between nationalism and languages and has shown that "movements working for national independence are regularly associated with movements for the establishment of national languages." He offers Québec as an example of a fight for independence that includes "a movement to resist French language loss" (175). According to Ebsworth and Ebsworth (2011), many have "persistently associated Spanish with Puerto Rican identity and English with a threat to all that is Puerto Rican" (100). For many in Puerto Rico, learning English is different from learning other languages. Learning English can signify an acceptance of US government and culture and a denial of Puerto Rican identity.

Education has been at the center of much of the politics regarding language. Those in favor of Americanization push for educating students in English, which results in opposition from some students when they encounter English in the classroom. Rosa M. Torruellas's research "found and described a student counter culture of resistance in the English class." She observed "a classroom atmosphere of apathy at best or outright hostile resistance at worst. . . . Students question teachers as to why they have to learn English if in the United States, people don't learn Spanish," and for these students, "English and Spanish are seen as being in opposition to each other and mutually exclusive" (Schweers and Vélez 1992, 28). In addition to students in the classroom, people of a variety of ages and from a variety of backgrounds join in the efforts to stop the use of English, according to Jorge Vélez's findings (2000). When students encounter disapproval of the use of English in all parts of their lives, those attitudes will almost certainly be adopted.

The director of the CCC, Dr. Helena Méndez, talked with me about this issue and said she found similar situations with the students who attend UPRH. She said, "I think the classes that have more problems with discipline are the ones that are teaching English because they are teaching something that [causes students to think] 'I don't care.' 'I don't think it's important.'" Torruellas's research also showed that "when students attempt to use English to communicate in class, they are met with *relajo* or ridiculing and teasing by their peers" (Schweers and Vélez 1992, 29). Alicia Pousada (2000) also found that many people "viewed English-speaking Puerto Ricans on the island as snobs or colonialists" (116). This pressure to avoid the English language adds to students' negative feelings toward it. Learning academic writing in any language is hard, and when students have to do it in their second language, learning is all the more difficult when they are made to feel, by some, that they are betraying loyalties.

Méndez explained that Puerto Rican students usually enroll in at least one English class from elementary school all the way through high school. She said, "When they come here to the university, they don't know [English]. So you ask, 'Why don't they know it?' They've been taught it for twelve years." She continued, "When they finish college, they don't feel confident to speak [English], so what's going on? So why after years, why don't they know the language?" Ebsworth and Ebsworth (2011) believe "it is not surprising that in light of the limitations of elementary and secondary settings, many students arrive at college with weak English skills, as demonstrated by their scores on the English as a Second Language Achievement Test of the PR College Board" (99). Méndez concluded, "I believe it is a relationship that students and the ones who teach the language have with the language." This negative relationship minimizes the chance for student success in achieving English-language proficiency.

According to Sylvia M. Casillas-Olivieri, writing center director at the Universidad del Turabo, students who study in private schools, which are more affordable than private schools in the States, are often better prepared in English than students who study in public schools. The private schools take different approaches to teaching their curricula. Some teach some subjects in English and others in Spanish, while other private schools make English the primary language of instruction in all subjects except Spanish and religion (in the case of parochial schools). In addition, private-school English teachers may have a better command of the English language. Some students who attended public schools report that their English courses were taught entirely in Spanish due to the teacher's deficient knowledge of English. As a result, parents who want their children to have a better opportunity to learn English, and can afford it, send their children to a private school.

In Puerto Rico, English is presented to the population as a second rather than a foreign language. According to Méndez, therein lies a major part of the problem. Since English is not needed to survive, she believes the population resists it. She said, "Here, they tell us that English is our second language, but that's not true. That's not true. I survive in my country by using only Spanish, so the second language is not true. To be a second language, that would mean that in certain areas of the country or certain administrative offices have to be in English, but that's not true. With one language, you can survive. So that's a lie." In this volume, Michelle Cox lists the many terms used to describe speakers who use a language in addition to English. She explains, "[ESL] is the term with the longest history on this list. Because of this longevity, it is the term that is the most recognizable but that also comes with the most baggage" (58). The students Méndez describes see inconsistencies with how the language is presented in school and what they see as the reality of their day-to-day needs. Méndez said, "Our radio, newspaper, TV, go around and mingle with the people, and see what language they are using. In this world in Puerto Rico, you don't need it. Don't lie. [English] is not important."

Though the reality may be that English is not important for day-to-day survival in Puerto Rico, Méndez is in favor of learning additional languages, English very much included. "It's good for you to have [English] because when you know a different language, your culture is expanded," she explained. "Your way to look at humans is different. The way you relate to humans is different, but the way they teach," she insisted, "stop lying about it being our second language."

Sometimes, the debate about various labels used to refer to speakers of English and other languages can feel like an abstract, academic exercise of little consequence, but Méndez clearly explains how crucial the ESL/EFL difference can be. A similar debate occurs in French-speaking Canada. There, many Canadian educators use the term *EAL* (*English as an additional language*) to sidestep the question of whether or not English is a second or a foreign language. Using the word *additional* takes the pressure off distinguishing the status of English.

BEING A LINGUISTIC FOREIGNER

When I arrived at the airport in San Juan, I was immediately reminded of what it feels like to be a linguistic foreigner. Even for an English speaker familiar with Spanish, it is quite different being in a place where most everyone is a native speaker of Spanish, talking fast, using slang, and picking up on nonverbal cues that go right by someone new to the culture.

Jorge met me at the airport. An employee of UPRH, he had been sent to drive me fifty minutes southeast of San Juan to my hotel, Palmas de Lucía. Jorge spoke almost no English, and my Spanish was severely lacking. It was a struggle to communicate; even covering the basics was exhausting. I was the other person from the other place speaking another language. I guess this was a fitting way to begin my trip. After all, the CCC consultants repeatedly told me that in order to really be effective as an L2 tutor, I needed to "get into their shoes" and "try to understand what it is like for them on a human level first."

During the drive, I was able to explain to Jorge that I was hungry and wanted "no *carne*, no *pollo*." I am a vegetarian. When he understood *ensalada*, he threw up his hands, smiled widely, and exclaimed "Ponderosa!" Not usually a fan of Ponderosa cuisine, I was grateful for the successful communication, and when we arrived, I approached the salad bar with appreciation.

By the time I made it to the hotel, I was exhausted. While interacting with Jorge and people at the airport and restaurant, I had been reduced to two-word phrases, hand gestures, and a lot of apologies. I was experiencing what many students must feel all day long in the States and in our writing centers. I can express myself well and with nuance in English, but in Spanish, I was working with the basics, and they felt inadequate.

By the second day, I was doing much better with the speed at which people were speaking to me, and I continued to appreciate the challenges L2 students face in our institutions. I had read and heard many times how tiring it is to work so hard to communicate and exist in a new culture, and I was truly experiencing it. When I was an undergraduate student, I studied abroad in France. However, I was with a group of English-speaking students from the United States, so I always had someone to talk easily with. In Humacao, I was alone and needed help with just about everything. I was reminded of how many of our international students are professionals with degrees and careers in their own countries before they come to the States to study. How frustrating it must be for them to be reduced to "basic writing." Being a linguistic foreigner is daunting, but it is also exciting because there is so much to learn. It is at once draining and illuminating.

THE CENTRO DE COMPETENCIAS DE LA COMUNICACIÓN

The CCC had a wall of windows so passersby could easily see in, and the center was painted with bright colors. There was a comfortable seating area in the front, private tutoring rooms on one side, small tables in the middle, and on the other side, an area was filled with computers students could use at any time. The only requirement was that they sign in so center usage could be tracked.

When they arrived at the center, the undergraduate and graduate student consultants all put on blue, collared polo shirts embroidered with the CCC logo. There were two tutoring teams, and depending on the assignment, students could sign up for sessions either in Spanish or English. Some of the consultants were bilingual, but not all. The consultants kept files on each student and recorded in them the date and details of every session.

While I was there, I observed a steady flow of people coming in and going out of the center. The students looked familiar to me in their blue jeans and Boston hats. There was the occasional returning student, and some just wanted to listen to their headphones.

The consultants got together every week at the same time to focus on some aspect of working in the CCC. I observed a staff meeting in which Maria, the senior consultant, used role-playing scripts she had gotten at an IWCA conference. She had translated them from English into Spanish so that all the consultants could use them together as a group. They sat in a circle in a small classroom on the ground floor of the *biblioteca* and went through each one. When they finished reading all the scripts, they further discussed the issues raised in the activity, and then they turned their focus to the other items on the meeting agenda, including scheduling and general center policies. They seemed to enjoy their time together.

Upon learning of the reason for my visit, several students and consultants were eager to share with me their opinions about language, culture, and the writing center. I appreciated their enthusiasm and listened to each of them as long as they wanted to talk. I also invited them to choose the pseudonyms I would use to accompany their quotes.

Nikki

When it was time for lunch on the first day, Nikki and a couple of the consultants showed me the way to the cafeteria. Nikki told me she enjoys hanging out at the CCC and is friends with many of the students who work there. She especially wanted me to understand the role language plays in her family. She said, "My dad wants me to sound Merengue, and my mom wants me to be totally American like Frank Sinatra." She explained her father's desire indicated that he believes her choice of language will determine her true national identity: "My dad wanted me to be more fluent in Spanish so that I could be pure Puerto Rican and just know a second language." Nikki's father rightly correlates language use with identity. Merengue is a Dominican rhythm, so it is possible Nikki's father wants her to retain some family connection to the Dominican Republic while also integrating fully into Puerto Rican society. On the other hand, her mother may see English as opening the door for future migration to the United States. As Spolsky (1999, 181) explains, "Language is a central feature of human identity. When we hear someone speak, we immediately make guesses about gender, education level, age, profession, and place of origin. Beyond this individual matter, a language is a powerful symbol of national and ethnic identity." For Nikki's father, language use equates to membership in their culture.

Nikki continued, "Some people I know think that learning English means that they're betraying their native language because the way they see it, we're a colony of the United States, and if we subdue to learning the language, it means that we are forsaking our natural language, our native language. They don't really see it as a benefit to learn another language." Students who internalize this struggle no doubt find it harder to succeed in their study of English, and they likely bring these feelings with them when they enter the writing center. This adds an additional dimension to the familiar consultant challenge of trying to work with the reluctant writer.

"They mind learning English," Nikki said, "because it is kind of like forced on us to learn English, and it really kind of pisses them off. It's like, 'Why do we have to learn it?' I know a lot of people who resist it." Ebsworth and Ebsworth (2011) make clear that "acquiring English in Puerto Rico is much more than learning another language. For the Puerto Rican learner, it involves not only acknowledging the power of English in local and global terms, but also confronting the complex psychological and social stresses and pressures that its history and associations entail" (96). Nikki said, "They don't mind learning French; they don't mind learning Italian; they don't mind learning any other language." She said students ask, "'Why can't we choose to learn it?'" and according to her, not having a choice causes resistance. Méndez agreed that this lack of choice leads to even more resistance.

Nikki wanted to tell me more about how Spanish and English work for her. She said, "I do speak both languages, but I have no clue which is my first language cause usually you know in your head, like, if you think in English, then that's your first native language, but I literally think with both. Like, I start a sentence in one language, and then all of a sudden, it just goes right to another, and I just say it in two languages at the same time." Nikki illuminates the problems that Cox points out when writing center and second language writing scholars try to categorize people by the number of languages they speak, or classify them according to whether or not they are native or nonnative speakers of a language. In Nikki's case, she is fully bilingual and does not think of her languages in terms of native or nonnative.

Edgar

The university participated in a bilingual initiative program. As a member of that program, Edgar came from the United States to study in Humacao. He told me about how language has affected his identity both in the States and in Puerto Rico. He said, "I was raised in the States, so I came over here just to learn Spanish because over there, I would be hassled a lot for not knowing Spanish by friends, family, church members, and everything. They all speak pretty fluent." He continued, "I wouldn't hang out with anybody that was from my culture, actually, because they were too arrogant to speak to me because I'm supposed to be Puerto Rican, and I don't know any Spanish. They thought I was like, false. Like they thought I was lying whenever I said, 'I'm Puerto Rican.' 'Oh? Well, speak to me in Spanish then.' And, I'm like, 'No. Why?' Because I could understand it completely, but it's just whenever I had to speak it, it wouldn't come out. Apparently, you can't be Puerto Rican if you don't speak Spanish. You need it to be accepted."

Edgar's experience in the States was similar to what he experienced when he began living in Puerto Rico. He said, "Whenever you speak [English] to [people here] in the everyday, they don't like it because they feel like, 'You're in my country, so please speak to me in my language.'" What Edgar describes matches Pousada's (2000) findings that "island-raised Puerto Ricans often mocked the speech and cultural values of US-raised Puerto Ricans" (116). When speaking English, Edgar could not fit in comfortably with the Puerto Ricans he encountered in the States or in Puerto Rico. Many saw him as different and did not accept him as a part of their culture because of his language use. In order to change this, Pousada (2000, 117) suggests competent bilinguals need "to demonstrate how one does not stop being Puerto Rican if one learns English." With this shift, people like Edgar would not feel shunned.

Similar to Edgar, Nikki spoke of encountering people who didn't appreciate being spoken to in English. She said, "I know a lot of people who are like, 'Speak to me in Spanish!' I'm like, 'If you understand me, what's the problem? I'm not forcing you to speak English.'" Nikki also experienced what Torruellas found when observing school students. "In high school," Nikki said, "some kids would taunt me. They would call me the *gringita*: the American girl." Nikki concluded, "I was just like, whatever." Speaking English was cause for bullying, and being called an American was a putdown.

Alexander, Juliana, and Daniel

Though there is a great deal of pushback against the learning of English, students and tutors repeatedly mentioned to me the importance of English. Ebsworth and Ebsworth (2011, 99) point out this "dichotomy in Puerto Rico," where "many individuals state the belief that learning English is important. Yet, they also respond to social and psychological forces that act against its acquisition." In other words, they say it is important to learn English, but they resist actually learning and using the language.

With the goal of becoming a computer programmer, Alexander often comes to the CCC for tutoring in English. He said, "The whole world speaks English, and studying it helped me a lot in opening my opportunities of jobs." While looking ahead to how English will be important in the future, Alexander knows it is also important to him now. He explained, "I study math, and almost all book is in English, so I need to find a tutor or a Spanish version of the book." While some textbooks are in Spanish, he said, "the versions in English are more advanced. Sometimes, you have a book in English the seventh edition, and in Spanish, they going from the five edition." When dealing with computers, currency is important. He continued, "The writers of those books know the books will be used in the whole world, so they have to write in English."

Méndez added, "If you get any book in science, it is going to be in English. When [students] open the book, what are they going to face? They aren't going to be using their own language to understand it because the books are in English." Méndez believes the students are being denied access to the information they need. She said, "I think it's horrible that the textbooks aren't translated. [Students] have to go through too many hurdles to get the knowledge. If the texts would be in Spanish, they would learn it. In Spain and in Latin America, they teach sciences in Spanish, so why they are not in Puerto Rico?" She mentioned some restrictions on doing business with countries besides the United States and believes those restrictions add to the lack of available materials in Spanish.

English-language consultants Juliana and Daniel also stressed the importance of English when it comes to textbooks. Juliana remarked on "the attitude" she finds in many students. She said, "Some people just say, 'I don't need English. I'm in Puerto Rico. I don't need English.' But, they do," she insisted, "they really do." Daniel added, "Basically, if you're going to study here, you need English. At the university, only a few books are in Spanish, and they aren't the original. They've been translated."

Isabella (translated by Maria)

A member of the Spanish-language consultant team, Isabella, talked with me about her goals of becoming an accountant. She said, "I would like to learn more English and better my Spanish because nobody's perfect in either language, and it's important to learn both." The CPA test is in English, and she also mentioned wanting to be able to communicate when traveling.

Isabella continued to talk, but Maria stopped translating for me. I wasn't sure why, and then they both started giggling. Maria looked at me and said, "I can't say it; she told me not to." I didn't know what was going on or whether they were planning to let me in on it, so I simply sat and waited. Then Isabella nodded, and Maria looked at me and further explained why they feel it is important to learn English. She said, "It's a thing that we kind of hope to, um, sort of . . . get an American boyfriend from the States." I said, "Oh, okay." She continued, "Okay, to explain. We sort of, I don't know, it's a thing we do, like, a culture thing. Like, a girl would normally, her stereotype of 'oh my god, that's the guy I want,' is like white, blonde hair, blue eyes. You ask any Puerto Rican girl, 'a pale American with blue eyes.'" She explained, "It's like what my mom says. She told me like, 'You need to get a guy with, like, straight hair, so you can better your race.'"

The dichotomy that Ebsworth and Ebsworth (2011) point out kept coming up in my discussions with the students. On the one hand, Isabella told me it is important for her to learn English in order to be successful, but she already is a successful university student who was even hired as a consultant at the CCC. She says she needs English, but she works in a place that tutors English, and she speaks almost no English. Nikki and Edgar spoke of the resistance to English, and yet, according to Isabella and Maria, an American guy is the ideal boyfriend.

WRITING CENTERS AS CHANGE AGENTS

Language is an integral part of identity, of what it means to be human. Both the students who work at the CCC and those who come in for tutoring bring with them attitudes that reflect their home and school experiences. That is the story at all writing centers. In an effort to make all people feel comfortable in a writing center, all languages must be welcomed. In this volume, Frankie Condon and Bobbi Olson explain that writing center directors, tutors, and scholars can't "fix" the world or our institutions. But we can move thoughtfully, experimentally, and with care to create and sustain spaces shaped by our shared concern for justice, for equality of access, and opportunity. Figuring out how to do that is, of course, the challenge.

Méndez, director of the CCC, also believes writing centers are in a unique position to work for positive change. She considers the tutoring session—the heart of writing center work—the place to open minds. "I believe that writing centers are not neutral," she said, "I believe that 100 percent. I think that writing centers are places for people to change their attitude. How you do that is not by politics or imposing things. It is by questioning and allowing that person to get into the process of thinking their own thoughts about what is written there." During a tutoring session, Méndez believes, a consultant should ask, "Why do you believe that?" She explained, "I'm not challenging that. I just want you to express it but in a clear way. 'Why do you think that?' Make that person think. So in that sense, change is going on. It's a challenge. Your comfort area is being challenged, and I think that's what has to happen."

In addition to challenging writers to open their minds, Méndez offered five ways writing centers in the States can create spaces that welcome all students.

1. Present a multicultural scenario.

   Méndez suggests placing phrases in different languages and posters representing different countries around the center. She said, "You might say, 'Well, that's a façade.' And it is, but it's important." If the writing center has words and images that reflect students' home cultures and languages, they are more likely to feel welcome. Méndez says some students see the center and think, "This is an environment that I don't like; it is challenging to me; it is scary to me." While it may seem simple, she believes "putting a phrase on the wall can help." She said, "Make that person special because that person every day is made invisible. Make it visible by some things on the wall that say, 'Hey, you are welcome. Your culture, your language is welcome here.'"

Special promotions and events can also be created to target specific populations. "If you want to target the Hispanic population," for example, Méndez said, centers should "put a Spanish phrase on the information, and when Spanish speakers see that, they will feel good. It's empathy."

2. Provide tutoring areas with some privacy.

Being completely alone might not be the best idea, but having an area that is somewhat private can, according to Méndez, help students feel less self-conscious about needing help and about others hearing their pronunciation. She said, "When [students] come [to the CCC], they are ashamed when they don't know [English] because they are supposed to know it. That's why they can come in these private rooms so that nobody is around, so they can feel comfortable." She added, "The consultants know not to laugh at you, but someone else might do it."

3. Learn to pronounce the student's name.

Méndez feels strongly that consultants should take the time to learn to say each student's name. She said, "At least the first name. Okay? It's important." She insisted, "Don't call me 'Helena;' call me 'Elena.' My name is important. At least know me by name. Know how to pronounce my name right. And what country I come from." She said if consultants take the time to do this, students "will come back because they will feel that they are accepted and respected and honored."

4. Develop sensitivity toward different content and beliefs.

Méndez reminds consultants that encountering different people might mean encountering different content. She stresses the fact that "we might not understand the content, but it is not wrong" because people from different cultures look at the world in different ways. She encourages tutors to be sensitive to difference. For example, "If a person is writing about how a woman should not go out because it will dishonor the family, which happens in some cultures, the consultant should be sensitive about that," even if the consultant has a hard time understanding that cultural norm.

5. Participate in multicultural education.

When consultants are not busy in sessions, Méndez believes, they should use some of their time to learn about the places the students who visit the center call home. The writing center should be a place where everyone is learning. She said consultants should think, "I learn as a tutor, and I'm learning even more now because I am learning about cultures." She believes tutors should "feel grateful for that learning" and even thank students at the end of sessions in which the tutors, too, learn something.

Méndez suggested writing centers include cultural sensitivity discussions in meetings and retreats. If each tutor learns about one country or culture and gives a presentation to the staff, Méndez asks, "What will happen?" She answers, "That tutor will be enriched, and the center will be a mecca for all students." Centers can gather their own information about what languages and cultures are represented on campus, or they can find that information through an office on campus that keeps those records.

When I expressed how difficult many people find it to work with L2 writers, Méndez said tutors should feel confident in their abilities and remember writing center work constitutes a learning opportunity for everyone involved. She said tutors should know "that person came to ask for support because they know you can give it." Tutors must have the confidence that they can do it. She said tutors should "mentalize it; put that uniform on. I'm the tool that he or she needs now, and I'm going to provide that, and I'm going to be learning because that person is going to give me something in exchange, and I'm going to be a richer person." She said tutors who learn to pronounce students' names and learn what country a person comes from are already "breaking down a lot of that intensity. There are two minds that have to be merged at some point," she said, "so know [you're] going to be supporting this person in this process" and "be thankful to have that opportunity."

LEARNING LANGUAGE, GAINING IDENTITY

Issues with Spanish and English are not confined to Puerto Rico. In the States, there are groups of people who fear the increasing numbers of Spanish speakers. While some people in both places are uneasy with shifts in demographics and languages used, others believe there is another way to look at these changes. Rather than losing identity, Aníbal Muñoz Claudio, English Professor at UPRH said, embracing multiple languages allows one to expand and enrich an identity. In fact, "Modern studies of identity," according to Spolsky (2010, 176), "stress that it is quite normal for an individual to share in several identities each associated with a different level of social organization and to switch between them in changing situations."

To illustrate this dilemma, Muñoz shared with me a conversation he had recently had with a colleague at UPRH. The colleague was critical of Muñoz's teaching of English. He said to Muñoz, "The more English that our students speak, the more identity they will lose." Muñoz said he disagreed and told his colleague, "If you learn another language, the more identity you gain." He then presented an analogy. He asked his colleague, "If you learn French or Italian or Portuguese, will that make you less Puerto Rican or more Puerto Rican?" His colleague answered, "Well, no. That's not the case." Muñoz said, "You see that? A Brazilian, a Chinese, and an Egyptian will be just pleased by learning English because they don't have any political attachments, any political ideologies, or any political mindsets involved in that equation." He said, "Many students believe that by learning English, they are relinquishing their Spanish, Puerto Rican identity," and to change that, he said, "we need to make English part of our culture. We need to invite the English language into our culture." He remarked as well on the fears that exist in the States. He said, "They take Spanish as a foreign language as well. Instead, bring it into your culture, invite in Spanish to belong." He spoke of Europe and how many people speak multiple languages there without feeling threatened. He said that to get past the barriers we have all created, people in the States need to embrace Spanish, and Puerto Ricans need to embrace English. He said if we can think of the languages as belonging to us, it would become a process of "gaining, not losing identity." He acknowledged the difficulty of this proposition but stressed that the more people who can see learning another language as "a linguistic phenomenon, not as a political phenomenon, then the more open minded we can be to eliminate that barrier."

In his work to change the minds of people who distrust learning English, Muñoz distributed a questionnaire to professors and students at his university in order to learn more about what they believe to be an authentic part of their culture. He said, "You usually cherish and you usually work with the things that belong to you. Right now, I think 90% of our population would say, 'No, English does not belong to me.'" The responses to the questionnaire confirmed what Muñoz had suspected: "A great majority did not consider English to be part of their culture." Interestingly, though, he said, "They do consider Thanksgiving and Christmas and Santa Claus and St. Valentine's and many other cultural elements. They do accept computers and shopping malls and Macy's and Sears, so it's very interesting to see that you have all those cultural elements embedded in our culture here, but not yet the language."

The situations in Puerto Rico and the States share some commonalities. In one, people are resisting the English language, while in the other, people are resisting the Spanish language. Each is trying to protect culture and identity and ward off what is perceived as a threat to an established way of life. Perhaps this is where the writing center can come in. The writing center could become the place where we dissuade fears of difference, particularly with language, and we can take that experience with us into our homes and classrooms and interactions with others. If we do as Méndez and Muñoz do in Puerto Rico, and Kevin Dvorak and Glenn Hutchinson and Paula Gillespie do in this volume—if we bring multiple languages into the center and believe they belong to all of us as a broadening of our identities, then perhaps we can all become more comfortable with the comingling of languages and seize the opportunity to gain rather than lose identity.

Questions to Consider

1. Méndez offered five suggestions for writing centers in the States. Consider each of her suggestions. How might they work in your center? Which ones would you like to try out? Do any of them concern you? What would you add to her list?

2. Professor Muñoz believes that learning any additional language, including English, adds to a person's identity. His colleague believes that learning English is different from learning other languages and that the learning of English can result in the loss of identity. Imagine you are standing with Professor Muñoz and his colleague, and they invite you into their conversation. What would you contribute to their discussion?

3. Have you experienced resistance to language and cultural change? Was this experience in an academic setting? How might you respond to people who do not think writing centers in the United States should move toward embracing multiple languages?

For Further Reading

The following readings are included on the PBS website to accompany the *Do You Speak American* documentary by Robert MacNeil. In the series, MacNeil travels around the United States and learns about the varieties of English spoken by people in different regions of the country.

Baron, Dennis. 2005. "Language Change: Language and Society." PBS.org. http://www
.pbs.org/speak/ahead/change/society/.
  Dennis Baron writes about language change and identity, and he also recounts the ways in which the United States has handled the controversial introduction of different languages into the educational system. After reading about Puerto Rico's issues with languages in schools, it is interesting to read about the United States' experiences.
Rohde, David. 2003. "Global American: Global English." PBS.org. http://www.pbs.org
/speak/ahead/globalamerican/global/.
  David Rohde explores the way the English language is spreading throughout the world. When English spreads, it both changes the languages it comes into contact with and is itself changed. This article provides insight into why Professor Muñoz's colleague fears the introduction of English into Puerto Rican culture.
Wolfram, Walt. 2005. "Language Change: The Truth about Change." PBS.org. http://
www.pbs.org/speak/ahead/change/change/.
  Walt Wolfram explores the connections between social groups and language change, explaining that some people resist change in an effort to maintain status and identity with certain groups. It may be helpful to consider this article alongside the stories from Nikki and Edgar.

References

Ebsworth, Miriam Eisenstein, and Timothy John Ebsworth. 2011. "Learning English in Puerto Rico: An Approach-Avoidance Conflict?" In *Handbook of Language and Ethnic Identity: The Success-Failure Continuum in Language and Ethnic Identity Efforts.* Vol. 2. Edited by Joshua Fishman and Ofelia Garcia, 96–112. New York: Oxford University Press.
Grimm, Nancy M. 2009. "New Conceptual Frameworks for Writing Center Work." *Writing Center Journal* 29 (2): 11–27.
Helton, John. 2012. "Romney, Santorum Continue Sparring over English in Puerto Rico." CNN.com. http://www.cnn.com/2012/03/16/politics/campaign-wrap/index
.html.
Marquez, William. 2012. "The Fight for English in Puerto Rico." BBC.com. http://www
.bbc.co.uk/news/world-us-canada-18501193.
Muñiz-Argüelles, Luis. 1989. "The Status of Languages in Puerto Rico." In *Language and Law: Proceedings of the First Conference of the International Institute of Comparative Linguistic Law,* edited by Paul Pupier and José Woehrling, 457–72. Montreal: Wilson and Lafleur.
Office of Intergovernmental Affairs. 2011. *Report by the President's Task Force on Puerto Rico's Status,* by Cecilia Muñoz, Thomas J. Perrelli, Tammye Treviño, Rick Wade, Cecilia Rouse, Patrick O'Brien, Eric Waldo, Brandon Hurlbut, Judith A. Enck, Paul Dioguardi, Juliette Kayyem, Mercedes Márquez, Anthony Babauta, Gabriela Lemus, Julissa Reynoso, Matthew Kabaker, Joanna Turner, and Hallie Schneir. Washington, DC: Government Printing Office. http://www.whitehouse.gov/sites/default/files
/uploads/Puerto_Rico_Task_Force_Report.pdf.

Pousada, Alicia. 1999. "The Singularly Strange Story of the English Language in Puerto Rico." *Milenio* 3:33–60.

Pousada, Alicia. 2000. "The Competent Bilingual in Puerto Rico." *International Journal of the Sociology of Language* 142 (3): 103–18.

Schweers Jr., William C., and Jorge A. Vélez. 1992. "To Be or Not to Be Bilingual in Puerto Rico: That is the Issue." *TESOL Journal* 2 (1): 13–16.

Spolsky, Bernard. 1999. "Second-Language Learning." In *Handbook of Language and Ethnic Identity*, edited by Joshua A. Fishman, 181–92. New York: Oxford University Press.

Spolsky, Bernard. 2010. "Second-Language Learning." In *Handbook of Language and Ethnic Identity: Disciplinary and Regional Perspectives*. Vol. 1. 2nd ed. Edited by Joshua A. Fishman and Ofelia García, 172–85. New York: Oxford University Press.

US Census Bureau. 2012. "Language Spoken at Home: 2012 American Community Survey 1-Year Estimates." http://factfinder2.census.gov/faces/tableservices/jsf/pages/productview.xhtml?pid=ACS_12_1YR_S1601&prodType=table.

Varela, Ricardo Julio. 2013. "Opinion: Is Puerto Rican Statehood the Next 'Latino' Issue for Conservatives?" NBCLatino.com. http://nbclatino.com/2013/01/30/opinion-is-puerto-rican-statehood-the-next-latino-issue-for-conservatives/.

Vélez, Jorge A. 2000. "Understanding Spanish-Language Maintenance in Puerto Rico: Political Will Meets the Demographic Imperative." *International Journal of the Sociology of Language* 142 (1): 5–24. http://dx.doi.org/10.1515/ijsl.2000.142.5.

PART TWO

Research Opportunities

Inquiry can take many forms when tutors stoke their curiosities, pursue them in a sustained and disciplined manner, and create new knowledge beneficial to themselves and others. The chapters in part 2 illustrate various approaches to inquiry and how tutors can become involved in their own projects. While examples of research may be found in every chapter, this section raises ideas for research that intersect with the everydayness of writing center work. In chapter 5, for example, a writing center director overhears a conversation between tutors about whether or not it's okay to use their L1, Spanish, when tutoring. With a bit of encouragement, the tutors and director turn this conversation into a research project. Chapter 6 shows how tutors in one writing center were able to examine the complicated dynamics of showing respect in tutoring sessions. The issue arises when tutors try to critique or challenge some Latino writers, who sometimes misinterpret the tutor's attitude toward their work. Video recordings allowed tutors to view their sessions multiple times and discuss what they observed and heard at granular levels. The last chapter in part 2 is devoted to research and speaks directly to tutors about ideas, methods, presentation, and publication. In this chapter, experienced tutors and professional researchers share stories about how they got started—and the mistakes they learned to avoid.

5

MULTILINGUAL WRITERS, MULTILINGUAL TUTORS
Code-Switching/Mixing/Meshing in the Writing Center

Kevin Dvorak

I walked into the writing center one quiet afternoon while Alezka was tutoring Stephanie; it was the only session in progress. They did not notice me at first. When they did, Alezka looked at me, wide eyed and worried, as if I had caught her doing something wrong. She had been speaking with Stephanie in Spanish. Alezka turned back to Stephanie and continued their conversation—in English. Recognizing that I had already disrupted their dynamic, I decided to disrupt it a little more.

"So, what are you two working on?" I asked.

"It's an essay for her basic writing class," Alezka responded. I had spoken with Stephanie on several earlier occasions, but she remained quiet.

"Okay," I responded.

"I was just explaining something to her in Spanish because I thought it would make more sense that way," Alezka continued. It was clear Alezka thought she was guilty of violating writing center policy.

"Okay. Did it help?" I asked Stephanie.

"Yeah," she replied shyly.

"Great, then keep doing it," I said as matter of factly as I could.

I walked out of the center wondering why Alezka thought she had done something wrong. Our writing center was at an institution where approximately 50 percent of the undergraduate population was Hispanic, most of whom spoke Spanish. In addition, the university was located in Miami-Dade County, which has the third largest Hispanic population in the United States (Pew Research Center 2012). According to the 2012 US Census Bureau report, Hispanics comprised 64.3 percent of the population in Miami-Dade, and 72.3 percent of overall residents spoke a language other than English at home (United States Census

DOI: 10.7330/9781607324140.c005

Bureau 2013). So, we were located in a cultural context in which using two languages was common. Alezka and Stephanie both spoke English and Spanish, and I knew they both used both languages frequently during conversations, so why would this one be any different?

"Because we're in the writing center," Alezka said to me afterwards when we discussed her session. "I wasn't sure if I was allowed to use both because we're supposed to be teaching English." Alezka was reinforcing the underlying assumption—and sometimes requirement—in US educational settings that English is the only language faculty, tutors, and students are allowed or supposed to use, especially when teaching and learning English.

Alezka and I talked at length about her session, and we brought up the issue at our next staff meeting. The staff consisted of six undergraduate peer tutors—all of whom could speak Spanish. Three were in favor of using Spanish during sessions and three were opposed, though no one was entirely convinced his or her opinion was right. The staff and I discussed how using Spanish might benefit a session and how it might detract from a session. We talked about how tutors reacted when students used Spanish first—and vice versa—and we talked about times when the tutors refused to engage students in Spanish. This conversation lasted for weeks without a definitive resolution, so we decided to investigate it more deliberately the following semester.

The next fall one of my undergraduate tutors, Aileen Valdes, worked with me as a research assistant to explore the pedagogical implications of code-switching among multilingual (English- and Spanish-speaking) students and tutors. Based on anecdotal data from our staff meetings, there seemed to be varying opinions on how and when to use Spanish during sessions and whether or not Spanish should be used at all. Therefore, we developed a project based on the following questions: When and how might code-switching be used during a tutoring session? What are students' and tutors' attitudes toward code-switching in the writing center? From these questions, we wanted to learn, is it possible that students and/or tutors prefer using both languages, since this reflects the culture surrounding them? Or do they prefer to work toward the exclusive target language since English is the language of the university and professional world? As writing centers become more linguistically diverse, these are important questions all centers should be examining as the answers will likely be different from one center to the next.

Developing a contextualized understanding of code-switching as a tutoring pedagogy is especially valuable because an increasing number of multilingual students and tutors, particularly those who speak English and Spanish, are populating our writing centers. Hispanic students are now the largest minority group on college campuses, comprising over 16 percent of all US college students, a number that increases to 25 percent for two-year colleges (Fry and Lopez 2012). Many of these students are bilingual, speaking combinations of Spanish and English at home, school, and work. In many sections of the country, particularly South Florida, Texas, Arizona, New Mexico, California, New York, and the Chicago area, the growing numbers of Hispanic students are reflected in the student demographics we see in our writing centers—both as student-writers and, in increasing numbers, as writing tutors (See Gillespie and Hutchinson, this volume).

As the number of Hispanic and multilingual students continues to increase, writing center tutors can expect to experience more languages within their daily work environments, whether those languages are for social, professional, or educational purposes. Tutors should be aware of how and when multiple languages can be used during tutoring sessions (see Liu, this volume), and tutors should expect to have more conversations and debates like the ones I had with Alezka and the rest of my staff. Writing center directors can expect some students and tutors to be in favor of a multilingual approach, one that accepts and promotes using mixtures of languages and language varieties; they can also expect some community members to resist multilingual approaches to tutoring writers, holding steadfast to an English-only approach that results in code-segregation (Guerra 2012); and directors and tutors should expect others to be ambivalent, perhaps because they can see both positive and negative outcomes of such an approach.

If writing centers choose to embrace multilingual approaches to writing center work, we can expect to disrupt some of the more traditional dynamics of our centers. As Nancy Grimm notes,

> When a writing center embraces multilingualism rather than monolingualism as a conceptual norm, many things change. Most importantly, the writing center begins to actively recruit tutors who speak other languages and varieties of English. Not insignificantly, the racial composition of the staff changes. The writing center becomes a place where multiple varieties of English are spoken rather than only historically privileged varieties of English. (Grimm 2009, 18)

Using Grimm's call as a starting point, this chapter discusses a research project that investigated what happens when "multiple varieties of English are spoken" in a center, not only for social conversation but also during sessions between multilingual tutors and students. The chapter defines key terms related to facilitating multilingual approaches to writing center work and shows transcriptions of tutoring sessions in which tutors or students used both English and Spanish during tutoring sessions. It then discusses tutors' and students' attitudes toward using both languages during writing center sessions. The chapter concludes by offering ways to build on this research and to bring languages other than English into writing centers. This research benefitted our work because it helped develop a contextualized understanding of our students' and tutors' attitudes toward and experiences with code-switching during writing center sessions.

CODE-SWITCHING AND CODE-MIXING

If multiple languages are going to be used in a writing center environment, there are several key linguistic terms worth noting in order to understand how people incorporate different languages into conversations. These terms—*situational code-switching, metaphorical code-switching, code-mixing,* and *code-meshing*—all offer us ways to envision how tutors and students can utilize multilingual approaches for pedagogical purposes. This section defines the first three terms, while the fourth will appear toward the end of this essay.

Code-Switching—Situational

Sociolinguist R. A. Hudson defines "code switching" as a situation in which someone "who speaks more than one language chooses between them according to circumstances" (Hudson 2001, 51). For many multilingual students, a US writing center is likely to be a place where they choose to speak English. Hudson calls this type of act "situational code switching," which happens when

> the switches between languages . . . coincide with changes from one external situation (for example, talking to members of the family) to another (for example, talking to neighbors). The choice of language is controlled by rules, which members of the community learn from their experience. (52)

The controlling rules of a typical US writing center would likely appear to be constructed by an English-only philosophy due to the center's being situated in an institution of higher education guided by, as Horner and Trimbur (2002, 595) suggest, "a tacit language policy of unidirectional monolingualism." This "tacit language policy of unidirectional monolingualism" may have been what scared Alezka when she realized I heard her using Spanish during her session. Her educational experiences, up to that point, were likely grounded in the implied understanding that English was the only language we used in the writing center. So, Alezka and her classmates performed situational code-switching when they shifted from speaking Spanish with friends around campus (external situation 1) to speaking English with student-writers once they entered the physical space of the writing center (external situation 2).

Code-Switching—Metaphorical

As the tutors became more comfortable using Spanish in our writing center—for either social or pedagogical purposes—more students began using Spanish in the center. This created a more multilingual environment, a change in dynamic that allowed tutors and students to engage in what Hudson calls "metaphorical code switching," which is when "the choice of language determines the situation" (Hudson 2001, 53). Based on our observations, it appeared to be common for our bilingual tutors and students to take a break from the "work" of the session—discussing an assignment or the immediate writing task at hand—to have a moment of general conversation. It was during these times that one of the two might code-switch from English, the language of "work," to Spanish, the language of conversation. This kind of switching should not be surprising since, as Hudson writes, "it is entirely to be expected that bilingual speakers will use their choice of language in order to define the situation, rather than letting the situation define the choice of language" (Hudson 2001, 52).

Code-Mixing

Hudson defines "code mixing" as a communicative moment "when one fluent bilingual speaker speaks to another fluent bilingual speaker and changes languages without any change at all in the situation" (Hudson 2001, 53). The major difference, then, between code-switching and code-mixing is that, for the latter, the situation does not change. As I will show in the next section, bilingual tutors and students may occasionally code-mix in the middle of sentences, using combinations of Spanish and English words, to discuss an assignment, for instructional purposes, or for general conversation. In these examples, the situation becomes one in which the languages seamlessly blend together, perhaps changing the sense of "unidirectional monolingualism" to one of "multidirectional bilingualism."

THE SOUND OF BILINGUAL SESSIONS: CODE-SWITCHING AND CODE-MIXING IN ACTION

To examine how and when bilingual tutors and students were employing Spanish during writing center conferences, Aileen and I decided to gather data via three primary research methods: observations, surveys, and interviews. We applied for a research grant from the International Writing Centers Association (IWCA), which we received, to purchase a recorder, transcription machine, and $10 gift cards for participants, and we applied for approval from our university's Institutional Review Board, which we also received.

For our observations, we decided to audio record tutoring sessions between tutors and students who could speak both English and Spanish. We asked staff members for their permission ahead of sessions, and then one of us asked for the student's permission at the beginning of each session, reviewing IRB protocol and asking the student to sign a consent form; therefore, all sessions were recorded with both the student's and tutor's permission. After the sessions, we asked the tutor if any instances of code-switching occurred during the session. Not all sessions included code-switching. The tutors and students discussed in this section, though, did use both languages during their sessions, as the observations captured instances of metaphorical code-switching and code-mixing.

Yessica and Ashley: Metaphorical Code-Switching

When Yessica entered the university as a first-year student, she was placed in a developmental writing course for which she needed tutoring. That semester, she became a regular at the writing center, and she continued to visit regularly into her junior year. While she worked with most of the tutors, she developed a strong rapport with Ashley. For their tutoring session discussed below, Yessica brought an assignment from one of her upper-level English classes, taught by Professor González, to the center hoping to get assistance with citations. In this session, you will see the student introduce an example of metaphorical code-switching in order to create a moment of solidarity between her and her tutor.

About six minutes into the session, Yessica and Ashley discussed the use of quotation marks when quoting a resource. Ashley explained how to use quotation marks and when Yessica should and should not use them. Here is an excerpt:

ASHLEY: And why is that italicized? You don't know? (laugh)

YESSICA: It's not a quote. Well, it is a quote from what I read but is not, you know, it's like a saying.

ASHLEY: You could just put quotation marks. You don't need to italicize, and this is part of your writing, so you don't have to italicize that either. None of that actually.

YESSICA: *González me tiene loca.* [González is driving me crazy.]

(mutual laughter.)

YESSICA: I swear to God. When this like . . .

ASHLEY: (laughing) Yeah, but you're almost finished.

YESSICA: Yes, I can't wait.

ASHLEY: Okay (speaks softly while reading the revised text). Okay, good.

YESSICA: (continues to read text)

In her moment of frustration, Yessica code-switches, initiating in Spanish a conversational comment to Ashley: "*González me tiene loca.*" Ashley acknowledges the moment of solidarity by laughing with Yessica about her feelings toward the professor. Yessica then code-switches back to English, transferring her emotional claim to her academic/ professional language ("I swear to God. When this like . . ."). There is a moment of conversational overlap, as Ashley speaks over Yessica during the second half of Yessica's complaint. Still laughing, Ashley interjects some reassurance in English: "Yeah, but you're almost finished." This may be in conjunction with Yessica's most recent language use, Ashley's understanding of her role as English tutor, or simply because she just chose to speak in English. Yessica's tension appears to have dissipated a bit, as she continues in English: "Yes, I can't wait." Ashley concludes this portion of their conversation, using English to move the session forward: "Okay, good." Yessica begins reading the text Ashley has started, and they refocus on Yessica's work.

In this particular case, Yessica provides us with an example of what Hudson refers to as "metaphorical code switching." The physical situation where Yessica and Ashley are engaged does not change—they are both sitting and talking in the writing center. However, the metaphorical situation does change. Yessica's use of Spanish changes their roles momentarily from tutor and tutee to one that is less formal and more casual in that moment. In this moment of tension, Yessica removes herself momentarily from her work mode. Ashley's laughter signals an acknowledgment of Yessica's comment, but Ashley quickly refocuses the conversation back to English and, thus, back to working on the assignment.

This was the only time Spanish was used by either during the session. Yessica initiated the usage during a moment of solidarity when she appeared to be trusting Ashley's judgment about her feelings toward her instructor.

Roberta and Stephanie: Code-Mixing—Session 1

Originally from Honduras, Stephanie moved to Miami after graduating high school so she could attend college in the United States. Stephanie had been in the United States for only a few months before enrolling in her first college classes. Stephanie was one of the writing center's most frequent visitors during her first three years at the university. She worked with almost every tutor at least once and formed regular working relationships with several of them. Stephanie worked with Roberta several times during the course of two years, and the two often code-mixed during sessions.

The following excerpt is from a session during which Stephanie needed help writing a research paper for one of her psychology classes. During the session, Stephanie uses Spanish mainly for questions and instructions, while she uses English mainly for reading, keywords, and some communication. Stephanie initiates Spanish frequently, but Roberta primarily uses English to respond.

About five minutes into the session, Stephanie and Roberta were using the Purdue OWL to determine the correct format for adding the date to a blog citation.

ROBERTA: Here we go. Blog post.

STEPHANIE: *Espérate, pues, creo que ya abrí aquí.* [Wait, then, I think I opened (it) here.]

ROBERTA: Okay, we need to include the title of the blog in the URL. Please, note that the title is online . . . Okay, so you're going to write *March*.

STEPHANIE: March, *¿qué?* [March, what?]

ROBERTA: March *el cinco.* [March the fifth.] What's the day that you got it?

STEPHANIE: August 10, 2009.

ROBERTA: No, that *you* got it.

STEPHANIE: *Ah, que yo . . .* [Ah, that I . . .]

ROBERTA: *Que viste el comercial.* [That you saw the commercial.]

STEPHANIE: *Ayer.* [Yesterday.]

ROBERTA: So put yesterday's date.

STEPHANIE: *¿Qué fue ayer? ¿El veintitrés?* [What was yesterday? The twenty-third?]

ROBERTA: 'Cause we don't know when it was put up, right?

STEPHANIE: *Bueno, allí sale.* [Well, it comes out there.]

ROBERTA: *No dice el . . . pero* does it say when that commercial was put up? [It doesn't say the . . . but does it say when that commercial was put up?]

STEPHANIE: *No, no dice nada.* [No, no, it doesn't say anything.] It doesn't say. *Entonces sería así.* [Then it would be like this.] March 2010 *y ¿qué más?* [March 2010 and what else?]

ROBERTA: *Espérate.* [Wait.] Put the other date—August 10. *Eso en paréntesis.* [That in parentheses.] There, start writing. *Pon el año primero.* [Put the year first.]

This is an example of Roberta using a code-mixing pedagogy to instruct Stephanie. Roberta code-mixes English to Spanish to clarify a suggestion she has made. She rephrases the colloquial English phrase *you got* it to a more specific phrase, in Spanish, *"Que viste el commercial."* ["That you saw the commercial."] Roberta used the colloquial "you got it" to ask Stephanie when she viewed the video, implying that the date Stephanie first saw the video was the date she "got it" from the Internet. Stephanie responds "August 10, 2009," which may be the date the video was either created or posted to the Internet. Roberta responds by asking Stephanie again about the date she "got it," emphasizing the word *you* in hopes that Stephanie would recognize that Roberta was not asking about a production date but about the date Stephanie first watched the video. Stephanie hears Roberta's emphasis on *you* and recognizes Roberta's intention, so she responds with *"Ah, que yo."* ["Ah, that I."] As Stephanie says this, Roberta clarifies her intention by stating *"Que viste el comercial."* ["That you saw the commercial."]

This was the first time during the session that Roberta used Spanish to clarify a language issue Stephanie had with English. The language issue in this case was not one related to the assignment; rather, it was related to a question Roberta asked. While a native English-speaking (NES) student may have been able to understand Roberta's intention (though that is not guaranteed), Stephanie was not able to recognize Roberta's intention by using "got it" in place of "watched it" or "accessed it" from the Internet. Roberta's explanation, then, prepared Stephanie for future experiences with the ambiguity inherent within a phrase such as *got it.*

Roberta and Stephanie: Code-Mixing—Session 2

Stephanie worked with Roberta on a second assignment about two weeks after the session discussed in the previous section. Stephanie's assignment was to write another short research paper, and, since Stephanie had already drafted and revised her essay, the two focused most of their time on lower-order concerns. During the session, Roberta noticed Stephanie had been translating some of the ideas expressed in the paper word for word from Spanish to English. The excerpt below shows two examples of this.

> STEPHANIE: . . . for example, Farmville. This webpage I always use it because I can communicate with my friends, family, and also it reminds me of birthdays from others.
>
> ROBERTA: Okay. This webpage I always use.
>
> STEPHANIE: Used?
>
> ROBERTA: No, not the tense. This webpage I always use. In Spanish, *sí.* [In Spanish, yes]. *Que tú digas que esta página siempre la uso, pero* in English, translating it doesn't work. [For you to say "this web page I always use," but in English, translating it doesn't work].You have to swap it. I always use this webpage.
>
> STEPHANIE: *Ya, ahora sí. ¿Así o . . .* [Ok, now I get it. Like this, or . . .]
>
> ROBERTA: *Así,* and you can take out that *it.* [Like that, and you can take out that *it.*]
>
> STEPHANIE: I always use this webpage because I can communicate with my friends, family, and also it reminds me of birthdays from others . . . *yo no sé si hay una coma aquí.* [I don't know if there is a comma here.]
>
> ROBERTA: No. Look, the same *cosa que pasó aquí* with "birthdays from others." [Look, the same thing that happened here with "birthdays from others."]
>
> STEPHANIE: It reminds me—ah. Okay.
>
> ROBERTA: It reminds you of what?
>
> STEPHANIE: It reminds me of date?
>
> ROBERTA: No. What you're doing is thinking about it in Spanish: *que es los cumpleaños de otros.* [What you're doing is thinking about it in Spanish: that is the birthdays of others.] And then you're translating it into English, but when you put it in English, "birthdays from others" doesn't make sense. You could say "it reminds me about other people's birthdays."
>
> STEPHANIE: It reminds me about other people's birthdays. *¿Con coma arriba o no?* [With a comma on top or no?]

In both of these situations, Roberta recognizes a Spanish construction written in English. Both of the clauses ("This web page I always use" and "reminds me of birthdays from others") are understandable, but they produce an accented English that may be labeled as problematic by an instructor reading Stephanie's work. For the first clause, Roberta quickly explains to Stephanie how the word order she used in English reflects a Spanish construction, and Roberta suggests a way to reorder it in a way that reads more like Standard American English. For the second clause, Roberta explains to Stephanie how the Spanish *de otros* can translate to either "from others" or "of others" in English, and that Stephanie was selecting the one that would sound awkward to her audience. Transfer errors, which occur when a speaker's L1 influences their L2, can be difficult to overcome, but the goal now is for Stephanie to incorporate these new English words and phrases into her own lexicon and apply them in the future.

THE CODE-SWITCHING/CODE-MIXING DEBATE— STUDENTS' AND TUTORS' OPINIONS

In addition to learning about how and when code-switching and code-mixing might occur during sessions, Aileen and I wanted to gauge our bilingual students' and tutors' attitudes about these approaches. During the first discussions I had with Alezka and other staff members, there were mixed opinions about code-switching and code-mixing. As we continued to discuss this approach over the course of a few semesters, more tutors began feeling comfortable using Spanish in the center for sessions and general conversation. If the writing center was gradually becoming more multilingual, would that encourage more students to work there, or might it make some students feel apprehensive about our tutors? Did the tutors think this approach was appropriate, or did they find that students were not comfortable speaking a second language in an environment dominated by English? To find answers to these questions, Aileen and I conducted formal interviews with thirteen bilingual students who frequented the writing center and five bilingual tutors who claimed they had used Spanish during tutoring sessions.

For each interview, Aileen and I met the participant(s) in my office. While most of the interviews were with individuals, one was with a pair of students and another was with a group of three students. The interviews were designed to be less a formal question-and-answer process and more of a discussion. Since we knew many of our students and tutors came from different areas of the United States and Central and South America, we began each interview by asking the participants to talk a bit about their backgrounds and learning both Spanish and English. We then asked about (1) their experiences in the writing center, (2) about specific times they may have experienced code-switching in educational settings, including the writing center, and (3) their opinions regarding code-switching during tutoring sessions. During each interview, we asked many follow-up questions as topics emerged during our discussions. The following sections provide examples of what were consistent opinions among the students and tutors we interviewed.

Yessica (student)

One of the first students I interviewed was Yessica, the student who had worked frequently with Ashley. Yessica immigrated to the United States from Cuba when she was four, and she lived at home with her parents, both of whom spoke little English. During her interview, Yessica stated that she spoke more Spanish than English during her time away from campus and university work.

I met Yessica several weeks into her freshman year when she stopped by my office to ask about the writing center. During our first discussion, she told me her writing professor had said he thought her English was not strong enough to pass his class and that she was better off dropping out of college. I explained to her that the writing center would help her as often as she needed assistance and that I hoped she would work hard to prove her professor wrong. She told me she was determined to do so.

Now a junior, Yessica stopped by my office for our interview, during which she recalled her first visit to the center. Yessica explained to Aileen and me that prior to entering the writing center for the first time, she was nervous because she thought she might not get the help she needed. She said, "I was scared that I was going to be judged, and when I left, they were going to be talking about me and criticizing me. That was really intimidating." However, Ashley made Yessica feel at ease early during their first session by addressing her in Spanish. This surprised Yessica, because, as she said, "I thought that Spanish was not used here. You know and probably I was going to get mistaken, and they were not going to help me." She then went on to say that being allowed to use Spanish in the writing center encouraged her to become a regular visitor.

Like many students, particularly nonnative English-speaking students who are relatively new to the United States and college life, Yessica was intimidated by the thought of visiting the writing center because she thought the tutors would judge her based on her ability to speak and write in English (Bruce 2009). This is a common perception that our writing center staff worked hard to dispel. By embracing a more multilingual approach, the tutors tried to create an environment that showed great respect for language and cultural differences.

Diana (student)

Diana had been a student in my second-semester English course, and she visited the writing center about once a week to work on assignments for a variety of her classes. Diana began the interview by telling Aileen and me that she was born and raised in Puerto Rico until the age of six-teen, when she moved to Maryland. She said she only took one English class while growing up in Puerto Rico, so she had little formal prepara-tion in English before her move to the United States. Two years later, Diana enrolled at our university and started using the writing center. The first tutor she worked with was Alezka, who helped ease Diana's anxiety during the beginning of their session. Diana reflected on their session: "I remember I got stuck explaining to her the assignment and she's like, 'Do you speak Spanish?' I was like 'Yes.' She's like, 'Explain it to me in Spanish and I'll walk you through.' 'Okay, *esto, esto, esto . . .*' [Okay, this, this, this . . .]. After I explained it to her in my first language, I was able to keep going with the progress of the assignment."

For Diana, her tutor's ability to code-mix provided her with a level of comfort that encouraged her to move forward with her session and feel productive. This level of comfort and productivity led her to become a regular visitor to the writing center. Diana explained why she appreci-ated being able to work with bilingual tutors.

> It's good to have a tutor that is bilingual or multilingual because some-times I get these mental blocks, or sometimes I'm not sure if this is the right way to say it. So, I rather discuss it with the tutor in order to pre-vent . . . my first language is Spanish so . . . instead of taking my whole time in the world trying to think in English, and in my head I'm thinking in Spanish, I would rather tell the person who speaks Spanish. I say it in Spanish, and if that person tells me how to say it in English, then at least I get feedback how to say it in English, and I'll apply it in my vocabulary. I wanna prevent that much stuttering and when if I say something like it won't make sense. I don't wanna make a fool out of myself.

Diana's attitude about the writing center changed from the one she had before her first visit. This change is important, as she said code-mixing helped her better comprehend writing in English. The bilingual environment made her more comfortable and had a positive impact on her attitude, which kept her motivated to visit the writing center rou-tinely. This willingness to visit the center had a positive effect on her English-language learning experience.

While many of the Hispanic students Aileen and I interviewed, like Diana, shared the notion that they enjoy having tutors who can code-switch between Spanish and English, some also stated it can occasionally be better to work with a tutor who only speaks English (or only speaks English during sessions). After discussing positive experiences working with a bilingual tutor, Diana acknowledged the benefits of working with tutors who only speak English: "It's a challenge. It will help me improve in English 'cause it's kind of reinforcing me or pushing me to think in English, speak English. It's like a challenge, but sort of like it's helping me, because sometimes when you're speaking in English, you have to think in English." Diana's conclusion was that both approaches have the ability to provide students like her with strong learning opportunities.

Courtney and Maria (students)

Courtney and Maria were good friends who often visited the writing center together. Aileen and I felt they would be more comfortable talking with us together, so we decided to interview both of them at the same time. Courtney was a twenty-year-old senior prelaw major who arrived in Miami from Cuba when she was thirteen. She explained that she believes that since the writing center is an academic environment, she should only use English. She said, "I pretty much come in with the mindset to speak English. I have a lot of friends that I speak Spanish to, but I try within the confines to speak English as much as I can." For Courtney, there is a clear distinction between using the two languages: English is for academic and professional purposes, and it is the language that will provide her with a better future. Spanish, on the other hand, is reserved for situations involving family and friends who do not communicate well in English.

Maria shared several of Courtney's opinions about using Spanish in the writing center, only Maria felt more strongly against it. Maria, who emigrated from Peru when she was four, explained that she did not think it would be appropriate for a bilingual tutor to use Spanish to discuss academic work with her. However, she would not mind if a tutor used Spanish during a more social moment, such as greeting her at the beginning of a session. Maria said,

> [The tutor] could speak Spanish to me if he's trying to be social and friendly, not when he's helping me with work, unless he's making an outside joke just to alleviate tension. Generally, I wouldn't like it because right now the standards are set by the people here in English, so if you're doing it for social reasons or to express yourself, then that's something different. But in academia right now, everything is in English. . . . I don't think [tutors] should speak to [students] in Spanish because their professors won't and the people that are gonna be in their field won't, so they're

gonna be like my dad. They won't feel the need to assimilate anymore, so they're just going to be that lagging thing behind that won't come along that won't catch up.

Similar to Courtney, Maria expresses a clear distinction between the functions of each language: English is for professional and academic settings, and Spanish is for socializing. She believes using Spanish in the writing center will hinder her professional progress.

Roberta (tutor)

While the students Aileen and I interviewed provided us with reasons they both liked and disliked code-switching in the writing center, we knew it was important to hear the voices of the tutors as well. What were their experiences using a bilingual approach to tutoring, and what were their experiences using two languages during one session? The first tutor we interviewed was Roberta, who had used code-switching techniques frequently with Stephanie and other students. We conducted the interview in my office, as it would be quieter there than in the writing center.

Roberta, a double major in professional writing and English, started working as a writing center tutor during her junior year, a semester after the staff had started discussing bilingual approaches to tutoring. Roberta was born and raised in Miami, but her family still had very strong ties to the Dominican Republic, where they lived prior to moving to South Florida. Roberta said she spoke English to her mother at home but that her mother "would still respond in Spanish." As the oldest child, Roberta said it was difficult at times while growing up because "everyone else got help from their parents on homework, and I had to stick it out on my own because [my family] could never help me with English or vocabulary, or explaining 'what does this mean?'" Roberta became the most fluent English speaker in her home and often had to translate conversations and documents for her mother.

Roberta favored code-switching and code-mixing as pedagogical tools, as mentioned earlier in this chapter. During her interview, she discussed how she approached situations when students produce problematic translations.

> Most students think in Spanish and write in English, especially if [they are] bilingual. Even I do that sometimes. Well, if I get stuck, the first thing that I can process is Spanish, so when they get stuck, the first thing they will process is Spanish. So, I say, "Okay, just say it to me in Spanish then." Then I'll even help them out. Sometimes you just cannot think of

the word in English, but you know the exact word you're looking for in Spanish. It'll just ease them because they don't have that language barrier where the tutor doesn't get where they're coming from, so it makes it a little easier because [students think] "she's just like me. She thinks in Spanish, or she knows what the word I'm looking for is because she knows it in Spanish."

While Roberta often had success with this approach, bilingual students she worked with were not always receptive to her introducing Spanish into sessions. Roberta reflected on one session when she spoke in Spanish and the student replied, "I don't want to hear it in Spanish because I want to improve my English." She said she complied with the student's request and only used English for the rest of their time together.

Roberta felt it was better to invite students to decide whether or not Spanish should be spoken during a session than to not allow Spanish at all. She said, "I understand the student has to learn English, but why [create] frustration. They know you speak the language, but you refuse to help them using their native language?" For her, "The only drawback is if the student only communicates to you in their native language and refuses to try to communicate in English" because then they "are using it as a cushion." As a tutor, "you have to know when to draw back and say, "Can you say it to me in English? How do you write it in English?" As Roberta mentioned toward the end of our discussion, her approval of code-switching and code-mixing went back to her earliest educational experiences when she struggled to learn English and had no one to communicate with in Spanish. She said her sense of feeling lost and hopeless was something she did not want her students to experience.

Marco (tutor)

Marco grew up in Rosario, Argentina, and started studying English there when he was around eight years old. He moved to Miami with his family when he was fifteen and enrolled in ESOL classes at a local public high school before being placed into gifted classes. Marco, a communications major, began working in the writing center during his junior year, and he was initially opposed to code-switching and code-mixing in the writing center. He said his opposition stemmed from his experiences in his ESOL classes, where he felt as if he needed to completely immerse himself in English in order to communicate with classmates.

As more tutors and students used Spanish in the writing center, Marco said he slowly started to speak Spanish more himself. He discussed his experiences with one student, a female from Venezuela whose frustrations with English prompted him to use Spanish during one of their sessions. Marco said, "I realized when I started talking with Natalia in Spanish, she felt more comfortable writing in English because she could go back to me and ask me in Spanish." Marco realized that building linguistic rapport with this particular student helped her feel more relaxed during sessions and, hence, more productive, so he continued to code-mix with her during subsequent sessions. However, that experience did not necessarily change his opinion on using a bilingual approach to tutoring. Even after experiencing success with Natalia, Marco said of his other sessions, "I make an effort to not speak Spanish because I really feel like I am not helping them fully."

After each interview, Aileen transcribed the session and the two of us reviewed it together. If we had any questions, we followed up with the participants and asked for clarification. Once we completed the interview process, we reviewed all the transcripts and coded them based on emerging themes.

These interviews reinforced our initial understanding that Hispanic students' and tutors' opinions about whether or not Spanish should be used during sessions can be quite complex. It appears there is no clear distinction between students who prefer one style over the other. We found that the amount of time spent in the United States did not determine whether or not a student preferred one style over the other, nor did family proficiency and educational background. These findings lead to a conclusion that, to paraphrase Hudson, we can be sure no two multilingual students have the same preferences for tutoring styles because no two multilingual students have the same educational and linguistic experiences with English or Spanish (Hudson 2001, 11).

CONCLUSIONS

The writing center mentioned in this essay exists in a highly multilingual, multicultural environment that operates within an overarching "general political climate that excoriates non-'standard' varieties of English and policy that mandates against bilingual education" (Rymes and Anderson 2004, 130). Even in this diverse region of the country, some schools promote an English-only educational system that marginalizes large numbers of students, especially Hispanics. The center we worked at quietly challenged that monolingual norm for almost two years before we began openly discussing and researching the potential benefits of using multilingual pedagogies during tutoring sessions. We decided to develop a more formal understanding of how and when code-switching and code-mixing could be used during sessions, and, perhaps even more important, whether students and tutors wanted to use two languages during their sessions. As Betsy Rymes and Kate Anderson continue, "The fact remains that every individual in the United States is entitled to receive an education. In order to ensure that the civil rights of every student are not violated, schools must be granted the authority to use students' home languages as paths to school language and academic content" (Rymes and Anderson 2004, 130). As a result of this research project, we granted our students and tutors the authority to use their home languages and to code-switch and code-mix in ways that helped them become more productive during sessions. In doing such, we engaged in many conversations about working in a highly diverse environment, a dynamic "contact zone" (Pratt 1991), which heightened our awareness about the academic and social environments in which we live and work.

We learned that code-switching and code-mixing can be used as pedagogical tools during tutoring sessions between bilingual students. They can be used to create a sense of solidarity between a student and a tutor (see Yessica and Ashley, Marco and Natalia) so the student may feel more comfortable working in an environment that has historically marginalized them due to their linguistic and cultural backgrounds. They can also be used to clarify moments of confusion when a student can think of a concept in her L1 but cannot adequately express it in her L2 (see Roberta and Ashley). Both of these methods allow students and tutors to move forward with their sessions.

Though many of these bilingual tutors and students found code-switching and code-mixing to be helpful during a session, some expressed a sense of ambivalence regarding whether or not they liked using both languages. Most of the tutors and students Aileen and I interviewed expressed a sense of optimism about having the ability to code-switch and code-mix during sessions because it increased their ability to communicate; however, several stated that they wondered if code-switching may, at times, slow down an individual's learning process, as it took time and experience away from the target language. Overall, though, it appears most have embraced the fact that they have the ability to think, write, talk, and teach in more than one language and that their work more closely reflects the multilingual reality that surrounds the university.

THINKING AHEAD: CODE-MESHING?

While code-switching and code-mixing during tutoring sessions may contribute to the creation of a more multilingual writing center environment, a realization of the prototype promoted by Grimm, it still does not address the fact that students—and tutors—ultimately are faced with the challenge of having to write in Standard American English. Thus, in academic settings, code-switching and code-mixing may be relegated only to the center, viewed as marginalized acts that can only be practiced as conversations, not as writing. While these linguistic acts can occur in the center, they are often not tolerated in texts produced for the classroom.

If we can achieve multilingual writing centers, ones that employ tutors with diverse linguistic backgrounds and who promote linguistic diversity on campus, we can take a step toward challenging monolinguistic norms found on many campuses. First, centers can promote code-switching and code-mixing as effective pedagogical tools in an effort to challenge assumptions about English-only education. "Code-switching," according to Ronald K. S. MacCauley, "used to be taken as a sign that speakers imperfectly controlled either or both languages. This turns out to be a misjudgment. In many cases, speakers who are fully fluent in both languages will switch back and forth for a variety of reasons, often connected to topic or attitude" (MacCauley 2011, 90). The tutors at our center often demonstrated great fluency when switching back and forth between English and Spanish, using each language for a variety of pedagogical purposes.

Next, if writing centers can challenge the ways we teach and tutor writing in multilingual settings, perhaps they can challenge the way writing is taught in classrooms. As Suresh Canagarajah states, "A classroom based on 'standard' English and formal instruction limits the linguistic acquisition, creativity, and production among students" (Canagarajah 2006, 592). Linguistically diverse writing centers can show how multilingual pedagogies can increase opportunities for learning, the way they did for Stephanie; for creative expression, the way they did for Diana and Yessica; and for production, the way they did for Marco's student, Natalia. Perhaps, then, these learning moments can be shared in an effort to promote Canagarajah's notion of code-meshing.

Similar to Hudson's *code-mixing*, Canagarajah offers the concept of *code-meshing* as an alternative to *code-switching*. Code-switching implies using different languages for different situations; for example, students may use Spanish for social interaction, but they still need to write in Standard American English. Code-mixing, then, blends languages together, but mainly for the purpose of conversation or writing informal texts. Taking this mixing of languages one step further, Canagarajah suggests that code-meshing is process of "merging the codes" into academic texts and environments rather than separating one from another (Canagarajah 2006, 598). The difference between code-switching and code-meshing, according to Vershawn Ashanti Young and Aja Martinez, "is that the former arises from traditional English-only ideologies that require multilingual/multidialectical students to choose one code over another while privileging codes associated with dominant races and further alienating the codes of traditionally oppressed peoples. However, code-meshing promotes linguistic democracy, as students are not called to choose but are rather allowed to blend language and identities" (Young and Martinez 2011, xxiv). If writing centers recognize code-meshing as a next step toward building a more multilingual educational environment, it may mean tutors and students, such as Yessica, Ashley, Roberta, Stephanie, and Marco, can transform their bilingual conversations into texts that become part of a classroom and academic norm that democratizes our educational systems.

Questions to Consider

1. What are the attitudes and perceptions of code-switching/mixing in your writing center? What do the tutors think about using multiple languages to tutor English? What do students think?

2. Record several tutoring sessions at your center and transcribe the conversations. Read through the transcriptions to note how and when tutors and students use nonacademic language during their conversations (see Babcock, this volume). What seems to prompt the use of nonacademic English?

3. Some writing centers, such as the one at Baruch College in New York City, have asked students who speak a variety of languages to contribute to projects for which they write expressions like *I write* or *hello* in languages other than English, which the staff then post somewhere in the center. These projects support multilingualism in the center as well as one of Dr. Mendez's recommendations in Shanti Bruce's chapter in this collection: "Present a multicultural scenario." These efforts show students the different ways writers speak and write at their institutions. If you were to do a project like this at your center, do you think it would make a positive difference?

For Further Reading

Horner, Bruce, and John Trimbur. 2002. "English Only and U.S. College Composition." *College Composition and Communication* 53 (4): 594–630. http://dx.doi.org/10.2307/1512118.

Bruce Horner and John Trimbur show how composition classrooms promote a "tacit policy of English monolingualism" (594). The authors examine historical reasons for this practice and invite readers to consider ways to incorporate multilingual approaches into teaching composition. Their essay provides a foundation for understanding how code-switching and -mixing in writing centers can be one way of resisting a culture of "unidirectional monolingualism," which Horner and Trimbur believe to be a "problem and limitation of U.S. culture" (597).

Newman, Beatrice Mendez. 2003. "Centering in the Borderlands: The Writing Center at Hispanic-Serving Institutions." *Writing Center Journal* 23 (2): 43–61.

Beatrice Newman claims that "little has been written . . . about Hispanic students and writing centers, and nothing has been written about Hispanic students at writing centers in borderlands institutions" (44). Over ten years later, Newman's claim still holds true. Though there has been a growing movement toward recognizing writing center work from multicultural perspectives, there is still little research and literature regarding Hispanic students' experiences in writing centers, as either writers or tutors.

Young, Vershawn Ashanti, and Aja Y. Martinez, eds. 2011. *Code-Meshing as World English: Pedagogy, Policy, Performance*. Urbana, IL: National Council of Teachers of English.

This collection examines the potential role code-meshing may have in the future of teaching English in a variety of contexts. Chapters focus on how code-meshing can be used to democratize educational settings and "help expand the ways in which students learn English" (xx). The essays in this collection can help tutors think about ways in which their writing centers can help promote linguistic diversity at their institutions.

Acknowledgments

Research presented in this chapter was funded by an International Writing Centers Association Research Grant. I would like to thank Dr. Joanne Pol for assisting with translations and Aileen Valdes for assisting with data collection and early translations.

References

Bruce, Shanti. 2009. "Listening to and Learning from ESL Writers." In *ESL Writers: A Guide for Writing Center Tutors*, 2nd ed. Edited by Shanti Bruce and Ben Rafoth, 217–29. Portsmouth, NH: Heinemann.

Canagarajah, A. Suresh. 2006. "The Place of World Englishes in Composition: Pluralization Continued." *College Composition and Communication* 57 (4): 586–619.

Fry, Richard, and Mark Hugo Lopez. 2012. "Hispanic Student Enrollments Reach New Highs in 2011." Pew Research Center. http://www.pewhispanic.org/2012/08/20 / hispanic-student-enrollments-reach-new-highs-in-2011/.

Grimm, Nancy Maloney. 2009. "New Conceptual Frameworks for Writing Center Work." *Writing Center Journal* 29 (2): 11–27.

Guerra, Juan C. 2012. "From Code-Segregation to Code-Switching to Code-Meshing: Finding Deliverance from Deficit Thinking through Language Awareness and Performance." *Working Papers Series on Negotiating Differences in Language and Literacy* 5: 1–12.

Horner, Bruce, and John Trimbur. 2002. "English Only and U.S. College Composition." *College Composition and Communication* 53 (4): 594–630. http://dx.doi.org/10.2307 /1512118.

Hudson, R. A. 2001. *Sociolinguistics*. Cambridge: Cambridge University Press.

MacCauley, Ronald K. S. 2011. *Seven Ways of Looking at Language.* New York: Palgrave MacMillan.

Pew Research Center. 2012. "Latinos by Geography." http://www.pewhispanic.org/2012/03/16/latinos-by-geography/.

Pratt, Mary Louise. 1991. "Arts of the Contact Zone." *Profession* 91:33–40.

Rymes, Betsy, and Kate Anderson. 2004. "Second Language Acquisition for All: Understanding the Interactional Dynamics of Classrooms in Which Spanish and AAE Are Spoken." *Research in the Teaching of English* 39 (2): 107–34.

United States Census Bureau. 2013. "Miami-Dade County, Florida." http://quickfacts.census.gov/qfd/states/12/12086.html.

Young, Vershawn Ashanti, and Aja Y. Martinez. 2011. "Introduction: Code-Meshing as World English." In *Code-Meshing as World English: Pedagogy, Policy, Performance*, edited by Vershawn Ashanti Young and Aja Y. Martinez, xix–xxxi. Urbana, IL: National Council of Teachers of English.

6

THE DIGITAL VIDEO PROJECT
Self-Assessment in a Multilingual Writing Center

Glenn Hutchinson and Paula Gillespie

Our campuses, particularly our urban campuses, are increasingly multilingual. Many colleges have large numbers of international students while others have populations that reflect our Miami demographics, so they are a mix of students who have studied English grammar abroad and those who immigrated to this country and have learned English without necessarily having studied it. At our growing urban campus, the majority of students are Hispanic, many speaking Spanish as a first language; our university has international students from over one hundred countries. Also, most of our tutors speak more than one language.

So how do we approach and best help our students learn English as a second or third language? How do we, as two writing center directors, help our staff best utilize their skills and resources? One effective way to study tutoring sessions involving two or more languages is to record and review them, followed by reflections and director-tutor conversations. This chapter describes a process approach to educating both tutors and directors through the use of video recording and analysis. After an explanation of the project, we explore three main ideas about what we as directors learned from our tutors and possible implications for writing center research.

1. Ongoing training: Directors have as much to learn from tutors' reflections and looking at videos as tutors do. Tutors trust us with segments of their videos that show their weaknesses as tutors, and their attitudes show an openness to ongoing learning. We are able to reflect on and revise our tutor education based on this project.

2. Diversity: A diverse tutoring staff, including multilingual tutors, can strengthen a writing center, particularly in working with multilingual writers. Many of our tutors use more than one language in a tutoring

DOI: 10.7330/9781607324140.c006

session. In addition, our tutors draw upon their own experiences as language learners when tutoring.

3. Politics of language: Tutors and center directors must continue thinking about their relationship with language and how that informs the way they interact with students. For example, our Digital Video Project often helps us explore our belief that there is no Standard American English, that all dialects are equal, and the possibility for the kind of code-meshing of different languages and dialects Kevin Dvorak discusses in this book.

FORMAT OF THE DIGITAL VIDEO PROJECT

Writing centers can use both audio and video recordings to help tutors reflect upon their work. For example, tutors at the University of Kentucky videotape sessions and reflect upon their body language. They then transcribe the dialogue of a section and write a reflection: "Self-conscious examinations of these texts teach them about their practices and their limits" (Rosner and Wann 2010, 9). In addition, these kinds of projects can make the writing center a place of research for tutors as they watch themselves on video: Who does the talking in the session? What body language do you see? What is working and not working? (Gillespie and Lerner 2008).

In our Digital Video Project, writing consultants in FIU's Center for Excellence in Writing videotape tutoring sessions, write reflections, and conference with the center directors. Writing consultants reflect upon what they learn from watching the videos and what they learn about themselves and the roles of tutor and writer.

The Steps to the Project

1. At least one time each semester, tutors choose one session to videotape. They ask the writer to sign a consent form. If writers do not agree to be videotaped, the session is not recorded and the tutor chooses a different session.

2. Tutors videotape the forty-five-minute session with a Flip, laptop, or phone camera.

3. Tutors watch the video and focus on a pivotal moment in the session.

4. Tutors write a one-page reflection about the session and focus on a clip.
   a. What did you notice from watching the video?
   b. What was the main goal of the session?

    c. To what extent were these goals achieved? Explain.

    d. What did you learn from watching the video? Would you do anything differently? Explain.

5. Tutors upload the video to the director's office computer.

6. The center directors schedule a forty-five-minute conference to discuss the reflection and video. They watch the five-minute clip with the tutor and then discuss what the tutor has learned or questions he/she has.

7. The directors reflect on the conference and discuss with one another what they learned from the session and how they can make use of this knowledge.

ONGOING TRAINING

All of our peer tutors complete a course on writing center theory and practice before working in the writing center, and the Digital Video Project gives us an opportunity for more tutor training in subsequent semesters after the course. Also, we as directors learn much from our tutors, their work with multilingual writers, and our writing center.

Prior to meeting with the tutors, we read their reflections. During the forty-five-minute conference, we first ask tutors if they want to add anything else to their reflection before we view their five- to ten-minute video clip. We watch the video and then have a conversation about the tutoring session. Following the conference, we, the director and assistant director, often have an e-mail exchange about how we can use what we learn, particularly during our weekly staff meetings. Over the past year, we noticed the following themes emerging in our conversations about working with multilingual writers.

Tutors Need Encouragement

Many tutors choose to show their five weakest minutes, a possible indication that they internalize the value of this kind of reflection and that they trust this process to help them become stronger tutors. However, we would not want to discuss only the negative, as sometimes happens when responding to student writing. We often refer to Donald Daiker's (1989) essay "Learning to Praise" and the importance of encouragement, particularly "for students who have known little encouragement and, in part for that reason, suffer from writing apprehension" (105). In a similar way, we need to help tutors identify what is working well in their sessions, for sometimes they do not notice the effective moves they are making as tutors.

Tutors Ask Questions about Being Directive/Nondirective

In our peer-tutoring class, we discuss what we have come to think of as a continuum along a line of directive or nondirective tutoring, and that we should be flexible, perhaps shifting within a session, as needed. Along with our textbook, *The Longman Guide to Peer Tutoring* (Gillespie and Lerner 2008), we compare essays such as Brooks's (1995) "Minimalist Tutoring" and Shamoon and Burns's (1995) "A Critique of Pure Tutoring." We emphasize that we do not need to approach every tutoring session in the same way. For example, international students from China may need direct guidance on the use of articles in their writing. However, at the same time, we do not want to take over a writing session and prevent the writer from expressing what he/she wants to say, and we definitely don't want to overlook issues or problems relating to the student's not meeting the goals of the assignment. We discuss Carol Severino's (2009) chapter in *ESL Writers*, different scenarios of working with multilingual writers, and the possible tutor roles of "assimilationist," "accomodationist," or "separatist." One of our tutors, Jennifer, reflected upon the danger of becoming too "directive" or "assimilationist" and that tutors can "risk removing the writer's unique voice from the paper." She added, "I would suggest always trying to keep in mind that you are trying to help the writer to more clearly convey their own voice rather than teaching them to say things in a way that you believe is better."

The videos help us as directors see what complex tasks the tutors face. We place a heavy emphasis on respect in our center. The research of Castellanos and Gloria (2007) on the retention of Latino students shows they succeed better and are retained to graduation if they find a community where they can be in communication with peers who respect them and are interested in their traditions and language use. Maintaining that respect, though, while perhaps disagreeing with a writer's immediate goals can create tensions for the tutors. Some students who were educated in countries whose writing conventions differ from Standard American English conventions, and even those multilingual writers who were educated in this country, have a hard time not falling into traps of novice writing: summarizing when they should analyze or defaulting to a five-paragraph organization when the assignment calls for something different. Some have also been severely criticized and underestimated by instructors when they hand in work that contains usage considered nonstandard.

Our tutors themselves, many of them, have experienced discrimination firsthand when they have ventured outside of Miami, discrimination based on skin color, hair texture, or the languages they might be speaking with their parents or friends. Within Miami, the most recent immigrants might have experienced shunning and ridicule on the playground, where they are taunted about their accents or lack of understanding. Because of their own experiences, our tutors often embrace Castellanos and Gloria's (2007) assessments of what makes Latino students succeed, and they are strongly motivated to help our students.

In a recent staff meeting, we asked our multilingual tutors how they balance ideas of respect with realistic goal setting. What follows are some responses to the question.

Some students come to Somaily very focused on grammar, and about such a student she says,

> I communicate to the student that if the paper isn't answering the intended prompt, then having perfect grammar won't prevent [the writer] from receiving a lower grade. Sometimes, if the student brings the paper's grading rubric, I show them what percentage of the grade is dedicated to grammar. Usually, grammar isn't one of their professor's main concerns. I assure them that we will come back to grammar once we fix other issues on the paper.

Jennifer writes,

> During sessions where the student and I have established differing hierarchies of problems we'd like to address, I find that letting the student be heard is extremely helpful. Allowing them to state why they are so concerned with a particular aspect of their paper may sometimes make them feel even more in control of their draft. If a professor has stressed the importance of using "correct" grammar, it's understandable that this would be a primary concern for the student. Once we establish what each of us feel are the most important things to address, I try to find a middle ground. If their organization is presenting a serious problem but they want to mainly focus on grammar, I will try to combine explanations for both. So, as we discuss how the order of certain paragraphs may hinder the reader's understanding, I may also inject discussions of sentence-level clarity. At the end of the session, if I feel that we have not addressed everything, I always give them a quick "wrap-up" of things they should still look for.

Luis writes about those students who focus more on whether something is correct rather than if it belongs in the first place. He listens to their concerns, but then asks them a question.

> "So what are you trying to say here in the first place?" This calls the student to think about not only the sentence at hand and their immediate goals, but also forces them to think of the topic they are handling at the moment and whether that sentence even addresses what they were

thinking. . . . This allows our goals that may be separate to align in a way that doesn't involve me forcing the student away from their concern, and keeps the session about the content. Sometimes students are insistent and respect is harder to control, so I sometimes back off and remind them that the time we have won't be enough if they try to tackle these minute issues yet that I am here to work with them.

Syed creates a bulleted suggestion list when there is "disagreement with expectations."

1. Create comfort.

2. Briefly mention "higher order concerns"

3. Praise—Something specific—so confidence is boosted—Everyone likes compliments + builds comfort

4. Address the concern

> If writer disagrees show genuine interest, ask why . . .
> Talk about it so it is "addressed"
> Try again (use "Polite Persistence") to help the writer see "errors"

Syed probably puts *errors* into quotation marks because we have made an effort to avoid this word since its translation into Spanish is a word with strong negative connotations. We are more likely to stress correctness than use the word *errors* for usages that many would consider nonstandard.

Common responses to the writing prompt include listening and asking genuine questions and respecting the writer's priorities by agreeing to work on what they value most, but also mentioned is incorporating minilessons on structure, organization, and other global issues while working on grammar or usage.

Our tutors must understand that what seems to them to be a first-order concern (the text is not doing what the assignment asks) might not be a first-order concern for the writer (I need help with correctness). Like Nancy Grimm (2011), we attempt to make less of a distinction between HOCs and LOCs.

However, navigating this continuum of being nondirective and directive requires continual reflection. Some videos show tutors not encouraging students to read their papers aloud, not reading the entire essay, and making changes on the students' papers or computers. And although each session is different and we avoid mandating that a tutor should never mark on a student's paper, these examples lead to discussions in our weekly staff meetings about other possible methods, like the practice of taking notes on a separate sheet of paper that can be shared with the writer.

VIDEO SCENARIOS

Tutors discover for themselves their own strengths and weaknesses in these complex situations. For example, watch Juan's video, a session with a multilingual student writing an essay about Habitat for Humanity. The transcript below is an excerpt of a moment in which the tutor helps the writer edit the essay; however, the tutor makes all the changes.

YOUTUBE LINK/WRITING CENTER LINK: http://goo.gl/uYG9Ar
TRANSCRIPT:

> JUAN: Okay. So, (reading student's paper) "I'm researching about Habitat for Humanity because I want to show people how the global housing needs can be reduced in this coming years." Okay. Do you see something wrong with that sentence?
>
> ALEXANDRA: No.
>
> JUAN: Okay. What I see is that when you say "in this coming years." . . . this would mean one thing, but you're referring to . . .
>
> JUAN/ALEXANDRA: Years.
>
> JUAN: So it will be "in these coming years."
>
> ALEXANDRA: These.
>
> JUAN: Okay?
>
> ALEXANDRA: Okay.

We pointed out the positive moments in the session as Juan helped the student find clarity with her ideas. However, when Juan watched his video, he also realized, "It was mainly me who ran the session" and noted there are times when he could be "less directive" and encourage the student to revise. For example, he noticed after watching the video that he was the one holding the pen and making all the changes on her essay.

Online Session: Somaily https://goo.gl/c9pP0I

Using Adobe Connect, you can review the above clip of a recorded online tutoring session in which the writer, Viviana, shares her screen with one of our tutors, Somaily, and they discuss the document through the computer's microphone. Somaily begins with positive feedback, discussing the memo's content, and then the session focuses on sentence clarity and questions about grammar. Viviana's first language is Spanish (her word processor commands are in Spanish as she composes the essay in English). Somaily, who is also fluent in both English and Spanish, comments to her, "You wrote it thinking in Spanish" (17:50 mark) and points out the need to reverse the words in English. She discusses the difference between *people is* and *people are*, and there is a lengthy discussion about the difference between *people* versus *family* and verb agreement (24:45 mark). Somaily points out that Viviana adds needed words when she reads the text aloud around the 37:52 mark and then assists her in adding these missing words to her document.

Somaily Reflects on Her Session

During an online session with Viviana, I noticed that I focused on grammar more than I probably should have, and at times I fluctuated from nondirective to directive tutoring. I came to this conclusion while focusing on the time frame between minutes 16:15 to 21:35. In that time frame, I work on Viviana's sentence structure and try the nondirective approach at first. I ask her what she meant to say in the sentence and guided her to a better structured sentence; however, toward the end of that time frame, I began to tell her how to fix her sentence directly. I was editing more than guiding or teaching.

Somaily's video shows the complexities of being directive or nondirective. Although Somaily worried that she was doing more editing than guiding, we highlighted that she was helping Viviana to be a close reader of her text and to make some necessary changes. Although this online session does not address every grammatical issue that requires attention, including the usage of commas, Somaily helps Viviana identify and clarify her meaning.

In "Looking at the Whole Text" (Staben and Dempsey Nordhaus 2009), the authors make a useful distinction between directive and direct tutoring. Directive tutoring says, in effect, "I'll decide how you should write this." Direct tutoring explains concepts the writer needs to know or ask about. Most of all, we want our suggestions to be direct and clear for students. One of our tutors, Laura, stresses the importance of being "much clearer in verbalizing[her] thoughts" when working with multilingual students. She says, "Sometimes I am guilty of being too vague in my feedback . . . ." However, Somaily adds, "I also think that it can become easy to focus on sentence-level errors instead of higher order concerns . . . [we] should avoid falling into that trap." The Digital Video Project can give us a chance to continue a dialogue about this complex issue.

Tutors sometimes use more than one language in a session. Watch this clip of one of our tutors, Jeanette, working with a graduate student, Jimmy, and using more than one language to help him compose. The session focuses on Jimmy's research project about mentoring. Jeanette reads sections of his essay aloud as they discuss it.

Youtube Link/Writing Center Link: http://goo.gl/PVgZ2J
Transcript:

JEANETTE: So comment on how the attitudinal variables . . . in reference to the model, right? So comment on . . .

JIMMY: Some comment on . . . on how . . .

JEANETTE: Maybe . . . are they related to the model?

JIMMY: Yeah. Comment on (typing) how the attitudinal variables . . .

JEANETTE: Uh-huh.

JIMMY: How the attitudinal variables . . .

JEANETTE: *Si no te viene en ingles, piensa en español.* [If it doesn't come to you in English, then think in Spanish.]

JIMMY: *Sí. Como ellas . . . que figura presentan . . .* [How they . . . what figure they present]

JEANETTE: Okay. Known variables.

JIMMY: Comment on how the attitudinal variables manifest themselves . . . (typing)

JEANETTE: Ok . . . so . . . (reading) "And fourth, the paper will interpret the results of the survey and comment on how the attitudinal variables manifest themselves as a result of the study."

When Jimmy searches for the right word, Jeanette advises him, "*Si no te viene en ingles, piensa en español* [If it doesn't come to you in English, then think in Spanish]." So he switches to Spanish and then back to English before writing how the "variables manifest themselves." Then the remainder of the session includes more Spanish as Jeanette asks, "*¿Que significa, por ejemplo* . . . absenteeism and employee turnover?" Jeanette tells him that he needs to discuss these terms more, and Jimmy makes a plan of action for revision ("*trabajar en esto*"). As Jeanette and Jimmy discuss his next appointment, they discuss "*este* paper" and "*el* meeting" for the staff every *miercoles* (Wednesday) at 1p.m.

Our other tutors comment that many of their sessions involve more than one language. Sometimes, as Katie notes, switching from one language to another can "help them bridge the gap" between their first language and English. Somaily explains, "This makes the students feel more comfortable and it helps me understand their intended meaning." Another tutor, Nazneen, who speaks Hindi, explains her use of more than one language.

As I reviewed the video, I realized that there was a session within the session. Prem has expressed the need to improve her speaking power . . . I often switch to Hindi and address an idea if I felt Prem is not really getting a concept. I used to do this more often, but as Prem excels in her skills I use language changeovers less.

(Watch a clip of Nazneen and Prem's video: http://goo.gl/2kL5sx.)

In Martha's session, she helps Ashley compose a movie review in Spanish. Both students are bilingual, but Martha has more experience writing in Spanish. Martha and Ashley discuss the composing process mostly in English and focus on the use of transitions. Ashley reads her paper aloud, and Martha reflects in her session notes.

> We were both comfortable with both English and Spanish in terms of speaking the language, but when it came to writing in it, our levels of "expertise" were different. As I've mentioned before, I don't believe a "bad" or "wrong" Spanish exists, so I wonder if this may also apply to writing—a lot of my advice to Ashley in terms of writing on her paper came from my experience with AP Spanish courses in highschool, where we used writing guidance from the Real Academia Española (http://www. rae.es/rae.html) and AP textbooks from College Board. I often wonder if these sources set the standard for "correct" writing in Spanish, and what effect that has had in terms of Spanish writings. In order to help her find words to convey her thoughts as accurate as possible, I asked her what she meant by saying certain things, discussing which Spanish words we thought worked best.
>
> In comparison to the style of the session, it became bilingual more conversationally, since we were both completely bilingual. I didn't feel the need to ask "Is it ok to speak to you in two languages?" because we were just speaking in two languages to understand the assignment. Usually, my bilingual sessions are done in an effort to get a student to understand something better in English, so this was a different experience from the norm.

(Watch a clip of Martha's session: https://goo.gl/bw8hqb.)

DIVERSITY AND TUTORS

The video project reinforces our valuing of our multilingual tutors. As the above examples indicate, our writing center is multilingual and diverse. In addition to our students being second language learners, most of our writing center staff speaks more than one language, and at least one-third were born in another country. We have found that our multilingual tutors not only perform at an extremely high level but also add value to our ongoing tutor education in our staff meetings as they contribute insights unique to them as language learners. Their role as learners gives them a peer status native speakers as well multilingual students value. We sometimes hear of requests for specific kinds of tutors but not for native speakers of English; the most frequent request is for a tutor who speaks Spanish.

And according to the last US Census, over the past thirty years, the number of people speaking a language other than English in the home has increased by 140 percent. Although this linguistic diversity is often framed as a problem or challenge for the writing classroom, more teachers are recognizing the opportunities possible for writing instruction and the necessity for multilingual instruction. For example, studies show that knowing more than one language can help strengthen the mind's ability to think and solve puzzles (Martin-Rhee and Bialystok 2008; Kovacs and Mehler 2009). In addition, Horner, NeCamp, and Donahue (2011) point out the limits to monolingual research in composition studies and argue for an increase in multilingual scholarship.

Our videos, then, show the benefits of a multilingual staff; however, we have taken steps to recruit a diverse staff, diverse not only in second language ability, but diverse in majors. We did not want our tutor preparation course to seem forbidding since it often takes time for some of our most promising students to see themselves as tutors. So our undergraduate students often sign up for The Processes of Writing without realizing the primary aim of the course is to prepare them to be tutors in the writing center. Fliers and other sources of information advertise the course and explain that successful students can apply to become tutors in our writing center at the end of the semester. However, the course also satisfies students' need for a writing requirement, and sometimes half of the enrolled students begin the semester never thinking of themselves as tutors. We had thought that eventually, when the course had plenty of applicants, we might make it by consent of instructor, but we are glad the ambiguity of its title allows us to attract and recruit students who take it to improve their writing but subsequently come to understand their potential as writing tutors.

For example, Diego moved to Miami when he was about ten from Colombia. He takes great pride in his "correct" use of Spanish but worries that writers would be concerned about his accent. He said, at the end of the course,

> At the beginning of the semester I didn't even know the purpose of this class was to train us for tutors. . . . Over the course of the semester I have experienced how great of an impact a tutor can have, not only in a paper, but in the student directly. . . . The thought of being a tutor does motivate me; I however, don't know if I am up for the challenge now. If sometimes my studies alone seem overbearing, how would I feel having someone else's grades somewhat depending on me? I understand that our goal is not to get the students good grades, but help them become better writers,

yet we all know that most visitors go with the primary purpose of getting a good grade. For now, I don't feel ready to hold that responsibility but would love to consider the thought at a later time.

It came as a surprise when Diego changed his mind suddenly. He went on to become one of our best tutors and a great contributor to our center.

Nancy Grimm has set the bar high for recruiting and retaining a diverse tutoring staff. Her university, she writes, is 95 percent white, but she and her staff have succeeded in creating a center that employs underrepresented students at between 30 and 40 percent (Grimm 2011). She has done this in part by encouraging students who use the center to apply to become coaches there. Grimm makes diversity a "core value" in her center; multiliteracy can be part of that commitment to diversity, as it is in Grimm's center; in our experience, multilingual students make great tutors!

Consider These Observations from Our Tutors about Their Own Relationship with English

GEORGIA: "It took me a while, a lot of reading, to familiarize myself with English. I used to think in French; now I think in English."

CAMILIA: "I've learned that patience is in order because even to this day, I still have issues with some grammar and other aspects of the English language."

THALIA: "Coming from the Dominican Republic to Florida to go to FIU was certainly a very big step for me. What most scared me was the fact that in DR everybody speaks Spanish and that's what I was used to. Therefore, when I had to go to FIU I was scared of people not understanding me and judging me because of my Spanish accent. I was also scared of not making friends. What made it get better was realizing that people could understand me and everybody was super friendly and welcoming at FIU."

How fortunate for our center that Diego, Georgia, Camila, and Thalia became tutors and can share their own experiences with learning a new language with the students they tutor. At the same time, tutors who have successfully adopted English as a primary language may be self-conscious about their ability to speak in their "first language." After conducting our conferences for the Digital Video Project, we started two new conversation circles in our writing center. The first circle is in English for those students who want to practice their English in an informal place, especially international students in the United States for their first semester. Also, we have a conversation circle in Spanish for students interested in practicing their Spanish, many of whom are children of immigrants to Miami. Our multilingual tutors, then, want an opportunity to improve their "first" language, as most of their schooling has been in English.

POLITICS OF LANGUAGE

In our conferences, we find ways to celebrate different languages and dialects. In the peer-tutoring class, we read essays about code-meshing and the CCCC's resolution, Students' Rights to Their Own Language, which explains, "Language scholars long ago denied that the myth of a standard American dialect has any validity. The claim that any one dialect is unacceptable amounts to an attempt of one social group to exert its dominance over another" (National Council of Teachers of English 1974). However, how do we challenge the idea that "there is but one tongue that must be mastered if those students before us are to succeed, the standardized American English, the conventions of an universalized Edited American English" (Smitherman and Villanueva 2003, 2)? So we want to continue asking how our multilingual writing center can be a place for code-meshing, or what Vershawn Ashanti Young calls the "multidialectalism and pluralingualism in one speech act" (Young 2011, 67).

One important way is for our staff to be respectful of different dialects and aware that as our world becomes more globally connected, we communicate in different ways and in World Englishes. As our tutor, Martha, explains, "[Multilingual students] can be amazing writers; they usually are. They have a lot to offer in terms of opinions from a fresh and different perspective, but sometimes lack the confidence to say things how they want to, due to fear of sounding silly or having 'bad English.' I've realized through all of this I don't believe a 'bad English' exists, just different versions of it."

Also, as we mentioned previously, our writing center is a place where we hear different languages being spoken. Students often communicate with receptionists in Spanish to make an appointment for a writing session. We have a conversation circle that encourages people to speak in Spanish. Some of our staff attend a Mandarin class organized by international students from China and report back words and phrases they learn to our weekly staff meeting.

Our tutors tell us that they ask students what they want to express in their writing. For example, Jeanette says her sessions sometimes explore that tension between different ways of communicating and the question of what is "standard and acceptable." Her advice to other tutors is "Listen. Discuss. Allow [students] to share their intended meaning and especially when you come across confusing or awkward syntax. Dialoguing helps students to find an array of ways to communicate what they mean to say and are experts on." Jeanette points out that students often know what they want to change in their writing, so why not ask them?

Besides a respect for different dialects, our writing conferences also explore the cultural and political aspects to language instruction. For instance, Carlos, too, often asks his writers, "How would you say it in Spanish?" when they are struggling with a passage in their writing. Of course, if tutors do not share a second language with writers, then tutors can ask, "How would you say this in—?" For instance, Carlos will ask a writer how she would write it in Japanese, and then they find the word in a dictionary. Therefore, tutors can help create a multilingual writing space even if they don't share a second language with the student.

In our conference, Carlos mentioned other ways he connects with students. For example, in his video clip, he works with a student on his personal statement. The student visited the center at least seven times as he revised his statement for his dental school application. Carlos helps him with removing unneeded repetition in the essay. Also, the student discusses how his parents immigrated to the United States by taking a dangerous boat ride, as many Cubans have done, to find freedom. Carlos shares some of his own family's immigration story. Carlos was born in the United States, but his parents were immigrants from Cuba. These tales of exile can create powerful bonds between tutors as well as between tutor and writer.

The experience of exile can be painful. In our conference with Carlos, we discussed the stigma often given to different dialects and languages. Carlos told us that as a child, there was a time when he didn't want to speak Spanish, perhaps because of all the negative terms he heard Hispanic people being called. However, now Carlos often helps lead our conversation circle in Spanish, and many of his fellow tutors praise his enunciation and fluency in Spanish.

CONCLUSION AND FURTHER RESEARCH

The Digital Video Project, then, gives us an opportunity for ongoing tutor training. The videos and conferences help us discover more about our center and learn more from our tutors. This project can encourage further research. First of all, the project can give tutors an opportunity to be researchers; two of our tutors, Asra and Nazneen, presented their videos at a recent writing center conference, analyzing the videos and the learning process they experienced as they watched themselves at work. Also, our tutors are often reluctant to separate multilingual writers into a different category since our writing center thinks of second language writers as the "norm" (as our tutor Bryant put it). In fact, many tutors stress the strengths of ESL writers.

Challenges for the project include time and technology. Some tutors complete their videos sooner than others. And although this project is part of tutors' job responsibilities for the center, we schedule our meetings with them in advance as a reminder for them to complete the video before the meeting. Though most students choose to use the camera on their laptop/phone or the center's Flip camera, we must make sure we have adequate equipment for students to record their sessions. Finally, we are discovering the value of typing up transcripts of the videos and reflecting upon the language used during the tutoring session. We now also appreciate the value of a quiet venue for these sessions, as our center's buzz can be distracting.

These videos show us how a writing center can work toward becoming a multilingual writing space, an important component for access to literacy. The multilingual writing space is a reflection of the United States, a place of different cultures, languages, and ideas. And for our students, who are often the first in their families to go to college, it is a crossroads: many struggle below the poverty line and see education as a chance for the American dream and a better future.

As Laura describes, "Sometimes those students are from countries far away from here, and their families have given up everything to enable them to come to America to study. They may not know the culture or the language well, and how you interact with them has the potential to make their experience, so far from home, a little bit easier and more comfortable."

Questions to Consider

1. Tutors may not always follow best practices or their center's policies (when helping students with grammar or editing, for example). If this were to occur while your session was being videotaped, would you be concerned about other tutors or your director seeing it? Explain.

2. Here are some questions to consider from our video clips.

   a. What did you notice during Juan's video? How could Juan both help the student with her writing and avoid being as directive?
   b. Somaily's video is an online session. How would you compare the experience of watching an online-session video versus a face-to-face session?

    c. Jeanette and Jimmy speak in both Spanish and English during their session. How do you think this code-meshing helped Jimmy compose his essay?

3. Our digital video project connects with the scholarship of Nancy Grimm and others about the importance of diversity in a writing center. If you were to videotape tutoring sessions at your writing center, what diversity would you see among the users of the center? Among the tutors/consultants?

For Further Reading

National Council of Teachers of English. 1974. *"Resolution on the Students' Right to Their Own Language."* NCTE Position Statement. http://www.ncte.org/positions /statements/righttoownlanguage.

    Each semester, we like to discuss this statement with our students and invite their reactions. If there is no Standard American English, then what changes do we need to make in our writing centers? We hope our chapter shows you how we attempt to address this issue by respecting different languages/dialects and creating a multilingual space.

Daiker, Donald A. 1989. "Learning to Praise." In *Writing and Response: Theory, Practice, and Research,* edited by Chris M. Anson, 103–13. Urbana, IL: National Council of Teachers of English.

    We often discuss this article in our tutoring class and staff meetings. We believe that sometimes as teachers and tutors we can focus too much on error and forget to praise students for the positive parts to their writing. One reason for giving specific praise is to help students identify the strengths in their writing so they can apply that skill in new writing tasks.

Young, Vershawn Ashanti. 2011. "Should Writers Use They Own English?" In *Writing Centers and the New Racism,* edited by Laura Greenfield and Karen Rowan, 61–72. Logan: Utah State University Press.

    Vershawn Ashanti Young's chapter asks us to think about the politics of race when we discuss language. This is a great chapter to discuss in your peer-tutoring course or staff meeting.

References

Brooks, Jeff. 1995. "Minimalist Tutoring: Making the Student Do All the Work." In *The St. Martin's Sourcebook for Writing Tutors,* edited by Christina Murphy and Steve Sherwood, 83–87. New York: St. Martin's Press.

Castellanos, Jeanett, and Alberta Gloria. 2007. "Research Considerations and Theoretical Application for Best Practices in Higher Education: Latina/os Achieving Success." *Journal of Hispanic Higher Education* 6 (4): 378–96.

Gillespie, Paula, and Neal Lerner. 2008. *The Longman Guide to Peer Tutoring.* 2nd ed. New York: Pearson/Longman.

Grimm, Nancy. 2011. "Retheorizing Writing Center Work." In *Writing Centers and the New Racism: A Call for Sustainable Dialogue and Change,* edited by Laura Greenfield and Karen Rowan, 75–100. Logan: Utah State University Press.

Horner, Bruce, Samantha NeCamp, and Christiane Donahue. 2011. "Toward a Multilingual Composition Scholarship: From English Only to a Translingual Norm." *College Composition and Communication* 63 (2): 269–300.

Kovacs, Melinda, and Jacques Mehler. 2009. "Cognitive Gains in 7-Month-Old Bilingual Infants." *PNAS* 106 (16): 6556–6560.

Martin-Rhee, Michelle M., and Ellen Bialystok. 2008. "The Development of Two Types of Inhibitory Control in Monolingual and Bilingual Children." *Bilingualism: Language and Cognition* 11 (1): 81–93.

Rosner, Mary, and Regan Wann. 2010. "Talking Heads and Other Body Parts: Documenting Writing Center Interactions." *Writing Lab Newsletter* 34 (6): 7–11.

Severino, Carol. 2009. "Avoiding Appropriation." In *ESL Writers: A Guide for Writing Center Tutors*, edited by Shanti Bruce and Ben Rafoth, 51–65. Portsmouth, NH: Boynton/Cook.

Shamoon, Linda K., and Deborah H. Burns. 1995. "A Critique of Pure Tutoring." *The Writing Center Journal* 15 (2): 134–51.

Smitherman, Geneva, and Victor Villanueva, eds. 2003. *Language Diversity in the Classroom: From Intention to Practice*. Carbondale: Southern Illinois University Press.

Staben, Jennifer E., and Kathryn Dempsey Nordhaus. 2009. "Looking at the Whole Text." In *ESL Writers: Guide for Writing Center Tutors*, 78–90. Portsmouth, NH: Boynton/Cook.

7

EXAMINING PRACTICE
Designing a Research Study

Rebecca Day Babcock

Writing centers are rich sources of data tutors can probe for new insights and better practices for working with L2 writers. Research in a writing center begins with an idea and a plan for gathering and analyzing data. This chapter discusses some of the many research methods tutors can use in exploring the data gathered in their writing centers.

Perhaps you have been working with a student and have noticed moments of disconnect or other moments when the session went particularly well. When you are working with students, you may notice that some respond well to open-ended questions while others just sit and look at you when you ask a question, waiting for you to answer it yourself. Perhaps you are a multilingual person and you find that you and your tutee feel comfortable conversing in a language other than English, but you feel that somehow using a language other than English is wrong (see Dvorak's chapter in this volume for more). Or perhaps you find yourself engaging in lots of small talk before the session begins and you feel that somehow this small talk is a waste of time, and you should be getting down to business since you are on the clock. All these are valid concerns. If you are a graduate or advanced undergraduate tutor, you probably already know that these types of concerns can be addressed by research, but you may not have experience with the exact techniques researchers can use to address them. The challenge for you is likely how to design a study and what methods to use.

Perhaps you are an English major and are mostly familiar with library research. If you have taken psychology, you may be familiar with studies using quantitative or qualitative methods. These **research methods** come in to answer the **research questions** that you develop through your experiences working with tutees. Many studies have been done already,

DOI: 10.7330/9781607324140.c007

but don't let that discourage you. All studies are opportunities to learn and to ask more questions. What are you interested in? This chapter will help you decide.

For example, I am interested in tutors who are nonnative speakers of the language they are tutoring, a topic that has been little researched. What learning takes place for L2 tutors? How do monolingual tutees perceive multilingual tutors? In studies of multilingual writers, the tutor is almost always situated as a monolingual native English speaker. Or if the tutor is bilingual, the researchers dismiss the tutor's linguistic status, saying it doesn't matter (see for instance Weigle and Nelson 2004). To me, an observation of a population of nonnative speaking tutors could produce worthwhile research questions, and from there, data collection and analysis could proceed.

Several scholars have discussed how interests, curiosities, or discomforts can inspire research questions. Nancy Grimm (1999) reported on a tutor's discomfort with a tutee's unconventional literacy practices, and this led eventually to a dissertation study. The tutor, Marsha Penti (1998), decided to study the practices of a local religious group and how they interacted with the expectations of the university. Likewise, Gesa Kirsch (1992) wrote that unease or embarrassment about a teaching or tutoring situation can lead to productive research questions:

> Research frequently begins with the urgency to understand events in the classroom or with a dissatisfaction with teaching methods. Instructional methods that work for one group of students may not work for another group. Mina Shaughnessy's seminal work, *Error[s] and Expectations*, for example, grew out of the need to understand the new student population entering New York City colleges after the open admissions policy was introduced. (252)

These moments of discomfort or unease or simple curiosity can engender productive research questions. For instance, when Terese Thonus (1998) asked, "What makes a writing tutorial successful?" she was on her way to her dissertation topic. To conduct teacher research, you can observe your practice for moments of confusion or hesitation and formulate these as research questions. Tutor accordingly and keep a log of your experiences. Reflect on them.

Perhaps you want to know how tutors feel about tutoring multilingual students. You could use surveys, interviews, or even stimulated-recall sessions in which you record the tutoring session and show it to the tutor later, stopping the video at intervals and asking the tutor how he or she felt.

Maybe you have found yourself in a situation in which you and the tutee really just didn't seem to click or didn't understand each other.

The main research question in the **grounded theory** approach is "what's going on here?" In this situation you could videotape your sessions and keep a log book of reflections. You could view your video and pick out moments of unease and share these with your tutee, asking what was going on for them at that moment. If you work together, this activity could also be a form of **action research**. You might learn a lot about politeness and cultural values as well. What to you is a polite request may be vague or meaningless to your tutee.

If I were to research the above topic, my research questions would be "how do L2 tutors benefit from their role and how do their tutees benefit?" I realize there is an element of evaluation in these questions because we must define *benefit*. Do I mean language learning? Satisfaction? Career advancement? I also need to determine how to best research this topic. I know I will need to interview or survey tutors and tutees. I probably must also observe their tutoring sessions. Perhaps I will design an action research study and involve tutors and tutees in determining the research questions, data collection, analysis, and write-up. If I decide to work with human subjects, I will need to contact the director of the Institutional Review Board (IRB) at my institution to inquire about the procedures involved for acquiring permission to do research, which may vary by institution. If I work in a writing center, or a university or college in general, I can likely recruit participants just by asking them. A difficulty would be if there are no L2 tutors at my institution. In that case, I can try to approach another institution about collaborating with me on my research.

EXAMPLES OF STUDY DESIGNS

In trying to get a handle on designing your own study, it might be useful to look at the design of a published study. Cumming and So (1996) wanted to know what languages were effective in tutoring sessions and whether sessions on English writing needed to be conducted in English only. In order to answer these questions, they designed a quasi-experiment. They proposed a 2×2 study design in which tutors who were fluent in the languages of the tutees they worked with were asked to modify their tutoring under four conditions: the language used in the tutoring session (English or other) and the tutoring approach, error correction or procedural facilitation (meaning the tutors took the tutees through a series of questions designed to get them thinking about their papers, such as "Is this the right word or expression?" and "Does this part fit with the other parts?" [203]).

Tutors fluent in the respective languages participated in the tutoring sessions in English or in the student's native language. Tutors were asked to conduct either a typical session of error correction or procedural facilitation with a focus on the writing process. Each of the tutees was assigned four tutoring sessions, one under each of the conditions. In all tutoring sessions, issues were identified, solutions were negotiated, and issues were resolved. The identifications were most often initiated by the tutors, but the negotiations were more equal, with 35–45 percent of the negotiations being led by students and 55–65 percent being led by tutors. Cumming and So (1996) found no real differences related to the use of English or the native language in the tutoring sessions. However, they observed that "utilizing the mother tongue appears to offer both tutors and learners a precise, meaningful way of guiding text revisions that is not available when tutors do not know learners' mother tongues" (220). This finding is important since common sense may tell us that tutoring students who have written papers in English must be conducted in English, but according to these study results, tutors and tutees can feel comfortable conversing in whatever language works best for them.

Further questions raised by this study are related to Socratic questioning versus simple error correction and these techniques' effectiveness or desirability. Future studies can look at the discourse itself rather than the language used, perhaps applying concepts from **conversation analysis** such as the IRF pattern (initiation, response, feedback) to transcripts of tutoring sessions (see Mackiewicz and Kramer 2015). This pattern was observed by Sinclair and Coulthard (1975) in their analysis of classroom talk as teachers often ask a question of a student, receive a response, and then evaluate the response.

Opportunities for research abound each time you have a question or observe something that makes you curious. I began the path toward my dissertation research when two deaf writers came into the writing center I was working at and no one knew how to tutor them. I even saw tutors shying away from tutoring them! A research question was born: how are tutoring sessions conducted between a hearing tutor and a deaf tutee? The answer was through interpreters, and our problem was that the interpreter we were using tended to intrude on the tutoring session rather than just interpret what was said by either party. I decided to conduct a **descriptive** study rather than an **evaluative** one since little previous research had been done on the topic. Before I could ask how best to tutor a certain population, I needed to know how they were currently being tutored as a starting point. In order answer this question, I needed to **observe** tutoring sessions, and as a memory device I decided to video record the sessions. I also knew I needed to **interview** the participants since I could not read their minds to know what they were thinking during the tutoring sessions. In addition, I decided to **collect** and **analyze** written documents such as student papers and tutor training manuals, first because **interview, observation,** and **collecting documents** are the "big three" data sources of qualitative research, and second because it would further enhance my understanding of what was going on (see Babcock 2012).

DATA-COLLECTION METHODS

Interviews can be **structured, semistructured,** or **unstructured**. In structured interviews, you ask all participants the same questions and do not veer from the script. In semistructured interviews, you have lists of topics to cover, but you can ask unscripted follow-up questions and follow the conversation if it veers in another direction. In unstructured interviews, you just talk and let the themes and topics emerge from the concerns of the participants. You can conduct your interviews in person, on the phone, by e-mail, or by text chat, Skype, or some other technology not yet invented! The ease of e-mail interviews is that you can just cut and paste your participants' responses into your paper. In-person or phone interviews can be audio or video recorded with permission. The drawback to recording interviews is that you may be tempted to transcribe everything rather than just the salient quotes you want to include in your paper. Also, you may use a method of analysis in which you must have transcripts in order to code them (see below).

Observation is important if you want to make general observations about the work that goes on in a writing center. Sit unobtrusively in a busy area and make notes. These will come in handy when you do your write-up. When you observe tutoring sessions, group sessions, or writing workshops, you may simply take notes or you may video or audio record the sessions. You may not even have to be present if you ask the participants themselves to start and stop the recorder for you. With camera uploads to Dropbox, you could get the videos instantly on your computer.

Collection of documents can enhance your research or can be its main thrust. You may include analysis of student writing in your study design, or you may want to enhance your analysis by looking at tutor-training materials and writing center brochures and websites. You can also make an entire study out of rhetorically analyzing promotional and educational materials. Make sure you save copies of documents found on the Internet, as these do not always stay put and it is frustrating when you want to go back to a document and it is no longer there.

RESEARCH METHODOLOGIES

Action research is one way to involve your tutees, other tutors, director, instructor, and other stakeholders (like the writing center receptionist) in the process of formulating research questions, gathering data, analyzing it, and writing it up. Finally, **case study** is a popular and important method used in writing center research.

Action Research

One way to begin action research is to keep a log of your tutoring sessions. As you read over your log, note moments in which things did not work as you expected. Terese Thonus (1999) noticed that sometimes tutors' politeness strategies backfired because nonnative speaker tutees did not understand what the tutor wanted them to do since the politeness strategies the tutors used served to make their communication vague.

Action research may be a good choice if there is an issue your writing center community feels strongly about because "practitioner-researchers do not attempt to hide the social and political goals of their research, which, ultimately, are liberation and equality. In action research, the researcher and participants are partners in the process, and research goals are mutually determined and relevant" (Babcock and Thonus 2012, 38).

The editors of the *Action Research Journal* have put together a manifesto in which they write,

> We acknowledge the complexity of social phenomena and the non-linearity of cause and effect and see that the best response to such complexity is to abandon the notion of understanding as a product of the enterprise of a lone researcher, and to engage local stakeholders, particularly those traditionally excluded from being part of the research process, in problem definition, research processes, interpretation of results, design for action, and evaluation of outcomes. (Action Research 2009)

This form of research is rare in the writing center world, although it should be more prevalent, especially since its view of collaboration reflects so strongly those of most writing center practitioners. In action research, all stakeholders participate in all aspects of the research. For instance, the action research team may consist of students who use the writing center, tutors, administrators, and professors. The team will collaboratively develop research questions together, collect data, manage and analyze it, and prepare the final write-up. Perhaps this type of research is rare in writing center contexts because of the difficulty of arranging the schedules of large numbers of people.

A true study of this kind has not been published in the writing center literature, although Horner and Jacobson (1985) conducted the initial phases of an action research project and published the report as an ERIC document. More recently, Cathy Hutchings (2006) conducted what she termed an *action research study* at a multilingual and multicultural university in South Africa. Her investigation focused on linguistically and culturally diverse students, her methodology was **new literacy studies**, and her method of analysis was **grounded theory**. Hutchings looked at session reports and coded themes that she then entered into a computer program (NVIVO) in order to connect student demographic information (languages spoken, gender, academic rank) with consultants' evaluations of student learning attitudes and behaviors.

In *Researching the Writing Center* (2012), Terese Thonus and I suggest a research study that focuses on L2 tutors themselves, on their knowledge and attitudes. Data collection could proceed through logs, journals, observations of tutoring sessions, interviews, observation of training sessions, and analyses of written materials. This would make a perfect action research study, with tutors driving the research and being involved in all aspects. An action research model would also include tutees, who could be interviewed alone or in focus groups and also asked to keep journals.

Action research can also be conducted by staffs who work together on a daily basis with writers. In *At the Point of Need*, Marie Wilson Nelson (1991) and a rotating group of graduate-student teaching assistants conducted teacher research in a program that paired small groups of basic and ESL writers with graduate-student tutors. Each semester, the graduate students met and discussed tutoring sessions and hypotheses about what went well and what did not, and from these meetings they brainstormed tutoring techniques such as the use of freewriting and putting students in charge of their own work. They then evaluated again, keeping what worked and rejecting what did not. The procedure went on for years, so the group slowly and steadily improved their practices. The group gathered data from comments from the students themselves, from log books, observations, phone calls, videotapes, discussions, research reports, and finally from Nelson's own meta-analysis of the findings each group produced in successive years.

Case Study

A case study is more than a story of what happened with a particular tutee, which would be an anecdote or a narrative. In a case study, you start with **research questions** and then gather data to help answer these questions. The research questions can be generated by your experience, as explained above. Once you have your questions, determine what would be the best kinds of data to answer them. Some types of data you might look at are actual tutoring sessions, written work, and interviews with relevant stakeholders. Data collection is bounded (which means you set limits on it; you don't observe and collect everything) and continues until you have satisfactory data to answer your question. The write-up of a case study is usually in the form of a narrative and includes ample examples and quotations to illustrate your points. A famous example of a case study in the writing center literature is "Whispers of Coming and Going: Lessons from Fannie" (DiPardo 1992). Although not an actual study of writing center tutoring (the context was a writing group connected to a basic writing class), this was one of the first published studies to include actual data of student and tutor dialogue. It appeared in the *Writing Center Journal*, the flagship publication of the International (then National) Writing Centers Association. It has also been widely anthologized.

METHODS OF ANALYSIS

Once you have collected data you will need to analyze it.

Close Vertical Transcription

When observing and recording tutoring sessions, tutors may want to use **close vertical transcription** as described by Gilewicz and Thonus (2003). In this system, tutoring sessions are transcribed not as a "play" in which the participants nicely take turns but rather as a real dialogue with pauses and overlaps. Close vertical transcription allows you to more realistically represent tutorial dialogue for analysis.

Here is an example from Gilewicz and Thonus's article in regular transcription:

M: See, I don't know if my conclusion really, I kind of like messed up.

F: I kind of like the essay.

A: I like the whole thing.

F: Like the essay was really good.

A: It's really good.

J: It's really, really good.

F: The only thing that . . .

M: I messed up like . . .

F: I like it because it actually flows along with it.

A: Yeah, and you can picture everything.

F: Yeah, but like . . .

M: I left out the winning. I forgot it. (37)

In the above example, although there are four speakers, the dynamic nature of the conversation is not evident. The same conversation in close vertical transcription would look like this:

1   M: See, I don't know if my conclusion really ***. I kind of like [messed up.

2   F: [I kind of like the essay.

3   A: I like, I like the whole thing.

4   F: Like the [essay was really good.

5   A: [It's really good.

6   T: It's really, [really good.

7   F: [The only thing that

8   M: I messed up, like

9   F: D—, I know, I like it, 'cause it actually flows along with it [(.) but like

10 A: [Yeah, and you can picture every[thing.

11 F: [Yeah, [but like

12 M:[I left out the winning. I forgot it. (37–38)

In the second transcript, you can see the overlap of conversation through the brackets. When two lines are bracketed it means that two people are speaking at once for as long as the lines are vertically aligned. In addition, this second transcript gives information on pauses. A short pause is symbolized by a period inside parentheses (.) and longer pauses are indicated by the number of seconds of the pause (2s). This exchange is lively, so it does not contain longer pauses. The series of three asterisks indicates an indecipherable word or phrase. You can see the rest of these transcription conventions by consulting Gilewicz and Thonus's (2003) article. To understand the difference in the methods, try reading each version of the transcript aloud in a group.

Close vertical transcription also allows researchers to look at backchannels (*uh-huh, yeah, OK*), which are different from overlaps or interruptions in that the speaker maintains the floor while the backchannel is simply affiliative. One investigator has found that L2 tutees tend to backchannel more than their native-speaking peers (Thonus 2002). Through the use of close vertical transcription, tutors could test this finding with their own data.

Coding and Analysis of the Transcript

Once you have transcribed an interesting portion of the transcript, you have a choice of several methods of coding and analysis. Two common methods are **conversation analysis** and **discourse analysis.** Close vertical transcription more closely resembles transcriptions used in conversation analysis, which is concerned more with speed, intonation, overlap, and repair, while discourse analysis looks more closely at *what* is said rather than *how* it's said. For instance, if you were to code the above excerpt for pronoun use (part of discourse analysis), you would note that all pronouns used are first-person singular except for the pronoun in line ten. This observation would lead you to ask about the relationship of the speaker to both the topic and the interlocutors. Why does everyone use *I* until A uses *you* in line ten? My analysis would be that here, A is invoking an audience, while in the other exchanges, the *I* is truly the persona of the speaker. I could look later on in the session and note whether the word *you* is used not to address the interlocutor but to invoke audience and would thus be a signal to the listener that audience was being invoked. If I were to code this segment for conversation analysis, I would look at overlap, latching, and interruption. In this segment I could look at lines four, five, and six with the echoing and overlap of "really good" and determine that this is an affiliative overlap, not meant to wrest the floor away from the speaker but to positively enhance and encourage the writer. Another coding example is F's attempts to take the floor in lines nine and eleven. F's attempts (twice saying "but like") were unsuccessful. In this case F had something to say but was not able to enter the conversation. Although traditional conversation analysis eschews the introduction of social, racial, and cultural elements into the analysis, the use of **critical discourse analysis** enables the researcher to point out instances of dominance and social oppression. For instance, if F were a woman, critical discourse analysis may point out gender bias as a reason she was unable to gain the floor. An understanding of these conversational moves can contribute ultimately to the evaluation of the overall effectiveness and success of a session.

POSTCONFERENCE SURVEYS

In this section I will discuss a couple of studies of L2 writers so you can see how they were put together and how to construct your own project. The first study I will discuss is "Learning More from the Students" by Kiedaisch and Dinitz (1991). Through **postconference surveys**, they learned that L2 tutees were less satisfied with their tutoring sessions than were their L1 peers. The initial research questions related to satisfaction and demographic details. In other words, the researchers wanted to know how satisfaction with the session related to factors like gender, linguistic status, and learning disability. After each tutoring session, researchers gave the tutee a satisfaction survey with Likert-scale items. For instance, one question read, "Were your goals for the session met?" and possible answers were on a scale of one to five with one being "not met at all" and five being "fully met." After one year of data collection, the data set consisted of 376 surveys, which had to be hand entered into a database. Jean Kiedaisch and Sue Dinitz did what many humanists would do: they turned to a statistician to analyze the data rather than attempting their own analysis. Although Cindy Johanek (2000) exhorted writing center and composition scholars to engage in statistical analysis, my personal comfort zone has not yet extended to performing with SPSS.

The authors found a significant difference in satisfaction among groups. Learning-disabled students gave their tutoring sessions the lowest ratings. ESL students also rated sessions lower than did other groups. From these results, Kiedaisch and Dinitz planned to focus on improving the training for tutors in working with ESL students. The strength of this type of survey research that gathers data directly from participants, is that it can be used to confirm hunches. If ESL students seem less satisfied, we can design a survey to confirm the phenomenon before formulating a plan of action. Plus, it's convenient to ask people to take surveys in the writing center after or before their tutorials, and it shouldn't take up too much of their time.

STIMULATED RECALL

Two decades ago, Janet Moser (1993) noticed that ESL students visited her writing center once or twice and then did not return. This observation caused her to wonder if the writing center was not meeting their needs and what could be done to improve the situation. She designed a study lasting two semesters in which she observed and videotaped tutoring sessions between Haitian undergraduates and US peer tutors and also interviewed participants about their experiences and suggestions. Moser's study participants included five tutees and two tutors, and each tutee was observed in one tutoring session. Moser used a technique called *stimulated recall* in which she showed participants the videotapes of the session and recorded their reactions, thoughts, and suggestions. We see this technique used sometimes in reality television shows when the participants react to events in "talking-head" segments interspersed with the action. The tutors noted that it was difficult for them to elicit answers from tutees, and they ended up answering their own questions after what they perceived as uncomfortable periods of silence. When tutees did speak, the tutors had difficulty understanding them. The tutees said they wished the tutors were more knowledgeable about grammar and preferred to conference with their professors rather than peer tutors. The Haitian students also reported forming study groups with their same-culture friends.

Moser suggested that this study could be expanded to look at tutees from various cultures and to explore possibilities in tutor training. For example, she suggested that a training program could be implemented to better prepare tutors to work with ESL writers. She also suggested that the writing center could offer a place for these study groups to meet, with a tutor available if questions arose. Moser acknowledged that without doing this study, she would not have been aware these study groups even existed.

In all these studies, the research questions were determined by moments of curiosity or unease. The methods were determined by the problem the researcher wanted to solve. In several cases, the researcher used **triangulation** to look at the data from various angles. For instance, Moser observed sessions and then asked tutors and tutees to go over their ideas and reactions with her. Keidaisch and Dinitz used the survey method, but they could also have expanded their data collection to include observations of tutoring sessions and interviews with participants.

RESEARCH ETHICS

It's important to remember that before doing any research with human participants, you should contact the office or person on your campus in charge of research that involves human subjects. Your research will likely be exempt from review since you will be studying normal educational practices, but you will probably be required to fill out paperwork concerning your study since you cannot declare your own study exempt. Some institutions such as community colleges may not have an Internal Review Board (IRB), but you still must gain informed consent from your study participants and also obtain permission if you plan to publish your research later. You also should ask them for their permission to share video and audio recordings of them or their written work in publications or at scholarly meetings. Most study participants are given pseudonyms by the researcher or choose their own. Some may ask that you use their real names. In any case, respect your research participants and do not do anything that may expose them to harm or embarrassment. Some researchers use **member checking** as a way to respect the ideas and opinions of participants. When I did my dissertation study, I submitted all transcripts of tutoring sessions and interviews to participants for vetting. In some cases I removed instances of *um* or *you know* at participants' request. Since I was not studying pause fillers, these changes were appropriate. Of course I could not have done that if my research focus had been on verbal hesitations. Once I had written drafts of my analysis, I submitted chapters to participants for their comments, and where their understandings of what was happening differed from mine, I included their analyses as well in order to give a more balanced treatment. Finally, guard your data very carefully, especially in cases in which you have not yet changed the real names to pseudonyms. Password protect your computer and any removable media you plan to use. Keep written transcripts in a locked desk drawer or locked office. Shred printouts once you are done working with them. All this is not to scare you but just to make you aware that laws protect human subjects from coercion and breaches of confidentiality. You will not be able to share your research in a public forum if you do not follow the policies of your school's IRB. For example, journal and book editors may ask to see your written consent forms before publishing your study.

SOME PEOPLE'S EXPERIENCES

A Mentor

I interviewed Libbie Morley of the University of Illinois at Urbana-Champaign, who requires research of the undergraduate tutors enrolled in her required course, Issues in Tutoring Writing. Most of the students in the class have never tutored before, although some have done tutoring in high school. The students are required to observe tutoring sessions in the writing center and read selections from *The Longman Guide to Peer Tutoring*, several articles such as "The Idea of a Writing Center" and "Peer Tutoring and the Conversation of Mankind," and a book on grammar. Then she requires them to come up with research questions based on their reading. Morley explains,

> I ask students to think about questions they have after reading for their training course and observing sessions. I emphasize questions rather than topics so they begin from an inquiry stance. The biggest obstacle to this project is the students' background in library research because this more qualitative project confuses and frightens them. (However, they love it once they get started.) That's why starting with questions disrupts their comfortable patterns of research. About half of the students also bring questions from outside the Writers Workshop itself—people they know or from other interests such as working with people with disabilities.

After the students have come up with research questions, Morley asks them to do a literature review and to create an annotated bibliography. She encourages them to do **case-study** research and to use the methods of interview and observation to collect data. She told me, "I don't want them to get so hung up on the methods that it affects their choice of research questions." Students read a chapter from *Fieldworking* (Sunstein and Chiseri-Strater 2011) about interview techniques. They audiotape tutoring sessions and are asked to transcribe and code two pages of text. Students use general qualitative coding rather than any special methodology. Students also look for themes rather than doing a technical discourse or conversation analysis in which they would look at turn-taking, word choice, qualifiers, grammatical constructions, and so forth. They are not introduced to theory at this point because Morley wants them to simply gain experience with the methods, do a straightforward qualitative analysis, and develop a thesis.

Morely told me that the "research projects have gotten them [the students] more invested in tutoring as opposed to thinking of it as a job." Many of her students are English majors and are not used to this type of research. She reported how one "anthropology major 'got it' and was helping teach the others." She went on to tell me that "a stumbling block is making generalizations from interviewing only two people! They need to come up with some sort of analysis without overgeneralizing." She and her teaching assistant work closely with the students over the semester to help them frame their research and understand their data. All of these students present their projects at the Undergraduate Research Symposium on campus in the spring and at a meeting for all Writers

Workshop staff. Fourteen projects have been presented at the Midwest or East Central Writing Center Association conferences, and one student presented at the International Writing Centers Association conference.

An Undergraduate Researcher

Undergrads have published research on L2 tutoring before, and with interesting results. Issue 32.1 of the *Writing Center Journal* focused specifically on undergraduate research and contained two papers on L2 writers (Brendel 2012; Nan 2012). However, in these studies, the authors published their results without enough attention to the methods of data collection or analysis. Both Frances Nan and Christian Brendel interviewed research participants but did not present research questions in the article. In this same issue, Jennifer Nicklay (2012) presented a more traditional research report in which she included her research questions, methods, and results. Although not a study of L2 writers, the format Nicklay used can serve as a model for researchers.

I interviewed Nicklay, a former consultant at the University of Minnesota Twin Cities writing center, about her research. Before she began tutoring in the writing center at the University of Minnesota, she had already been working as a tutor for five years. She started working in a writing center at Normandale Community College while she was in high school and went on to work in a more general academic tutoring center at the university, tutoring students in subjects varying from politics to calculus, from microbiology to global studies. She told me, "Throughout this time, I'd had some training in tutoring strategies, but the U of M writing center training course was by far the most extensive."

I asked Nicklay how she came to this research, which focused on consultant guilt in the writing center.

> The discussions in this course led to my interest in researching why writing consultants often feel guilty following consultations. I actually can't remember ever personally feeling guilt about sessions—frustrated, disturbed, or exhausted yes, but not guilt. So, all of us new consultants were having discussions in class about sessions that hadn't gone well, about situations with students that we wish we had handled better, I was really shocked at how much guilt my fellow consultants felt.
>
> Thus, when it came time for us to conduct research, I knew that exploring what caused this guilt—which I really felt actually hampered our ability to work with students effectively—was going to be the focus of my research. I worked a lot with other consultants—both my fellow new consultants in the class, and more experienced consultants in the center—to come up with the questions I asked.

While the focus on consulting principles and methods, and feelings of guilt in relation to these, remained my central focus throughout the research, my goals changed. At first, I hoped to compare the Writing Center consultants' experience of guilt with the consultants in the general academic tutoring center I also worked in, but I did not receive any responses to the survey from the other center. Then, I focused really heavily on exploring writing center literature—but, right at the end of the project, I discovered a new thread that I really wish I could have explored. There's this subtle link between how consultants experience guilt, inequities in power, ideals of individual authorship, and the tenants of academia. I only spent a paragraph exploring this in the final article—but I really, really wish I could explore it more, because it is a link that both needs and deserves more attention.

I went on to ask Jennifer how she chose her methods and what role mentors played in her research process:

Kirsten Jamesen, our writing center director, was a source of amazing support and guidance throughout my research. She had all the new consultants conduct research because she firmly believed that, as consultants, we should take part in the writing center discourse, even from the very beginning of our work in the writing center. I discussed my ideas with her often, and she provided wonderful feedback. Katie Levin, the assistant director, was also pretty amazing at listening to my ideas—and then pointing me to great resources.

My methods—to have the questionnaire—were largely determined by three factors.

- First, the topic of guilt lent itself to asking questions. Observing consulting sessions would have been interesting, but I would have had to sit in on too many to happen upon one that the consultant might feel guilty about. It could have been interesting to get the perspective of our students, but I wasn't sure how to tactfully and effectively go about that. Therefore, questioning consultants seemed to be the best approach.

- Second, as I mentioned, I had originally hoped to compare the writing center responses to those from another academic tutoring center I worked in. The sheer number of people between the two was too large to interview each person personally.

- Finally, I was limited in time. I had hoped to further interview some of the respondents, but the amount of time I had to complete the project—in conjunction with the two other jobs and course load I had—prevented me from actually conducting those interviews.

Finally, how I actually wrote up the report, using APA style, was just the most natural way for me to write it. I was a biology major in the College of Biological Sciences at the U of M, and, as a result, writing scientific research papers has become second nature to me. When it comes to writing up any kind of research—qualitative or quantitative—it is a structure that makes sense to me. I was very excited in my writing center research, though, to be able to bend the rules of such a style, though. For example, it was a rare pleasure to put myself into the paper—to be able to use the word 'I' and include my own, personal observations.

I asked Nicklay about the process of writing up research for publication as an undergraduate and she told me that writing up her research for publications was "so exciting!" She added, "I think I literally bounced off the walls of the center when I found out that I had been accepted for publication." She further explained to me that

this was, of course, nearly a year after I had actually completed my research, and to get it ready for publication, I had to go back to my research and back to my writing, and basically learn it all over again. I worked really closely with Kirsten and Katie to revitalize and restructure the whole paper, largely because my audience was now the wider writing center community, rather than just my fellow new consultants. The final version for publication had to be a lot shorter and a lot more to the point than the original—in other words, I had to get it to pack a lot more "wallop" in a lot less space. It was a really phenomenal experience to go through the editing, review, and submission process.

Finally, I asked Nicklay for any advice she had for other undergraduate researchers.

My advice would be to really be open when you start analyzing your research. Go in with your question, be focused—but be ready to find connections you would never expect. I ended my project in a place I never anticipated, and that I wish I'd left myself more time to explore. Also, talk to people—the best ideas come from being able to bounce your ideas off people. Finally, the writing center literature has great breadth and is pretty easily accessible—utilize the knowledge that's already there, and then use it to branch out and bring us new ideas!

Also, relish your time in the writing center! I was lucky to work in such an amazing environment for the time I did, and I will consider myself blessed if I ever find myself in such a supportive work and learning environment again in the future.

A Professional

Terese Thonus, the writing center director at the University of Kansas, did her dissertation research in response to the question, what is a successful tutorial? This study spawned several articles, and the one she decided to discuss with me is "Triangulating the Key Players: Tutors, Tutees, Instructors, and Collaboration in the Writing Center" (Thonus 2001). As part of her data collection she wanted to investigate all perspectives of all roles in the tutoring system. She explained it this way.

One of the hardest things about this study was narrowing the research topic. As a new researcher, I wanted to know what each person in the triangle thought about the role of every other person in the writing process. I soon realized I had to focus on what everyone thought about the role of one person, the writing tutor—and I could find more discussion and even research about this role.

Because I'm basically an introvert, I really looked forward to recording, transcribing, and analyzing tutorials much more than I did the interviews, especially because I had not met most of the instructors. But the combination of solo and interactive work ended up being great, keeping me grounded in interaction myself while I was analyzing others' interactions!

I asked her what prompted her to do this research and she responded,

I was working at Indiana University Writing Tutorial Services as a Graduate Assistant and was enchanted by all of the possibilities for research on speaking and writing that surrounded me. I decided I would write a dissertation using the everyday learning conversational data these interactions provided.

I asked Thonus how she went about collecting her data.

I collected data for over a year, amassing many more than 10 tutorial transcripts as well as hours of recorded interviews. As a researcher, I've always been fortunate to collect more data than I could possibly use for one project! At some point I made the decision to exclude the instructor voice from the dissertation data analysis and write-up.

Here are the details of the study from the informed consent form.

Information

- This study is based on the tutorial and three separate conversations between the researcher and the student, the tutor, and the student's instructor.
- Within 5–7 days of the tutorial, you will be asked to meet with the researcher at your convenience for a 60-minute session to discuss your impressions of the tutorial.
- Within several weeks of the tutorial, you will be asked to meet with the researcher again to read and comment on her report of your earlier interview.
- Ten students, their tutors, and the students' instructors will be participating in the study.
- The tutorial and all three of the conversations will be taped, although only the tutorial will be transcribed in its entirety.

Benefits

- The research study will "triangulate" systematically for the first time the opinions of students, tutors, and instructors about the "success" of specific tutorials.
- It will also for the first time permit students to participate in the definition of "success" and its consequences.
- Results of this research study may inform colleges and universities in the training of tutors, implementation of writing tutorial centers, and administration of academic writing programs.

I then asked Thonus about any findings related to L2 tutors and tutees. She explained that she studied two international tutees, one from Thailand and one from Malaysia.

> Tutee D was male, 20 years old . . . a junior majoring in computer science. In addition to English, he spoke Cantonese, Hokkien, Mandarin, and Bahasa Malaysia. Tutee E was female, 20 years old, from Thailand. . . . She spoke only Thai and English. Both tutees had visited the writing center before, and one (Tutee E) was making a repeat visit to the same tutor.

Thonus found that in tutorial D, the tutor had misunderstood the content of the student's paper. In this tutorial, both tutor and student had "high rates of overlap and self-suggestion" and "high incidence of evaluations and suggestions." Both tutor and tutee were Asian, and Thonus thought perhaps there were cultural factors involved when the student received a bad grade on a paper and then stated that he did not "blame" the tutor for this outcome but felt that it must have been his fault.

Thonus went on to tell me that "tutorial E was a pleasure to observe because the tutor and tutee were obviously comfortable with each other" as this was the second time they had worked together. Tutor E also introduced laughter into the tutoring session, prompting Thonus to investigate laughter in another study (Thonus 2008).

When I asked Thonus what advice she had for researchers, she responded:

- Find allies and support in your research context.
- Try new research methods in an attempt to answer perennial questions.
- Choose methods that match your personality and interactive strengths.
- Don't be afraid to critique ideas of other researchers.
- Be acutely aware of how research participants' perceptions of you will (not might) influence your access to and the quality of data you collect.

NOW THAT I'VE DONE MY RESEARCH, WHAT DO I DO WITH IT?

Here are suggestions:

- Get lots of feedback on your study as you go along. Make sure you have a mentor, but also ask naïve readers for their input. Sometimes people who know little about your topic can give you fresh insights.
- Try presenting your research at undergraduate- and graduate-student research forums and conferences. The National Conference on Peer Tutoring in Writing is also a great venue to present your research. Regional writing center conferences give tutors the opportunity to present closer to home, even if home is Europe, North Africa, or Asia. Look at the IWCA website (writingcenters.org) for information on these conferences.
- If you are ready to publish your research, consider submitting it to the *Writing Lab Newsletter* or the *Writing Center Journal.* There are also journals that cater specifically to undergraduate and graduate student researchers. For instance, *Xchanges,* based at New Mexico Tech, publishes research on rhetoric and composition, technical communication, and writing across the curriculum written by students of all levels, undergraduate to PhD. *Young Scholars in Writing Undergraduate Research in Writing and Rhetoric* is published by the University of Missouri Kansas City and features articles by undergraduates. *Southern Discourse* is a publication disseminated by the Southeastern Writing Centers Association and welcomes article submissions by undergraduates, graduate students, and professionals. *The Peer Review* is published by IWCA and promotes scholarship by graduate, undergraduate, and high school practitioners and their collaborators.

On a final note, one of the editors of this volume commented that not only can students "conduct research to learn and improve their writing centers, but it is also possible that they could propose those projects for classes in which they are required to conduct research, and of course, they can become the topics of master's theses, dissertations, and eventually, articles and books."

Here's wishing that your project may have such an illustrious future!

Questions to Consider

1. Reflect on a recent instance of discomfort, confusion, or unease in one of your tutoring sessions. How can this feeling be turned into a research question? If all your tutoring sessions have been "smooth sailing," talk to your fellow tutors about any negative or curious experiences they have had and brainstorm how these can be turned into research questions. Look back at Frankie Condon and Bobbi Olson's chapter (27), in which they discuss "pedagogical failures" and how these can be turned

into moments "that both tutors and writers can learn from and out of which tutors might produce new tutoring scholarship."

2. Conduct a mini research study, such as those mentioned by Glenn Hutchinson and Paula Gillespie (in this volume), in which you audio or video record a tutoring session (your own or someone else's) and transcribe according to Gilewicz and Thonus's (2003) "Close Vertical Transcription." Analyze a short exchange based on conversational analysis or discourse analysis. Choose only one factor to look at, such as discourse markers, overlap/latching, or pronoun use. What patterns do you see and what do they say about the relationship of the participants in the discourse?

For Further Reading

Babcock, Rebecca, and Terese Thonus. 2012. *Researching the Writing Center: Towards an Evidence-Based Practice.* New York: Peter Lang.

    Chapter 2 gives a full overview of different types of research and chapter 8 gives several sample research questions and study designs. Throughout the book we offer examples of research conducted in writing centers, broken down by topic.

Denzin, Norman K., and Yvonne S. Lincoln. 2011. *The SAGE Handbook of Qualitative Research.* 4th ed. Los Angeles: SAGE.

    Although this book would be quite pricey to buy, most libraries have a recent copy in the reference section and may even have an older edition you can check out. Beginners will find chapter-length treatments of research methods and methodologies written by experts in the field.

References

Action Research: Transforming the Generation and Application of Knowledge. 2009. http://arj.sagepub.com/site/author_resources/Action_Research_manifesto.pdf.

Babcock, Rebecca Day. 2012. *Tell Me How It Reads: Tutoring Deaf and Hearing Students in the Writing Center.* Washington, DC: Gallaudet University Press.

Brendel, Christian. 2012. "Tutoring between Language with Comparative Multilingual Tutoring." *Writing Center Journal* 32 (2): 78–91.

Cumming, Alister, and Sufimi So. 1996. "Tutoring Second Language Text Revision: Does the Approach to Instruction and the Language of Communication Make a Difference?" *Journal of Second Language Writing* 5 (3): 197–226. http://dx.doi.org /10.1016/S1060-3743(96)90002-8.

DiPardo, Annie. 1992. "'Whispers of Coming and Going': Lessons from Fannie." *Writing Center Journal* 12 (2): 125–44.

Gilewicz, Magdalena, and Terese Thonus. 2003. "Close Vertical Transcription in Writing Center Training and Research." *Writing Center Journal* 24 (1): 25–49.

Grimm, Nancy M. 1999. *Good Intentions: Writing Center Work for Post-Modern Times.* Portsmouth, NH: Heinemann.

Horner, Annette, and Karen H. Jacobson. 1985. *An Action Research Proposal: Identifying and Addressing Problems Related to RACC's Writing Laboratory.* Title III curriculum enrichment activity: Faculty development project. Final report. ERIC Document No. 261718e.

Hutchings, Cathy. 2006. "Researching Students: Lessons from a Writing Centre." *Higher Education Research & Development* 25 (3): 247–61. http://dx.doi.org/10.1080/07294360600793002.

Johanek, Cindy. 2000. *Composing Research: A Contextualist Paradigm for Rhetoric and Composition.* Logan: Utah State University Press.

Kiedaisch, Jean, and Sue Dinitz. 1991. "Learning More from the Students." *Writing Center Journal* 12 (1): 90–100.

Kirsch, Gesa. 1992. "Methodological Pluralism: Epistemological Issues." In *Methods and Methodology in Composition Research*, edited by Gesa Kirsch and Patricia Sullivan, 247–69. Carbondale: Southern Illinois University Press.

Mackiewicz, Jo, and Isabelle Kramer. 2015. *Talk about Writing.* London: Routledge.

Moser, Janet. 1993. "Crossed Currents: ESL Students and Their Peer Tutors." *Research and Teaching in Developmental Education* 9 (2): 37–43.

Nan, Frances. 2012. "Bridging the Gap: Essential Issues to Address in Recurring Writing Center Appointments with Chinese ELL Students." *Writing Center Journal* 32 (2): 50–63.

Nelson, Marie Wilson. 1991. *At the Point of Need: Teaching Basic and ESL Writers.* Portsmouth, NH: Boynton/Cook.

Nicklay, Jennifer. 2012. "Got Guilt? Consultant Guilt in the Writing Center Community." *Writing Center Journal* 32 (2): 14–27.

Penti, Marsha. 1998. "Religious Identities in Student Writing: Understanding Students of Difference." PhD diss., Michigan Technological University, Houghton, MI.

Sinclair, John McHardy, and Malcom Coulthard, 1975. *Towards an Analysis of Discourse: The English Used by Teachers and Pupils.* London: Oxford University Press.

Sunstein, Bonnie, and Elizabeth Chiseri-Strater. 2011. *Fieldworking: Reading and Writing Research.* 4th ed. Boston: Bedford/St. Martin's.

Thonus, Terese. 1998. "What Makes a Writing Tutorial Successful: An Analysis of Linguistic Variables and Social Context." PhD diss., Indiana University, Bloomington, IN.

Thonus, Terese. 1999. "How to Communicate Politely and Be a Tutor, Too: NS-NNS Interactions and Writing Center Practice." *Text* 19 (2): 253–79.

Thonus, Terese. 2001. "Triangulating the Key Players: Tutors, Tutees, Instructors, and Collaboration in the Writing Center." *Writing Center Journal* 22 (1): 57–82.

Thonus, Terese. 2002. "Tutor and Student Assessments of Academic Writing Tutorials: What Is 'Success'?" *Assessing Writing* 8 (2): 110–34. http://dx.doi.org/10.1016/S1075-2935(03)00002-3.

Thonus, Terese. 2008. "Acquaintanceship, Familiarity, and Coordinated Laughter in Writing Tutorials." *Linguistics and Education* 19 (4): 333–50. http://dx.doi.org/10.1016/j.linged.2008.06.006.

Weigle, Sara Cushing, and Gayle L. Nelson. 2004. "Novice Tutors and Their ESL Tutees: Three Case Studies of Tutor Roles and Perceptions of Tutorial Success." *Journal of Second Language Writing* 13 (3): 203–25. http://dx.doi.org/10.1016/j.jslw.2004.04.011.

PART THREE

Words and Passages

Like a road or bridge, language helps people and their ideas move through the world, but the path can be winding and uneven. Striving to understand how the words we speak and write create or block opportunities is one way to promote personal growth and social progress. The authors in this part offer personal stories of inquiry and discovery. The first chapter in this section asks, how do tutors experience matters of social justice in their tutoring sessions? To answer this question, the author asked tutors to create a concept map, rank order a list of topics, and then discuss these with her. The results of her inquiry illuminate some of the deeply interpersonal aspects of tutoring. Chapter 9 describes a problematic session that pitted the tutor against a faculty member. In this chapter, language and culture come together around the question, when a tutor learns something about student that the student's professor ought to know, what is the tutor's responsibility? In chapter 10, the author tells about one of the participants she met while gathering data for her dissertation research. This participant struggled to hold on to her voice in her writing, despite being part of a culture that urged her to lose it. In the last chapter of this section, the author writes about learning English—the discipline and perseverance it took him to achieve a level of proficiency that allowed him to become a writing center tutor. His story is especially revealing for monolingual speakers who may wonder why their L2 writers don't learn the rules of writing faster.

8

INVESTIGATING SOCIAL JUSTICE IN THE WRITING CENTER

Elizabeth (Adelay) Witherite

As an elementary English teacher in South Korea, I took satisfaction in knowing that my students participated cheerfully and did well on their assignments. After a while, however, I began to doubt. Was I unknowingly exercising favoritism or discrimination in the classroom? Had I fallen into habits I was only vaguely aware of and could not fully identify? My interest in such questions led me to my graduate program and, eventually, to my MA thesis. What I had not foreseen at that time in Korea, however, was that a writing center would be the context of my study.

My interests (and passion) led me to develop a thesis proposal focused on tutors' perceptions of social justice issues. Though I knew incidents involving social injustices could arise in tutoring sessions, I wanted to test my intuitions by exploring how other tutors perceived and reflected on these incidents. My research question was, how do peer tutors experience and conceptualize social justice issues within the context of tutoring sessions in the writing center? Broadly speaking, the process involved drafting a review of the literature, writing a chapter on my methodology, and submitting my research plan to the university's IRB. I collected data from eight participants using semistructured interviews and two tasks: concept mapping and category ranking. I analyzed and systematically condensed the data, wrote the results chapter, and then critically examined what I had found as I wrote the final discussion and conclusions chapter.

If this sounds like smooth sailing, it wasn't. I encountered the usual obstacles—conflicting advice, drama at the defense, and panic attacks. Nevertheless, what has really challenged me is the reflection I've been doing in the weeks following graduation. As I prepare to reenter an EFL teaching career, I am just beginning to appreciate the interdisciplinary skills I have gained. Writing the thesis was as complex as any

DOI: 10.7330/9781607324140.c008

life-changing experience. I had tutored students from all over the world and felt they had made a real difference in who I was and might become. International students taught me more about my own attitudes as their perspectives highlighted alternatives to my own; in that way, my tutoring experience complemented the lessons I learned in coursework. I saw my master's degree, and specifically my thesis, as an important step into my future, and I am still excited by what I learned from it.

Perhaps the main finding of my thesis was that tutors experience social justice issues as obstructions that sometimes make the goal of the session difficult or impossible to achieve. In addition, after analyzing my data, I concluded that

- tutors tend to acknowledge some forms of injustices more than others,
- they see oppression as manifesting in language,
- some tutors seek causal explanations for injustices, and
- most tutors view their roles as submissive in a larger academic context.

My first conclusion resulted from category-ranking data. I presented each participant with category cards: race/ethnicity; gender; sexual orientation; class/economic status; nationality; language; religion; physical or mental abilities; age; weight; and [blank] (for participants' suggestions) (Witherite 2014, 148). I randomly selected each card and read it aloud as I placed it among the other cards scattered on the table. I then asked the participant to "organize the cards in order of how often the topic has been relevant in tutoring sessions that [he or she] experienced" (Witherite 2014, 41).

Based on the average results of the ranking task, I found that the most common form of social injustice tutors had noticed in tutoring sessions was, by far, discrimination based on race and ethnicity. Participants tended to recognize issues related to gender and class/economic status second and third most often. In comparison, participants considered discrimination based on weight, religion, and physical/mental abilities to be less relevant than the other given categories; some participants made it clear they felt these categories were not relevant at all to social injustices they experienced in tutoring sessions. Finally, most tutors rated the categories of language, nationality, sexual orientation, and age to be moderately relevant in tutoring sessions they had experienced. These results are associated with tutors' perceptions of working with second language writers, as the categories of language and nationality may be viewed as less likely to involve social justice issues than race or ethnicity. However, I also found that participants' stories about social injustices did not correspond to the categories they considered most relevant. While a tutor may be on guard for issues involving race or gender, for example, social injustices often arise in unforeseen circumstances involving multiple interrelated identity categories.

Second, because they indicated examples of social injustice as it emerges in statements or written sentences, I found that participants see oppression as manifesting via language in their tutoring sessions. For example, on Julia's concept map, she indicated in quotes, "Asians are the hardest to understand" (Witherite 2014, 112). She explained that she intended to illustrate the kinds of things she might hear or read in a student's paper in a session, and each of the other participants offered similarly spoken or written examples. This finding is consistent with Suhr-Sytsma and Brown's (2011) study, in which the authors explore "the everyday language of oppression" in sessions.

Half the tutors in my study speculated about the causes of social injustices in tutoring sessions. Elliot noted circumstances that "influence . . . demonstrate . . . [and] complicate" social injustices; Lucy offered environmental factors, "such as university culture, social backgrounds, media, and peers"; Syd traced injustices to "overgeneralizations"; and Claudia considered "power dynamics and consequent text negotiation" (Witherite 2014, 114). In my thesis, I posited that tutors' explanations indicate their understandings of social injustices as systematic effects of social norms rather than spontaneous and individual phenomena.

My last finding, that tutors view their roles in terms of submission, is based on participants' allusions to the assignment, the required format style, and the professor's preferences as being, most often, the highest priorities of the session. Tutors see their own concerns, including a sense of being discriminated against, as secondary. When tutors' uneasiness coincides with a professor's expectations, as in the case of perceived injustice, tutors tend to cite the professor's possible reaction as a reason the student may want to revise, but when the tutors perceive an injustice not directly related to the assignment (such as a stereotype), they often just try to forget about it.

These findings have shaped the way I understand tutoring and tutors' roles in relation to social justice issues in sessions, but my thesis conclusions were only part of the knowledge I gained through my experience. In the remainder of this chapter, I would like to share with readers some of the things I learned about doing research on a topic that required me, sometimes, to step back from it.

LESSONS LEARNED

One of the most challenging and rewarding undertakings of my academic career, writing my thesis led me to reconceptualize my assumptions about tutoring and its broader academic context. This outcome was not something I had foreseen while I was busy taking classes, learning theories, reading journal articles, and getting too little sleep. The changes in my assumptions occurred slowly and often as a result of the mundane aspects of conducting empirical research. They happened as I struggled to effectively and justifiably reduce large amounts of information, to create conceptual "anchors," to maintain focus, and to meet unexpected challenges with innovation.

Condensing Information. In many parts of the thesis, I had to take an overwhelming amount of information, whether literature or data, and systematically narrow it into more practical, workable abstractions. As I brainstormed the first draft of my literature review, for example, I was daunted by the number of topics that related to my study, including hundreds of social justice research articles. My colleague Jocelyn suggested that I draw a diagram with three circles. "Your research question," she said, "should be in the center of all three." Based on this visualization, my three foci were tutoring, social justice, and writing centers. I wasn't doing a study *on* research, for example, so I decided to exclude literature on social justice research. Small decisions like this added up and helped me to move things along.

Jocelyn's recommendation allowed me to choose the main subheadings of my literature review, but another problem remained. I still had hundreds of books, articles, and other sources I needed to organize in a cohesive way. While cutting up a printed list of journal abstracts, I realized that organizing small pieces of paper was much easier than trying to shuffle piles of books and articles, so I printed and cut up my entire references list. On many of the paper slips, the title was enough to jog my memory, but I wrote brief notes on the ones that seemed obscure. I sorted piles according to the three main topics, and consequently, it was easier to find subthemes. With my references on a more manageable scale, it was much easier to envision how themes and subthemes related to one another.

After I had met each of my participants, I had to turn eight and one-half hours of audio-recorded interviews into a written source. To transcribe the data, I found a Chrome browser add-on, aptly named *Transcribe*, which allowed me to use keyboard shortcuts to manipulate the audio as I composed my transcriptions. When I was finished, I had 145 pages, including too many details about participants' experiences.

As a systematic means of reducing data, I established clear parameters for what would be included.

> First, data were drastically reduced by excluding generalized impressions or examples (e.g., "Lots of white males come in who . . .") and examples outside the one-on-one tutoring session (e.g., instances before or after sessions). At this point, 34 total anecdotes remained, which concerned only singular, specific experiences (e.g., "I worked with one particular student who . . ."). (Witherite 2014, 43)

When I attempted to code the remaining thirty-four anecdotes, however, not all the content helped to answer my research question. To be sure the results could provide insight on how tutors experience social justice issues, I developed a second parameter: only anecdotes in which "the tutor mentioned how the social justice issue affected that particular session" would be included (Witherite, 2014, 43). In the end, I retained eleven anecdotes, which appropriately paralleled my research goals. Reducing information made it possible to manage a long list of sources and a novel's length of transcribed data, but several sources and most of the data I gathered didn't make the final cut. What was included in the final draft of my thesis depended on whether it fit the study's focus.

Conceptual Anchors for Maintaining Focus. While writing my thesis, I didn't fully realize the importance of the research question and the interview protocol script. In hindsight, these were landmarks by which I could have measured the usefulness of data and ideas swirling around me. Though the research question evolved as I further understood what and how I wanted to explore, it was a constant means of evaluating my decisions. For example, when I revised the interview questions, I considered whether they would help answer my research question or were merely interesting. In my MA classes, I had heard conflicting perspectives on research questions. Some professors said determining research questions from the start is too constricting, while others contended research questions are important to keep a researcher on the right track. As I was conducting empirical research for the first time, the research question reminded me of the main goal while I navigated toward countless secondary goals.

Along with the research question, what I was learning about characteristics and sources of social injustice helped me to compose my interview questions. For example, I came to realize favorable discrimination is also injustice. When it came to the interview script, I knew it had to be reviewed by the IRB, but I didn't realize how indispensable it was until I met my participants. Social justice issues such as racism, sexism, and other discriminations based on identity categories are inherently charged topics, and though I tried to respond evenly to participants' responses, my mind occasionally reacted to their statements with judgment, vindication, or even self-righteousness. Ironically, my own presumptions could have gotten in the way of studying tutors' ideas about presumptions; for example, I caught myself thinking that one participant was oversimplifying race by speaking only of black and white people. With a set script, I was able to ask each participant the same questions, using the same phrasing and often in the same tone of voice. Glancing at the script recentered me in my role as an investigator. If I had not prepared the interview protocol to keep me centered, the resulting data would have been less valid, as I would have revealed my reactions to each participant. If they had felt I judged their responses, participants might have become defensive or apologetic, and this would have changed the dynamics of our communication and their subsequent responses.

Challenge as Opportunity for Innovation. When I chose to study matters of social justice, there was one obstacle I didn't anticipate. Although I had been aware of emergent *forms* of social injustices, such as racism and sexism, prior to my graduate studies, social justice and its inverse, social injustice, are abstract umbrella *concepts* that extend far beyond my own experiences. As I compiled sources for my literature review, I found there is not a single accepted definition of social justice; the boundaries of this ethical notion can change as much as the experiential phenomena it describes.

I managed to sidestep most of the problems caused by the ambiguousness of the term until I created the interview questions. At that point, I required a clear definition for the prompt. As I searched again through my sources, I noted recurring terms used to describe social justice issues, and I synthesized these existing classifications to construct a comprehensive idea that worked for my purpose. Social injustices, in my synthesized definition, were "oppressive, unfair, or offensive issues . . . [that] could include stereotyping, discrimination, or prejudices" (Witherite 2014, 39). I couldn't find any sources that contained a usable definition; therefore, I drew from reliable, recent, and seminal sources to construct my own.

When I shared the first draft of my interview questions with my advisor, he warned me that my questions might reflect answers I expected to hear. In the questions, he was able to see my personal opinions about social injustices, which would hinder my chance to learn about my participants' attitudes and beliefs by constricting their answers to coincide with my own. To step outside of my own biases, including my persistent sense of righteous indignation, I asked for recommendations from my advisor and several colleagues who were also developing their own studies. It was a lesson in rhetorical precision as I began to see how the wording of a question might affect the response. With the help of several mentors, I gradually developed questions that welcomed responses I could not foresee. One of my participants, Lucy, suggested that people tend to make immediate character judgments based on predominantly visible characteristics. Her statement intrigued me, but she could not have said it if my questions had been limited to what I had expected. Around the same time, I began listing categories I encountered in the literature review since I would need to approach the abstract idea of social justice indirectly through participants' specific experiences.

At the National Conference on Peer Tutoring in Writing in 2013, I presented my research proposal, and I asked for attendees' feedback on the nine categories I had identified to create the category-ranking task. The response was positive; the audience agreed that these categories encompassed nearly any social injustice they could envision. Moreover, I sensed that by placing equal emphasis on each category, I was creating a means for social injustices to be conceptualized collectively and thereby collectively challenged (Bell 2007).

These events expanded my viewpoint, but another issue remained. If I presented categories in a certain sequence, the order could affect participants' responses. The first draft of my questions would have either led participants to give particular answers or constricted their responses according to what *I* perceived to be the most relevant social justice issues in tutoring sessions. When I brought this concern to Becky, a volunteer tutor in the writing center, she suggested I invite the participants to choose the order themselves. I initially flinched at the idea of a significant change to the methodology, but I realized the benefits outweighed my hesitations. In the exchange, I not only ended up with a more innovative methodology that yielded numerical rank-order data, I was able to recognize my own preconceptions that may have weakened the study.

My last major challenge arose while I drafted the results chapter. Each of my participants created a concept map, so it seemed natural that I should present each participant's data separately. However, the second part of my research question corresponded to the participants' reported experiences. I reduced the data to eleven anecdotes, but they did not proportionately represent the participants. I therefore decided to present my results chapter in two main sections. The first section detailed each participant's conceptualizations of social justice issues based on their concept maps, and the second section presented themes from their combined anecdotes. It seemed to me to be an unusual approach compared to most theses I was familiar with, but it worked.

RESULTS OF MY EXPERIENCE CONDUCTING
RESEARCH IN THE WRITING CENTER

Though my thesis defense felt like a grueling succession of criticisms and caused me to doubt my work, I was welcomed with congratulations after the committee's private deliberation. I am proud of this accomplishment but perhaps even more so of the internal validation I have earned. Now that I can reflect upon my work, I realize the experience changed the way I see tutoring, matters of social justice that arise in tutoring, and the writing center as a place where all of these can be brought into focus for research. The writing center is a place where I can observe phenomena I read about and closely examine stories and insights fellow tutors share with me. One insight I've gained is that seeking input from others can be frustrating when their advice doesn't coincide with your vision, but it can also open doors you wouldn't have noticed on your own. When others offer suggestions, they offer a scaffold for me to build upon their experiences.

The research question limited the scope and content of my thesis, but the information my participants shared with me could have easily answered hundreds of research questions, such as questions about how tutors see their roles in tutoring sessions, what they personally gain as tutors, and how their perceptions of tutoring have changed over time. That information remains in my mind and continues to inform my everyday decisions. On the topic of social justice, the tutors in my study shared with me forms of injustice I usually overlook, and each of them presented possible solutions or other helpful concepts to enact their own visions of social justice. Many of these ideas may not make it to publication, but they have led me to become a more informed tutor, teacher, and scholar.

Although my name is the only one under the title of my thesis, I have come to realize many people held central roles throughout the process. On my mission to explore social injustices as they affect all individuals, I had more support than I expected. I began this journey so I could increase my understanding of issues important to me, and in the process, I found a way to contribute to existing knowledge I deeply value. As I transition from being a tutor to being a teacher once again, I know I have learned to see my actions and many responsibilities as an educator with much greater awareness and understanding.

Questions to Consider

1. Describe a tutoring session in which you believe an issue of social justice arose. What was the issue? How did that session go?

2. Tutors often recall sessions in which an issue of social justice was suppressed by the writer, the tutor, or both. Have you experienced this?

3. Make a list of three tutoring sessions that felt out of the ordinary. What details do you remember about the sessions? Why do you think those sessions are memorable?

4. Tutoring may be associated with writing centers, but the skills tutors enact are frequently applicable to other circumstances that can involve dealing with social justice, such as conflict resolution and playing "devil's advocate." Have you ever used tutoring techniques in interactions that involve social justice?

For Further Reading

Bawarshi, Anis, and Stephanie Pelkowski. 1999. "Postcolonialism and the Idea of a Writing Center." *Writing Center Journal* 19 (2): 41–58.

The authors present an analysis of writing center history and norms through a critical theoretical lens. Anis Bawarshi and Stephanie Pelkowski's seminal essay problematizes writing center work as it is bound to existing academic hierarchies. In their essay, the authors argue that the way writing centers are conceptualized and positioned within the academic context leads to manifestations of social injustices.

Suhr-Sytsma, Mandy, and Shan-Estelle Brown. 2011. "Theory in/to Practice: Addressing the Everyday Language of Oppression in the Writing Center." *Writing Center Journal* 31 (2): 13–49.

Through focus groups and interviews with tutors, Mandy Suhr-Sytsma and Shan-Estelle Brown explore ways social oppression can manifest in sessions through students' speech and writing. The authors present a two-list heuristic that includes ways tutors can identify oppression as well as ways tutors can challenge social injustice when it arises in tutorials.

Wilson, Nancy E. 2011. "Bias in the Writing Center: Tutor Perceptions of African American Language." In *Writing Centers and the New Racism: A Call for Sustainable Dialogue and Change*, edited by Laura Greenfield and Karen Rowan, 177–91. New York: Routledge.

Nancy Wilson describes 144 faculty members' and tutors' perceptions of three English writing styles: African American language (AAL), English language learner (ELL) writing, and Edited American English (EAE). Wilson found that participants tended to respond positively to EAE sentence constructions and sympathetically to ELL language, but they primarily responded to AAL examples with blunt contempt. This chapter raises crucial questions about ways language perceptions and social justice issues are intertwined.

References

Bell, Lee Anne. 2007. "Theoretical Foundations for Social Justice Education." In *Teaching for Diversity and Social Justice: A Sourcebook*, edited by Maurianne Adams, Lee Anne Bell, and Pat Griffin, 3–15. New York: Routledge.

Witherite, E. L. 2014. "Writing Center Tutors' Perceptions of Social Justice Issues: A Multiple Method Qualitative Study." Master's thesis, Indiana University of Pennsylvania, Indiana, PA.

9

BUILDING A CULTURAL BRIDGE BETWEEN GHANA AND THE UNITED STATES IN THE WRITING CENTER

Jocelyn Amevuvor

The Republic of Ghana is located on the west coast of sub-Saharan Africa, bordering Togo, Cote D'Ivoire, and Burkina Faso. Because the country was colonized by the British, English is the official language in Ghana. As a result of their background in English, some Ghanaians specifically choose to study in the United States because it is an English-speaking country; they believe the linguistic commonality will prevent language barriers.

Much of the knowledge I have gained about the Ghanaian culture comes from my experiences as the wife of a Ghanaian. At the writing center, I attempt to use my knowledge to connect with students from Ghana or neighboring countries. Consequently, when a Ghanaian international student came to the writing center looking noticeably distressed, I hoped my background would enable us to build a trusting relationship and result in a more successful tutoring session. Before getting into the specifics of that session, though, here is some background information on Ghana that could help you know the Ghanaian students of your writing center better. It should be noted, however, that this information describes only one aspect of Ghanaian culture and, like all descriptions of culture, does not apply to everyone. The Ghanaian student who enters your writing center is someone you should get to know as an individual.

Most people who have heard of Ghana think of it in terms of the *Kente* cloth they see mainly black students wearing during graduation. The cloth is often worn because it represents the pan-African community, which is fitting as Ghana's first president, Kwame Nkrumah, was one of the great leaders in the pan-African movement, alongside others like W.E.B Dubois and Marcus Garvey. Within the *Kente* cloth, *adinkra* symbols are sometimes woven.

DOI: 10.7330/9781607324140.c009

Kente cloth is not the only place to find *adinkra* symbols, though. Above the couch in my room hangs a flour sack painted with blues, reds, pinks, yellows, and greens. Even though it may look like a bunch of meaningless swirls, the picture actually contains three symbols, like the ones in the *Kente* cloth, and each one has an expression or proverb attached to it. One represents humility and strength while another declares *Gye Nyame*, which means "Only God." The final symbol is a familiar one, a heart; however, it symbolizes more than love because it means tolerance and patience (MacDonald 2007). The designs on the painted flour sack provide a window into key parts of the Ghanaian culture. Ghanaians value intellectuality, which is often realized through proverbs and sayings. Furthermore, Ghanaians are known for being religious, whether they are Christian, Muslim, or followers of the traditional religion; however, unlike other countries where people clash over religious beliefs, they are very tolerant and peaceful with one another.

Not found in the painting in my room are facts about Ghanaians it would probably take being with Ghanaians to understand. For example, the Ghanaian culture relies heavily on respect. Even offering the wrong hand when greeting someone can be interpreted as disrespectful since the left hand is considered dirty. Likewise, passing by acquaintances and not greeting them with a "hello" or "how are you doing" is considered rude and even immature. Once, when watching *Givers Never Lack*, a Nigerian movie also popular in Ghana, I was surprised to see a driver stop his car, get out, and individually greet all the elders meeting outside. Had the man just driven by, as I often do in the US context, he would have been considered rude.

One of the biggest ways to disrespect a Ghanaian, though, is to insult his or her intellectuality. Ghana is a country that strongly values knowledge and intellectual ability. Insulting the point a Ghanaian is trying to make, calling him or her stupid, or pointing out that something said does not make sense is considered a slap to the face.

Since many Ghanaians value intellectuality and wisdom, Ghanaians often take their time getting to a main point. Therefore, when Ghanaians make arguments, it is not uncommon for them to begin indirectly. At times, elders might get together over a local dispute, and as they begin their arguments, they open implicitly, oftentimes with a proverb. Likewise, indirectly entering into an argument or a point is common in Ghanaian writing, which brings me to my tutoring session with the distressed Ghanaian.

The Ghanaian who came to the writing center was my brother-in-law's roommate. Therefore, we were acquaintances, though we did not know one another well. Like other Ghanaians, he was exposed to English at a young age through government procedures, the media, and school. At the same time, he was exposed to local languages, such as Twi or Fanti, used by his family and community, making him multilingual. He came to the United States to obtain his bachelor's degree in safety sciences. He wrote a three-page response paper for one of his safety-science classes. His professor commented on it and asked him to go to the writing center for help revising the piece before resubmitting.

When we began our session, the student was mostly concerned about his teacher's feedback. So, we read the first sentence the teacher had commented on. The student wrote, "The need for Mr. Crankmout to say again to everyone of the planned visit by the Fire Department on their usual annual site assessment in order to put things right is a serious indication that all is not well with respect to the safety culture of the organization." The professor labeled the sentence as a run-on, though syntactically it is not. It is, however, a sentence with a long subject containing many prepositional phrases. Since the professor seemed more focused on grammar, I felt she was indicating that the student wrote the sentence in a very indirect manner, which is indicative of Ghanaian English. So, I talked with him about how to make the sentence more direct. By providing him with knowledge about how to make the sentence more direct, I became a cultural informant in that I explained the writing expectations of US academic culture to the student (Blau and Hall, 2002; see Cox, this volume).

As we continued through the teacher's comments, I could tell the student still seemed wounded by the teacher-feedback experience because he appeared crestfallen. Looking back at his paper, I saw another sentence that could have explained further why he seemed so dejected. The comment stated, "This doesn't make sense." Seeing that sentence took me back to when my husband and I were having a friendly debate that quickly turned less amicable when I said, "That doesn't make sense." Immediately, I could tell I had crossed a line as my husband shot back, "Oh, so you think I'm stupid." It was then I realized that, in Ghana, making sense is equated to intellectuality. Therefore, saying a Ghanaian's point does not make sense is like calling that person stupid or unwise.

Perhaps insult was added to injury with the teacher's comment, "A graduate of this program should have at least a basic command of the written language." This comment was probably particularly hurtful because it stated that the student did not have even a basic grasp of written English. However, he grew up hearing, speaking, and writing

English. He speaks many different languages, one of which is English (see Cox, this volume). His English is just as valid as any other speaker's.

The student was caught in a broader political issue about what varieties of English are acceptable. McArthur states that we often find ourselves between two ideas when it comes to what is acceptable in English. The first idea is that acceptable English "norms have long been with us, are clear, and need only be applied, and it is perverse or pigheaded to pretend otherwise" (McArthur 2001, 10). Such norms are often enforced by our institutions and teachers, like the Ghanaian student's teacher. They are seen as necessary in order to ensure writing is comprehensible for everyone as well as to have a standard by which to grade.

Not everyone in the institution feels such norms and standards are good, however. Others stand on the belief that there should be "much less authoritarianism and an alleviation of prejudice in gender, race, culture, language, dialect, and accent" (McArthur 2001, 10). Such prejudice separates some Englishes as Other and deems them unacceptable.

In the Ghanaian student's case, I felt his teacher's belief that his English was something Other than what was acceptable was based on assumptions about race and African cultures (see Balester, this volume). For instance, there is a pervasive notion that most African countries do not use English when really English is an official language in twenty-one[1] of the fifty-four countries on the African continent (CIA World Factbook n.d.). Such an assumption separates the English users of these twenty-one countries from the mainstream and deems their English less valid in the Western institution.

As a writing center tutor, I was in a position of power and could take one of two sides. On one side, I could agree with the professor's comments that the student did not have a basic command of written English. On the other, I could completely reject the teacher's comments. I did not want to side with the professor because I felt doing so would only promote the belief that the student was not a valid English writer when really the student could create complex English sentences, such as the first sentence his teacher had commented on. However, I was also aware the student's grade would suffer if he did not understand his professor's comments.

I chose to compromise. First, I did what was asked of me and helped the student revise according to the teacher's comments. However, I also tried to stay true to my beliefs by explaining to the student that the teacher wanted him to use some form of American academic English and emphasizing that his English was just as valid. To this day, I am still not sure whether the benefits of this compromise outweighed the negative outcomes of reinforcing potentially harmful presumptions about where students come from and how that relates to their academic abilities.

However, even in the midst of my uncertainty, I have hope that my knowledge about Ghanaian culture and writing enhanced our session. Through that knowledge, I was able to explain to the student where the gap was between his writing and his teacher's expectations of the writing while at the same time reassuring him that he was a valid and proficient user of English. My hope is that by sharing this story as well as some of my background knowledge about the Ghanaian culture, you may also be better prepared to help the Ghanaian students who walk through your writing center's doors.

Questions to Consider

1. In this chapter, the tutor attempted to help the student appease his teacher by working to make his writing meet US academic expectations. However, the tutor felt unsure about whether her choice to help the student change his writing actually reinforced discrimination against other Englishes. Do you feel the tutor made the right choice? What other ways could she have helped?

2. Some policies on course syllabi can have the effect of discriminating against students based on their language. Do such policies exist at your school? In what ways might they cause discrimination? How can the writing center be a part of promoting different Englishes in students' writing?

3. This chapter was meant to provide you with some background knowledge on Ghanaian international students who may come to your writing center. However, there are probably many other students whose cultures you know little about. With so many diverse students using writing centers, how can tutors become familiar with students' backgrounds and use that knowledge in tutoring sessions?

Note

1.   Botswana, Cameroon, Eritrea, The Gambia, Ghana, Kenya, Lesotho, Liberia, Malawi, Namibia, Nigeria, Rwanda, Sierra Leone, South Africa, South Sudan, Sudan, Swaziland, Tanzania, Uganda, Zambia, Zimbabwe. For updated information, go to CIA World Factbook.

For Further Reading

Canagarajah, A. Suresh. 2006. "The Place of World Englishes in Composition: Pluralization Continued." *College Composition and Communication* 57 (4): 586–619.

Suresh Canagarajah argues for embracing World Englishes in academic writing. His argument provides insight into all sides of the debate and explains how enforcing the idea of Standard English, enforced primarily by countries like England, the United States, Canada, Australia, and New Zealand, marginalizes students who use different varieties of English. He also presents the challenges associated with embracing different Englishes in academic composition.

Keim, Curtis. 2008. *Mistaking Africa: Curiosities and Inventions of the American Mind.* Boulder, CO: Westview.

Curtis Keim provides further insight into common misconceptions about African cultures. His book highlights where such misconceptions originate, such as the media, and helps to deconstruct those misconceptions. This book is a very good tool for tutors who desire to be better informed about common misconceptions about students from the African continent.

References

Blau, Susan, and John Hall. 2002. "Guilt-Free Tutoring: Rethinking How We Tutor Non-Native-English-Speaking Students." *Writing Center Journal* 23 (1): 23–44.

CIA World Factbook. n.d. "The World Factbook." https://www.cia.gov/library/publications/the-world-factbook/fields/2098.html.

MacDonald, Jean. 2007. "*West African Wisdom: Adinkra Symbols and Meanings: Adinkra Index.*" West African Wisdom: Adinkra Symbols and Meanings. http://www.adinkra.org/htmls/adinkra_index.htm.

McArthur, Tom. 2001. "World English and World Englishes: Trends, Tensions, Varieties, and Standards." *Language Teaching* 34 (01): 1–20. http://dx.doi.org/10.1017/S0261444800016062.

10

"THESE SENTENCES SOUNDED LIKE ME"
Transformative Accommodation in L2 Writing

Pei-Hsun Emma Liu

As a tutor while I was in graduate school in the United States, I regularly faced a dilemma with international students who brought their own cultural heritage to academic writing in the United States. This cultural heritage represents values learned over many years and may consist of the rhetorical norms they were taught in schools back home, the ideology about privileged languages, and the aesthetics of nonacademic discourse they bring with them from homes, communities, nationalities, and races (see also Amevuvor, this volume). Should tutors encourage international students to accommodate fully to US norms, or should we permit second language writers to express their individual cultural values in writing? Posed in this way, the question assumes *either/or*, but as Suresh Canagarajah (2006) suggests, "Rather than simply *joining* a speech community, students should learn to *shuttle* between communities in contextually relevant ways. To meet these objectives, we should perceive 'error' as the learner's active negotiation and exploration of choices and possibilities" (593). Canagarajah's idea of shuttling gives tutors and writers a way to think beyond the *either/or* of accommodation versus individual expression. As a tutor, it helped me to see the pedagogical possibilities of negotiating language differences and using first language (L1) writers as a resource.

As a researcher, I investigated how second language (L2) writers bring their cultural and linguistic identities into English composition. I found that one of my research participants, Angela, was a great example of what Canagarajah calls "active negotiation." Angela was a Taiwanese exchange student in the United States from whom I collected data for my dissertation. Based on my experience interacting with her, in this

DOI: 10.7330/9781607324140.c010

chapter I share Angela's story and discuss writing strategies an L2 college writer adopted to reconcile the academic English requirements with her Chinese linguistic identities. This strategy, which I call *transformative accommodation* following Canagarajah (2004), illustrates how Angela successfully negotiated a space that integrates native cultural rhetoric with US academic conventions.

Angela was twenty years old when I first met her. She is the kind of woman who makes people smile, laugh, and feel comfortable. Upon her arrival in the States, Angela was not confident in her English proficiency, and she was placed in the beginner level in a language institute. When we talked about her experiences learning English, she seemed frustrated, telling me she tried as hard as she could to avoid using English when she was in Taiwan. Despite her lack of confidence and low proficiency in English, she was comfortable and confident in Chinese writing. Her investment in Chinese writing was strong. Angela's parents taught her Chinese composition when she was little and sent her to private schools for extra lessons in Chinese composition. She developed an interest in Chinese writing after that. She enjoyed reading Chinese books to learn how to write, as well as practicing writing. Angela constructed her identity as a good Chinese writer based on her parents' influence and her investment in Chinese composition.

Angela continued to construct her identity as a good Chinese writer when she was taking an ESL composition class in the United States. When I asked her about the differences between Chinese and English composition, her eyes started to sparkle when she told me about how she was in favor of Chinese ways of writing in comparison with English ones.

E: How is [English writing] different from Chinese composition?

A: Ha, very different. Chinese composition pays attention to the FULLNESS of the whole article. That means English composition only has . . . if you use English and Chinese to write about the same topic, using English to write, I'll only ask for getting words as graceful as possible; also, I'll try to be *simple*, try to get to the main idea as soon as possible, and not [make the composition] too long. On the other hand, Chinese composition requires a certain number of pages, as well as structure like *qi-cheng-zhuan-he* [beginning-transition-turning-synthesis]; it also requires using a variety of words or different implied meanings, such as analogies, to strengthen the main idea again and again.

This excerpt shows Angela's positive attitudes toward Chinese composition. She begins by pointing out the "fullness" of Chinese composition and the "simplicity" of English writing. For Angela, English writing is all about using beautiful words, mentioning main ideas at the beginning, and making it brief. Chinese composition, however, is sophisticated in a way that is very organized and requires many writing devices, such as use of analogy. Her knowledge and experience with Chinese composition allowed her to construct a positive and strong identity as a writer in the English composition class, where she was paradoxically less competent and confident.

While Angela preferred Chinese ways of writing over English ways, she tried to be obedient and respectful and follow the teacher's instructions in class. She constructed her identity as a good and smart student in the writing class. She was one of the few students who interacted with the teacher. She enjoyed answering the teacher's questions. She was also a helper in the class. When her Japanese classmates did not understand the teacher's instructions, they asked Angela for help. For her, being a good student meant being obedient to and respectful of teachers. Usually Angela followed the teacher's instructions and was a good student. But she modified the instructions when they conflicted with her identity as a good Chinese writer.

When the teaching instruction was different from her writing habits or styles, Angela tried to include her own writing style. She accommodated to the teacher's instruction in a transformational way so she could maintain her identities as both a good Chinese writer and a good student. In other words, Angela wanted to include her Chinese identity in her English writing without violating the teacher's expectations. When I asked how she could manage to do that, she said,

> Mmmm, first, I needed to know exactly what she wanted . . . for example, she wanted the main idea in the first paragraph, so after that, I could add some of my own sentences to extend. In other words, she wanted a topic sentence; main idea was what she was asking for, so for those supporting details, I felt that I could include a bit of my own style, yeah. The way of describing things wouldn't be that direct, like the main idea.

Angela was able to negotiate her identities between being a good student and a good Chinese writer. She realized she had to make a point in the introductory paragraph, and she tried to follow that instruction. She was also able to find space to include her own writing style. I was curious about how she managed to do so. When I asked her for specific examples, she became excited and spoke quickly about one of her compositions she wrote in a transformative way:

> Like this one I wrote the main idea she wanted. She asked us to come up with a topic sentence first. So I wrote, I wrote about how I enjoy each time

passing by the trees because they're lovely. When those leaves falling from the trees . . . I mean these sentences sounded like me. Ha-ha, yeah. It's a bit like Chinese writing. But she'd think that I should write specifically. Like English writing requires you to write down your point first. But after my topic sentence, I wrote something poeticized, like Chinese.

The following textual example, previously referred to by Angela, shows the transformational accommodation of her L1 identity in her English writing.

> *Grant Street is my favorite side in IUP.* I enjoy every time I go through it. Because it is beautiful when those leaves fall from trees. Sometimes I saw those fallen leaves to fly about a bus passing the street. And I stop by footsteps to observe those people who pass away or those leaves change their colors. It is a romantic thing to stop my steps and be with trees. That doesn't matter that people are busy or leisurely, when they pass Grant Street. The street is always quiet and smile to people (italics added)

Although the piece of writing is not 100 percent clear, I think it is poetic, and in fact, this is the writer's intention mentioned above when she explained how she managed to maintain her L1 identity without violating the teacher's instructions. Angela tried to point out her main idea in the first sentence by saying, "Grant Street is my favorite side in IUP," and then she applied her poetic Chinese writing style in the rest of the paragraph. She tried to depict an image of tree leaves falling gracefully and peacefully. She strategically accommodated the teacher's instructions in a transformational way. She was able to make her point and at the same time satisfy her desire to be both a good student and a good Chinese writer.

All in all, despite Angela's low confidence and proficiency in English, she was able to negotiate and validate her identity as an English learner through the strategy of transformational accommodation in the ESL composition class. Her engagement in the imagined community of good Chinese writers empowered her investment in Chinese composition (Norton 2001). That is, she did not blindly accept whatever her teacher asked her to do; she negotiated between English and Chinese writing styles, constructing her L1 in the process as a resource that helped her gain confidence in learning to write in English.

The story of Angela suggests tutors can collaborate with multilingualism by accepting the transformational accommodation of L2 writers' native rhetoric and aesthetics in English composition (see also Cox, this volume). Academic discourse and experience can either empower or silence L2 writers. It empowers them when it includes students' cultural practices and silences them when it excludes those outside the mainstream (Liu and Tannacito 2013). Also, Angela's case indicates that a developed L1 identity can help L2 writers negotiate in the midst of conflicting/different rhetoric. L2 writers ought not be faced with the Hobbesian choice of giving up their native premises in order to adopt new situational norms. Instead, tutors should empower L2 students by helping them appreciate their own cultures and languages. Tutors should help L2 writers become empowered to better appreciate their own cultures and languages by encouraging them to express themselves freely, bringing their own identities into their writing.

Questions to Consider

1. Angela's story shows that her strong L1 identity helps her *shuttle* between L1 and L2 communities and eventually helps her gain confidence in L2 writing. Think about those who do not have a strong L1 identity or those who are eager to be assimilated into L2 conventions. As a tutor, how would you help them appreciate their own cultural heritage and how would you help them to view their L1 as resource instead of limitation?

2. Imagine an L2 writer came to you for help with his or her writing. How would you address and acknowledge the written language that deviates from Standard Academic English? How would you respond to "errors" that might be the writer's effort to include his/her own L1 writing style?

For Further Reading

Canagarajah, A. Suresh. 2002. "Multilingual Writers and the Academic Community: Toward a Critical Relationship." *Journal of English for Academic Purposes* 1 (1): 29–44. http://dx.doi.org/10.1016/S1475-1585(02)00007-3.
    While contending each model has its own value, Suresh Canagarajah criticizes several dominant models in ESOL academic writing that treat multilingual writers' vernacular discourse and cultural practices as "problems." The author proposes that instead of switching or infusing discourses, appropriating dominant discourses empowers L2 students, in a way allowing them to negotiate with dominant discourses critically and to bring their experiences, interests, values, and identities to their writing projects.

Canagarajah, A. Suresh. 2006a. "Toward a Writing Pedagogy of Shuttling Between Languages: Learning from Multilingual Writers." *College English* 68 (6): 589–604. http://dx.doi.org/10.2307/25472177.
    The author argues that teachers and researchers of English writing use an inference model from native language (L1) and native culture (C1) in reacting to the linguistic and cultural difference in the essays they read. He proposes a negotiation model that considers how multilingual writers move between texts.

Acknowledgment

I would like to express my gratitude to Dr. Dan J. Tannacito, who has served as my dissertation director and writing mentor in preparing this chapter.

References

Canagarajah, A. Suresh. 2004. "Multilingual Writers and the Struggle for Voice in Academic Discourse." In *Negotiation of Identities in Multilingual Contexts,* edited by Aneta Pavlenko and Adrian Blackledge, 266–89. Clevedon, UK: Multilingual Matters.

Canagarajah, A. Suresh. 2006. "The Place of World Englishes in Composition: Pluralization Continued." *College Composition and Communication* 57 (4): 586–619.

Liu, Pei-Hsun Emma, and Dan J. Tannacito. 2013. "Resistance by L2 Writers: The Role of Racial and Language Ideology in Imagined Community and Identity Investment." *Journal of Second Language Writing* 22 (4): 355–73. http://dx.doi.org/10.1016/j.jslw.2013.05.001.

Norton, Bonny. 2001. "Non-Participation, Imagined Communities and the Language Classroom." In *Learner Contributions to Language Learning: New Direction in Research,* edited by Michael P. Breen, 159–71. Harlow, UK: Pearson Education.

11

SOME THINGS I DID TO HELP MYSELF LEARN TO WRITE

Jose L. Reyes Medina

Deeply rooted in me is the passion to share knowledge and the determination to help others. As a tutor at the writing center at Bronx Community College, I work with a diverse population of students who come from different places around the world. We have students from Latin America, in particular the Dominican Republic and Puerto Rico; West Africa, in particular Ghana and Nigeria; South Asia, in particular Bangladesh and Pakistan; and Eastern Europe, in particular Russia and Albania. You can imagine how many languages are spoken on campus. I specialize in helping L2 writers at the center and work as an imbedded tutor in classrooms assisting English professors in a tutorial intervention program to help developmental students pass their assessment exams. I have also participated in roundtables sharing my frustrations and resilience as an English learner.

My first language is Spanish. I began learning some basic English when I was in high school in the Dominican Republic, my native country. Learning English was important to my family and me because once my mother emigrated to the United States, there was the possibility that I, along with my two sisters, would come to this country. Therefore, I needed to be equipped with the English language.

The English I learned, however, was not adequate when I arrived in this country. Soon I realized that I barely spoke English. Short answers, "Yes, I do" or "No, I don't," were the most common words in my nascent vocabulary. Sometimes I thought I had articulated a few complete sentences in a given conversation, but people misunderstood them because in reality I had mispronounced some words or had not organized my ideas in a logical order. Even worse, I did not understand what people said. My listening skills were poor. And I did not write well. When I was in my first ESL class at Bronx Community College

DOI: 10.7330/9781607324140.c011

(BCC), my instructor's correction marks, spread all over my essays, looked like the blacks spots on the skin of a fully ripe banana. I really struggled with the language.

Still, my desire for learning the language was stronger than any shameful moment I experienced for not knowing how to speak or for not understanding what people said, and I kept trying. While trying, I practiced some specific strategies, besides writing and correcting essays in class, to improve my learning experience. The following are some of the "tips" that helped me to be fluent in English.

First was carrying a dictionary (or using an online dictionary) that gave me example sentences. I know many students do not like the idea of carrying a dictionary in their bags the whole day because it's a little heavy. Plus, they say, "I have to bring my textbooks and food. It's too much!" I understand that. However, as I was learning English, I needed to look up definitions of words constantly. Looking up definitions was really necessary. When, for instance, I started attending BCC back in 2005, you could see me around campus with a green Barnes & Noble bag, a yellow dictionary inside. I used a dictionary (Longman) for English-language learners in particular because when I began to read novels, textbooks, and articles, I found many idioms (e.g., *out of the loop*) and phrasal verbs (e.g., *put up, take out*) I did not understand. And unfortunately, my English professor was not around me all the time to tell me the meaning of those words. But I could always grab my dictionary to get the definitions of those idioms and comprehend clearly the phrasal verbs.

There were also some example sentences that showed how to use the words. To illustrate, take the word *respect*. If you look it up, you will find a combination of features that distinguish an English-language learner's dictionary from a common one. Here are three usages of the first entry.

> **respect**[1] /rɪ'spɛkt/ n. **1** [U] the attitude of believing that something or someone is important, and so being careful not to be rude or not to harm him, her, or it. *In Japan, people show more respect to the elderly. These kids have no respect for other people's property. Out of respect for the flag, you should stand.* **2 in one respect/in some respects/in every respect** used in order to say that something is true in one way, in some ways, or in every way: *In some respects, very little has changed.* **3 with (all due) respect** (formal) used before disagreeing with someone when you want to be polite: *With all due respect, I don't think that will work.*

Right after the definition of the word, there are *examples* (in 2 and 3) *of the most common fixed phrases* in which the word is often used. Next, there is an *explanation in simple language* of the fixed phrase; then, a *complete example sentence* follows. This threefold format helps non-native speakers not only comprehend the word but also record its different usages in various contexts that are alien to them.

In fact, this threefold format is extremely helpful when it comes to using prepositions (e.g., *into, on, up, over*) before nouns or after certain verbs because there is no set of specific rules for how to use all prepositions. It all depends on the context. The preposition *on*, for example, always goes after the verb *focus*, as in the sentence *Today we focus on that project.* Nevertheless, you cannot use *on* after the verb *invest.* For the verb *invest,* you need the preposition *in*, as in *How much time did we invest in that project?* Why do we use *in* instead of *on* with the verb *invest?* Nobody really knows. That is why having a dictionary with examples of the proper usage of prepositions was crucial for me. Nowadays, however, thanks to the latest technological advances, L2 writers and language learners in general do not need to carry a print dictionary all the time. They can download this dictionary (or any other that has the features mentioned above) to their smartphones or tablets, or they can simply access it online.

Next, I listened to an all-news radio station when I had free time at my job. 1010WINS is a 24/7 radio station with a group of female and male anchors, along with a team of reporters, who alternately report news stories, weather forecasts, sports updates, and traffic conditions on the roads of the tristate area around New York City. In the beginning, although uncomfortable and sometimes desperate because I did not understand most of what the reporters were saying, I restrained myself from translating. I just listened to it. After roughly six months of listening to it for approximately forty-five minutes per day, four to five days a week, I started understanding them clearly.

Listening to 1010WINS sharpened my listening skills significantly. How did that happen? Let me explain. Every time I listened to these anchors and reporters, I developed two important skills that strengthened my fluency. The first one I call *acoustic discernment of different tones of voice.* As I listened more and more, my sense of hearing was getting better, and I was able to understand other people more clearly, including my high-pitched history professor and my manager who was a rapid speaker with a bass vocal timbre. The second skill was recognizing various ways to explain coherently the same event. That means that I learned reporters' distinct styles—different ways to say the same news—and absorbed well-organized sentences because every single sentence anchors say is edited carefully so listeners can get a clear and concise message.

Furthermore, listening to an all-news radio station was highly beneficial because it forced me to rely on meaning to process the news. For example, when I listened to a reporter describing a car accident, I had to construct mentally an image of the accident based on the description I heard. This was a productive, yet painful, cognitive process for me because, first of all, my brain had to get the meaning of the word and then search for an image that matched the meaning. Because I did not know the different words one anchor used in the description of the car accident, I had to listen to other words other anchors used to describe the same accident. As I listened repeatedly to a variety of words with the same or similar meanings, I expanded my vocabulary and created a more accurate mental image of the accident.

This process is different from watching television. On television, we can easily know about the car accident because we not only hear about the accident but also see images of it. Once we L2 speakers see the images, we do not make any effort to know the meaning of words used by the reporter in order to create a mental image. Why? Because our eyes decode those images for us, using vocabulary from our native language, NOT English. Consequently, we learn less English when we watch news on television than when we listen to it on the radio.

Besides carrying a dictionary and listening to an all-news radio station, I spent time on RIC—**R**eading, **I**ncorporating and **C**ontemplating. I was eager to learn more about how the English language works. So, I basically read two books that taught me how to structure and develop my writing better and correct my grammatical mistakes. The first is a concise handbook by Ann Raimes (2011) that focuses on the process of writing, research documentation styles, and grammar. The sections titled "Style," "Common Sentence Problems," and "Writing across Cultures" are particularly helpful for L2 students. The second is a booklet by David Blot (2007) with a set of exercises that deal with some of the most common grammatical mistakes L2 writers make. Both of these texts helped me become proficient in English.

Once I had read these books, it was time to (1) incorporate knowledge while contemplating or (2) contemplate while incorporating knowledge (it works both ways).

Incorporating knowledge meant applying knowledge (e.g., using grammatical rules) as I wrote the first draft of my essay or as I revised other drafts. At the same time, I thought seriously for some time (fifteen to twenty minutes) about my writing and how to enhance it. I know I may be just describing what a natural process of writing and revising is, but I do not think many L2 writers actually take time to look closely at what they write and how they write it. But, as an L2 writer, I know that every time I spent time contemplating a piece of my writing for twenty minutes or more, I was able to provide relevant supporting details, come up with more concise and coherent ways to structure my sentences, and get rid of unnecessary repetitions. Simultaneously, I incorporated some knowledge about grammar, correcting fragments and mixed constructions.

Further, I read the *New York Times*. I bought it on one day of the week and then read one and sometimes two articles of that same issue the other days of the week. I did not have time to read the whole paper. Still, whenever I needed up-to-date information, I checked the paper's website. The importance of reading a newspaper such as the *New York Times* is that the information you get in those pages is diverse and well written. A group of experienced journalists write different columns in different styles, using a sea of vocabulary that was challenging for me, as I'm sure it would be for most L2 speakers and even for some native speakers, but once I began to read it constantly, the vocabulary became less of an issue.

Finally, I decided to speak up. I participated in conversation circles and spoke a lot with my ESL instructor. I am grateful I had such an attentive and humble professor. I gossiped (oh yeah!) with my English-speaking friends, telling them about my culture, interesting incidents at my job, and issues from my personal life. While I did so, I constantly reminded myself that I need not be afraid of my accent. I needed to SPEAK UP. At the same time, I was mindful of the areas I needed to improve. For example, I sometimes did not pronounce the *t* sound of the *ed* ending of some past-tense verbs (e.g., *talked*); therefore, I practiced pronouncing it out loud. If anybody corrected me when I mispronounced a word, I listened to them and made an effort to repeat the correct pronunciation they gave me. I have also practiced the pronunciation of words online dictionaries provide.

Becoming fluent in a second language is not easy, but if one has hunger for learning and tenacity to keep studying, one will master the language. These strategies helped me build and solidify the foundation upon which my fluency in English stands. They are powerful tools anyone can use in language acquisition. English-language learners will certainly develop and strengthen their language skills should they practice these tips. They have helped me to know how to write.

Questions to Consider

1. If you are an international student now enrolled in a US college or university, you probably took English-language classes in school back home. How would you describe these classes? What do you think teachers and tutors in the United States would be surprised to know about the classes you took?

2. L2 writers can usually recall periods of time when they feel they made a lot of progress in learning to write and speak in English or another language. Describe one of these periods. What did you get better at doing? How did you gauge your success?

3. Many times, college students have a favorite go-to book that contains useful information about a subject that is important to them. Writers often have a favorite reference or style book. Choose one of your go-to books and study how it organizes information. Does it give you any ideas for ways to effectively organize the information provided in your writing center?

For Further Reading

Horst, Marlise. 2005. "Learning L2 Vocabulary through Extensive Reading: A Measurement Study." *Canadian Modern Language Review* 61 (3): 355–82. http://dx.doi.org/10.3138/cmlr.61.3.355.

Extensive reading as a way for second language learners to build their vocabulary seems to make sense, but how can we be sure it does? Marlise Horst studied adult immigrants with different language backgrounds in Montreal, Canada, and gave them various books to read that interested them. She then measured how much these readings added to their vocabulary, over and above the language classes they were enrolled in. Reading the books made a significant difference, Horst concluded, provided the adult learners read more than one or two per semester.

Bruce, Shanti. 2009. "Listening to and Learning from ESL Writers." In *ESL Writers: A Guide for Writing Center Tutors*, edited by Shanti Bruce and Ben Rafoth, 217–29. Portsmouth, NH: Heinemann.

Tutors can learn a lot by listening to second language writers as they talk about their language-learning experiences. Their stories move back and forth between language, culture, and personality. Shanti Bruce's recorded conversations with L2 writers dig beneath the familiar feedback sheets and reveal issues of privacy, age, maturity, and preconceptions about the purpose of a writing center.

Pickard, Nigel. 1996. "Out-of-Class Language Learning Strategies." *ELT Journal* 50 (2): 150–59. http://dx.doi.org/10.1093/elt/50.2.150. eltj.oxfordjournals.org/content/50/2.toc.

Nigel Pickard discusses a study that focused on the out-of-class language strategies a small group of German speakers of English used to help themselves become proficient in English. Listening to an English-speaking radio station and reading newspapers were the two strategies this group of participants used the most, the study reported.

References

Blot, David. 2007. *Grammar Study and Practice.* New York: Linus.
Raimes, Ann. 2011. *Keys for Writers.* Boston: Wadsworth.

PART FOUR

Academic Expectations

Tutors are often mediators between students and their instructors as they help writers read and write critically, navigate through disciplinary conventions, and polish their sentences. In this section of the book, the authors confront some of the challenges tutors face when they try to help writers meet readers' specific expectations. As students go from one discipline to another and then into their majors, they encounter shifting notions of critical thinking. Chapter 12 shows how these notions change and offers suggestions tutors can use to help students from different cultures. This chapter also reminds us that when tutors assist international and L2 students, they are helping them learn not the right way, necessarily, but the dominant way in colleges and universities in the United States. Chapter 13 offers a different perspective on critical thinking, one based on discipline-specific ways of writing and the anxieties tutors often feel about working outside their own areas of expertise. What are the limits of tutors' expertise? How do they signal their limits without undermining their credibility with those they are trying to help? Three vignettes toward the end of this chapter can provide a spark for lively discussion in staff meetings. Finally, chapter 14 draws upon the coauthors' ten years of experience as learners and now teachers of English in ESL and EFL contexts in Thailand and elsewhere. They take up the extended debate in applied linguistics over whether and how to correct errors, along with the cultural implications that infuse error correction. Also included with this chapter are three appendices that illustrate patterns of error in writing—a useful guide for all tutors.

12

TUTORING AGAINST OTHERING
Reading and Writing Critically

Valerie M. Balester

When international students come to the Texas A&M University writing center, we assume we will be working on a paper draft, but they can surprise us. A few years ago, we regularly worked with Shu Fen, a dissertation-level student. In the last ten minutes of each session, she pulled out a list of words she had heard on television, and we discussed their meanings. More recently, our tutor Julia blogged on *Peer Centered* about her experiences with Yashvant, an international student taking first-year composition.

> Yashvant was told to choose a campaign as from the 2012 presidential election and analyze it, and therein laid the problem: He didn't know who Mitt Romney or Barack Obama was. He didn't know the difference between a Republican and a Democrat. He didn't know how American government was set up or how election systems functioned. And these gaps in knowledge made him feel that he couldn't write the paper. (Medhurst 2013)

Although it may not be apparent, Yashvant and Shu Fen were both using their writing center conferences to improve their critical thinking skills. In this essay, I examine expectations about critical thinking faced by international students, especially (but not only) second language writers and speakers of English (L2 writers/speakers). Effective tutoring should start from the premise that critical thinking is a social construct, not always well defined, tied in complex and sometimes opaque ways to cultural and disciplinary rhetorical practices. Writing center tutors are in a powerful position to help international students overcome or deal with unrealistic expectations about critical thinking they may face in US classrooms. Most important, writing center tutors can go beyond helping international students assimilate to American ways of thinking;

DOI: 10.7330/9781607324140.c012

they can contribute to an intercultural understanding of critical thinking that will be more useful in an increasingly global academic climate.

Within higher education in the United States, critical thinking typically means employing judgments of quality, validity, reliability, or truthfulness and is usually applied to judging written or spoken texts. It is described as providing sound evidence to support claims, questioning experts and authorities from a skeptical stance, and contributing one's own thoughts or ideas to a discussion. It is widely believed that "students must learn to read textual statements as the beliefs of the writer"—beliefs that should be received with skepticism (Olson 1997, 506). Adjusting to the demands of critical thinking means learning to question authority and to participate in putting forth our own contributions to knowledge.

US academics often assume they share a common definition of critical thinking. It falls into the category of tacit knowledge; in other words, these scholars think of critical thinking as something they do not need to define because it is a universal aspect of human thought. However, there is dispute over the details of what constitutes critical thinking (Atkinson 1997; Moore 2013; Olson 1997). What a history professor means when asking for critical thinking may not match what a biology professor means. Moore found that although academics from different disciplines whom he interviewed were able to discuss their own understanding of critical thinking, and even convey it to their students, "the notion is a complex one, and . . . in this complexity there is potential for a fair degree of confusion for students in the way they engage with the ideas in their studies" (Moore 2013, 519).

In this essay, I look at critical thinking from an intercultural rhetorical perspective (Connor 2011). I assume critical thinking is culturally specific. As a construct, critical thinking varies between disciplines or genres, and between cultures as more traditionally defined, by language, geography, and sociopolitical boundaries (Ramanathan and Atkinson 1999; also, Atkinson 1997; Lun, Fischer, and Ward 2010). Dwight Atkinson states that "critical thinking is cultural thinking" (Atkinson 1997, 89). What he means is that critical thinking is a social construct and a social practice. For example, it is well established that some cultures associated with Confucian heritage operate by foregrounding the group and collaborative cooperative over the Westernized habit of foregrounding the individual. Westerners put a premium on the lone, dissenting voice or the creative genius revolting against the norm, like Copernicus or Martin Luther. The Confucian-heritage perspective, however, values the sharing of a strong tradition rooted in important texts (such as the wisdom of the Buddha), coming to consensus, and building relationships and solidarity with others. Atkinson explains how socialization into these views can affect self-expression: "The direct expression of ego via language seems to be substantially proscribed in many cultures" (Atkinson 1997, 82). Foregrounding personal opinions in a critical analysis, then, may feel awkward to some students.

Some of the best-known research in this area was conducted by Geert Hofstede (2001), who describes cultural characteristics reflected in the ways people communicate, think, and learn. Hofstede describes one cultural cluster of characteristics found in numerous cultures as large power distance, low individualism, and high avoidance of uncertainly; in contrast, the cluster that predominates in Western European cultures and the United States includes low power distance, high individuality, and low avoidance of uncertainty. Power distance describes the extent to which the least powerful in society accept that the power of those over them is unequally distributed, so high power distance means, essentially, that people accept a more rigid, autocratic power structure. Individuality describes the extent to which individuals are integrated into groups, and it is compared to collectivism; in collectivist societies, the individual's interests are subordinated to the group, often the extended family, and individuals may not have much choice in their affiliations. Uncertainty describes how much tolerance a society has for ambiguity; a society with high avoidance of uncertainty tolerates less ambiguity and may use rules or procedures such as politeness conventions to minimize it (Hofstede 2001). Think about how writers in the United States learn to compose academic essays; they do conform to Hofstede's pattern because the author is considered the authority (something we often have to urge novice writers to recognize) whose personal views are important and allowed even when they do not conform to the majority view, and who is expected to put them forward confidently.

If critical thinking is a central concept in US higher education, and if most faculty view it as a universal aspect of human thought, it stands to reason academics have complex expectations about how to express that thought in writing or about what sort of behaviors in classes or conferences students who can think critically should display. Sometimes these expectations are explained to students, and sometimes they remain unstated. But even when expectations are spelled out, meeting them can be a challenge for some international students. For example, overt debate, taking a strong pro or con stance, or contradiction and questioning of authority are valued behaviors that "have been frequently found to be problematic for L2 writers from more interdependently oriented cultural backgrounds" and are based on our cultural ideas about the individual's civic duties or about the reasonableness of dissent (Ramanathan and Atkinson 1999, 61; also see Durkin 2008).

Expectations may begin with faculty in the classroom, but they inevitably spill over into the writing center. Like faculty, tutors, who have been well socialized into US academic discourse, have expectations about how students should write or talk, ways that evidence critical thinking as we define it in a US academic setting. Tutors may wonder why some students they work with hesitate to question authority or to take strong "ownership" of ideas. They may feel frustration when a student resists taking a stance that even slightly contradicts a professor's favored theory, especially when the tutor can help provide a solid argument. What the tutor may see as an intellectual challenge, the student may see as disrespect.

OTHERING AND CRITICAL THINKING

Clearly, students run into difficulty when they do not display the kind of critical thinking expected. Worse, faculty or tutors may judge students who do not conform to their notion of critical thinking as having a deficit. One of the most common moves we make, when confronted with someone who does not meet our expectations, is Othering, that is, placing that person in a category we find is distinct from our own so we feel comfortable in discounting or even subordinating everyone in that category. Othering is a power move that pits *us* against *them* and that uses rhetoric to assert superiority. When confronted with college students who do not meet their expectations as critical thinkers, faculty may employ Othering by placing students in categories such as "not college ready" or "unteachable."

Adrian Holliday's (1999) concepts of small and large culture apply here. He describes the dominant culture—in this discussion the US academic culture—as the "large culture," and groups defined by "cohesive social behavior" are ethnographically described as "small cultures." The large culture is the social construct, the abstraction, while the small cultures are where we actually live, work, and act. The large culture prescribes our norms, sets rules and boundaries, and defines us by ethnicity, nationality, or other features we might have in common. In the large culture of the academy, "foreign students" may be lumped together and stereotyped as deficient in English. Small cultures more carefully describe their actual language and literacy practices. Small cultures are based on our social grouping, maybe our occupation or our identity with or membership in a group. In the academic context, a class or a writing center might constitute a small culture. Within a small culture, individuals navigate and negotiate the sometimes conflicting demands of the social groups with which they are affiliated (Bruce, this volume; Connor 2011). So while we may stereotype foreign students as a group, in the one-to-one interaction of a writing center session, we face an individual from a specific country with a unique language background and with unique educational experiences, preparation, and attitudes. Most important, we face an individual who is trying to solve a specific rhetorical problem, the problem posed by the assignment or the task they are addressing when they come for our help.

Amy Winans, who calls for a critical understanding of race, makes a point about othering that we can also apply to nationality (Winans 2006, 483). Winans identifies three beliefs held by the white students she worked with in Pennsylvania, and she explains why these beliefs are ripe for critical deconstruction: "that the United States is a meritocracy that rewards all individuals' hard work; that their identity is individual and can be chosen and shaped by them alone; and that they are not affected by history or racism" (Winans 2006, 491). We can easily enough identify more strongly held beliefs about "Americanness" that push international students into the Other category, such as that the United States has the best educational system, lowest level of poverty, highest level of material comforts, and strongest military in the world. If we accept these notions uncritically, we may think of "foreigners" as culturally or materially impoverished. In this respect, we might think of American (US) identity as the norm and other national identities as a deviation from the norm. If it's not American, it's not important or maybe just not quite right. The resulting attitude can be indifference, ignorance, or hostility toward international students' home cultures and languages (Leki 1992, 47).

Tutors can see how we might also extend this concept to language or thought. Michelle Cox in chapter 3 of this volume notes our tendency to lump all L2 students into a category based solely on linguistic identity. Shanti Bruce gives a detailed account about Puerto Rican identity and the complex ways it is tied to competency in English in chapter 4. As she explains, writers can be burdened when students who are learning academic English are "made to feel, by some, that they are betraying loyalties" (85). Puerto Rico's colonial past makes learning English more than a simple linguistic endeavor. We may further place international students who fail to display the type of critical thinking we expect into this category of "needs to learn better English." Those who do not speak or write Standard American English like a native need to learn it to become normal, and as teachers and tutors, we are doing our international students a favor by helping them be like us. Further, if they speak perfect, error-free English, they will think like we do (critically, of course). When we categorize all writing problems that face L2 writers/speakers under the category of "English language problems," we think of the support we can provide in a writing center primarily in terms of lower-order concerns like grammar, vocabulary, or sentence structure. Our assumption, one faculty may support and urge us to adopt, is that focus on individual sentences and words, rather than working from the top down and starting with the gist of a text or working with pragmatics, as discussed by Pimyupa W. Praphan and Guiboke Seong in this collection, is what L2 writers/speakers need to develop their critical thinking.

There *is* some truth to that assumption in that language proficiency has been tied to skill in critical thinking of the Western type. A 2010 study by Vivian Miu-Chi Lun and her colleagues Ronald Fischer and Colleen Ward attempted to sort out whether difficulties L2 students in New Zealand seemed to be facing with critical thinking were due to differences in thinking styles or just the result of a lack of proficiency in the English language (Lun, Fischer, and Ward 2010). They hypothesized that L2 writers/speakers would have more difficulty on objective measures of critical thinking than would mainstream New Zealand students (native speakers of English). They tried to isolate the causes for these differences as coming from either language proficiency or from differing cognitive styles. Ultimately, they found that the differences they uncovered could be traced significantly to language proficiency, and most especially to vocabulary, but not to cognitive styles. However, they cautioned that there could still be a connection between English proficiency and adoption of mainstream New Zealand culture, including cognitive styles, and they noted the need for further research.

We might conclude from this research that working on language proficiency is helpful, but we should not conclude that it is helpful for every student in every case. In truth, no single approach works, and applying a single approach to all L2 writers/speakers regardless of their needs, desires, or learning preferences, simply because we assume learning English grammar means learning English rhetoric, would constitute Othering.

Another form Othering can take is to assume all international students operate from culturally different rhetorics. When I interviewed ten Texas A&M writing center tutors in 2011, a few hinted that they applied contrastive rhetoric uncritically and broadly. For example, one stated that "Asian cultures have a totally different organizational strategy." I believe in practice she was not applying this statement to all Asian students, but I also believe she was theorizing from Kaplan's (1987) version of contrastive rhetoric, which asserts that organization patterns arise from cultural norms that interfere with writing in English as a second language.

Tutors who adopt a more critical and more accurate view of contrastive rhetoric can correct this stereotypical assumption (Connor 2011; Kubota and Lehner 2004; Matsuda 1997; Leki 2007; Severino 1993; Thonus 1993). Kubota and Lehner (2004) and Matsuda (1997) provide a way to view the differences in rhetorical strategies and knowledge writers bring to a task that avoids Othering. In Paul Kei Matsuda's terms, literacy learning is dynamic—not a matter of simply decoding or encoding a text but "the result of the encounter of the writer and the reader—an encounter mediated through the text" (52). The background of the writer and the reader must be considered, including what languages they speak, their educational and cultural backgrounds, and the discourse communities they share—that is, their large culture—but in understanding what a writer is trying to do, the small culture must also be considered. The rhetorical strategies any given writer brings to creating a text or expects readers to bring to that text include far more than organizational structures—they might include tone, level of formality, diction, choice of rhetorical figures or tropes, or the depth or style of argument, among other things. Every writer is situated within a fluid and dynamic rhetorical situation. This dynamism makes the writing center a particularly potent place to address the writer's choices because in the writing center we can take the time to individualize instruction.

So to the tutor who believed "Asian cultures have a totally different organizational strategy," we might offer a few observations. Asian students may have no issues with organization because in many Asian cultures students are taught to write scholarly texts in a US academic style. Or Asian students may be struggling so much with diction and understanding a topic that the difference in their organization comes not from the interference of another rhetorical strategy but from the fact that so much attention is being paid to meaning that they have not even worked on organization. It is even possible an Asian student wants to improve on or challenge US academic style by bringing the flavor of Asian rhetoric to a text. This critical view of contrastive rhetoric helps tutors remember that there is no one correct rhetorical style, and that what seem to be errors may just be differences in strategies or in understanding of the rhetorical situation.

LOCAL VERSUS GLOBAL APPROACHES

Sue Hum recognizes our sometimes well-intentioned tendency to deal with difference in reading multicultural texts by one of two moves: we may read locally or we may read universally. We can apply this to reading international student writing. In a local reading, we concentrate "on the particular, contextual difference-centered details of a text" (Hum 2006, 462). So, for example, we notice differences in the use of articles, prepositions, or vocabulary. In a universal reading, we focus "on the commonalities we all share as members of the human race" (Hum 2006, 462), and thus we tend to read more globally for content and gloss over the local differences.

Helping students read and write critically, however, requires a more complex approach than simply deciding to work at either a global or a local level. A more balanced approach would be intercultural: it would search for individualized solutions guided by the goals and learning/cognitive preferences of the student and respect for the student's starting place, the cultural and rhetorical traditions that may affect the writing. As one of the tutors at my writing center put it to me, "You're going to have to adjust your tutoring style to every person that walks in the door." Remember, too, that writers make choices, and sometimes the choices involve using language that resists the academic and English norms or that purposefully mixes or switches codes or language varieties, as described by Kevin Dvorak in this volume.

In writing centers, our bias is to work globally, sometimes at the expense of local issues, although when we work with L2 writers/speakers, doing so can be a struggle. Manuals often caution tutors to avoid starting with lower-order, or local, concerns (generally, sentence-level issues, grammar, and word choice) (Bickford 2006, 85), partly so tutorials do not get bogged down in editing before global issues are addressed. However, advice to the contrary, tutors often feel pressured to work on local issues. And maybe that's okay. It's natural for L2 writers/speakers to ask for help with the basic language skills usually associated with local concerns. Without skills such as the ability to read closely and quickly, students cannot meet the demands of their faculty to think critically. In a 1994 survey, L2 writers/speakers revealed they wanted to learn to process language more quickly and become more efficient readers and writers (Leki and Carson 1994, 91). Local work on vocabulary helps students learn to express the nuances of meaning available to fluent speakers.

Lun and others have suggested that a focus on vocabulary can help students who are experiencing problems with critical thinking tasks

(Lun, Fischer, and Ward 2010). Sarah Nakamaru points out the importance of addressing lexical problems.

> Attention to language is often presented as editing or proofreading and is almost always equated with "grammar," despite the fact that having access to and being able to effectively use English words and phrases (i.e., lexical knowledge/skills) is crucial to creating meaningful written texts in English. (Nakamaru 2010, 95)

David Olson (1997) explains why knowledge of English vocabulary can have a direct impact on critical thinking skills. Since critical thinking demands a reflective stance in which we use judgment to evaluate someone else's writing (or speech) or thought, we need specific vocabulary that can express our attitudes, what Olson (1997, 500) dubs "talk about talk and thought," and such verbs are to be found aplenty in English. His list of thirty includes verbs like *believe, know, mean, say, tell, assert, assume, claim, criticize, explain, imply, interpret, observe, prove,* and *suggest* (502). They are verbs that "provide the basic vocabulary for characterizing others' mental states" (503); for example, *think* and *know*

> can be used to indicate agreement or disagreement with the cognitive state of another person—if we agree, we say he knows; if we disagree, we say he thinks—the choice of the assertive verb does not depend purely on the attitude of the person whose speech is being characterized but also on the attitude of the reporter of the speech act. (503)

As Olson (1997) explains, "To think about what another thinks and why is one important aspect of critical thinking" (496), so students need a more nuanced lexicon.

Because the concept of global and local can be so thoroughly integrated for L2 writers/speakers, prioritizing global concerns and dealing with them first may not be a productive approach (Blau and Hall 2002; Cogie 2006; Myers 2003; Taylor 2007; Nakamaru 2010). The assumption that local issues are extraneous and not as important to meaning as global issues was contested by Sharon Myers, who found that providing a word or "fixing" a tangled syntax both potentially affect meaning: "Whether or not an error is global or local depends first and foremost on its context" (Myers 2003, 62). Virginia Taylor found that tutors in her study did something along those lines as they moved between the local and global "fluidly and flexibly." They "moved back and forth from rhetorical to linguistic foci in their discussions" (Taylor 2007, 61). According to Taylor (also, Cogie 2006), tutors must perceive the necessity of moving between the local and global and must understand that word choice, syntax, and other issues often considered local can affect meaning and thus be more than surface features.

I interviewed six international graduate students in 2011, all former clients at the university writing center and all English language learners. None of them was interested in passively sitting back while a tutor corrected their work. They all wanted to learn to write acceptable, even excellent, English prose. All of them said working on local issues was helpful, although one of them had assumed the writing center could not help with global issues since with him, tutors never did, and another said that although he would have liked help with global issues, tutors often did not get there. He was reluctant to be too "aggressive" or "rude" in interrupting and redirecting the session (even though we stress that the client's needs should come first). He explained that the best tutors provide "very direct feedback that gives options" and concluded that "one of the keys things I think for the consultant is to recognize the needs of the student. Because there are different things the student is coming in for, maybe flow . . . is the argument logical? . . . is the paper saying what they want to say or not? . . . If a consultant will be able to recognize the need of the student then this . . . would further elevate the writing center." Taylor (2007) also found that undergraduate L2 writers/speakers she studied requested work on global issues and local issues in a somewhat balanced ratio.

Sometimes, tutors default to local issues because of pressures they put on themselves. When the tutor is an undergraduate and the student is a graduate student, the tutor may not feel capable of providing global advice because of a lack of expertise in the graduate student's discipline. As Judith Powers warns, "In a situation where neither party fully understands the expectations of the discipline, working on sentence-level issues may be the only kind of work possible" (Powers 1995, 15). I interviewed ten experienced tutors in my writing center in 2010, and they told me they often moved flexibly between local and global issues when working with international graduate students. More than half of them described a process whereby a few sentences to a few paragraphs (with most favoring the paragraph unit) were read aloud, usually by the student, the same strategy noticed by Blau and Hall (2002, 42) in their study. Then the pair went back and identified and corrected errors, with the tutor explicating and guiding as needed. Tutors sometimes used this opportunity to bring attention to global or rhetorical issues such as audience, organization, or thesis support.

Unfortunately, the tutors sometimes felt anxiety about whether this was the sanctioned technique, and some did not recognize that focus on the local might be as significant as focus on the global. One tutor was aware that some errors affect meaning more than others; she described a technique whereby she regularly asked students to explain orally what they wanted to say in writing at the beginning of a tutorial. Then, they began reading aloud and working on local issues as they went. The tutor used what she knew about the student's local errors to clarify meaning. For example, if the student had particular trouble with definite articles, the tutor did not just provide the "right" one but used the process of collaboratively deciding on the proper article to ensure the student was saying what they really meant, a process that encouraged moving between the local and the global. The tutor saw the two as interdependent.

> They need a lot of help with sentence structure, verb agreement, articles, those are very common things, but those things help them express themselves to say exactly what they want to say . . . sometimes even the verb tense or the agreement. Is that word really plural or not? . . . So it may sound like grammar but it really is the communication in particular in sentence structure, and if they have trouble getting sentence structure clear and concise, I often ask them, "Can you put the big idea right at the beginning, a simple subject-verb construction and then add what you need to it to get that across?"

Another tutor reported focusing every tutorial on global concerns by engaging in discussions about the content to set the tone and provide context for working on local issues since editing at every level depends on understanding the writer's goals. A third tutor tried to avoid line-by-line editing with a questioning strategy.

> With students who are unclear about their assignments or their organization or that sort of thing I'll ask them first . . . "Do you want to read through this whole paper or do you want to just talk about it?" . . . I notice that it keeps me from line-by-line editing . . . and it allows me to focus on their thesis and their organization, so I'll ask them to tell me what their thesis is and then ask them . . . to break it down into their arguments and then we'll look through the paper for that.

In the end, letting the student guide the tutor is the best strategy. Do students need to fill in cultural background or work on enhancing those verbs that help them talk about the text?

It helps to take a little time at the outset of a tutoring session to get to know the student's language and literacy background, learning preferences, and goals. Tutors also need to take a few minutes to understand the writing task and the writer's approach. Tutors are often working on very tight schedules, and that can put pressure on them to Other students—assuming Asian students will defer to authority or

Arabic-speaking students will avoid directly stating a thesis up front can come from time pressure. It is important to skim over the draft and get the gist of the argument before delving into a sentence-by-sentence discussion of local issues. Tutors should also determine whether the writing is argument based or if the assignment requires critical thinking. Even reflective writing is often expected to display attributes of critical thinking, such as questioning the status quo or imagining a new perspective. Tutors should be looking for the elements of critical thinking in student writing while being aware that their presence or absence does not speak to the student's intellectual ability alone but also to US academic expectations.

EASING CULTURAL AND RHETORICAL ADAPTATION

The National Council of Teachers of English recently advised instructors to make their assignments more culturally sensitive.

> When designing assignments, instructors should avoid topics that require substantial background knowledge that is related to a specific culture or history that is not being covered by the course. Instructors should also be aware that sensitive topics, such as sexuality, criticism of authority, political beliefs, personal experiences, and religious beliefs, are subject to differing levels of comfort among students of different cultural and educational backgrounds. We encourage instructors to provide students with multiple options for successfully completing an assignment, such as by providing multiple prompts or allowing students to write in a variety of genres for completing the assignment. Instructors should provide clearly written assignments so that expectations are not left tacit. (National Council of Teachers of English 2001)

Writing centers have a central role to play in supporting students faced with assignments that do not follow these guidelines. When Yashvant and Julia discussed politics, Julia was serving as what Judith Powers (1993, 41) calls a "cultural informant," a term explained in more detail in this volume by Michelle Cox.

Christine Fox's 2003 case study of Ming, a junior-level Chinese immigrant student at the University of Rhode Island, illustrates another way tutors can help—by serving as cultural ambassadors. Ming received an assignment in a sociology class in which she was to discuss Buddhism as a "subversive science," something that caused her to "struggle for weeks with the notion that Buddhism might be seen in U.S. culture as subversive" (Fox 2003, 71). Fox explains that understanding American culture was an ongoing struggle for Ming (also see examples cited by Leki 2007). A sympathetic tutor could help Ming accept that not all of us believe such a statement and that, in fact, questioning it might be just the sort of academic move her professor would applaud.

The tutor can also help students tease out hidden expectations for critical thinking in assignments. Academic writing is almost always linked to critical thinking, even when it is not explicitly invited. In visiting various classes around our university to talk to students about journal writing, some of us in the writing center have discovered that when faculty are asking for "reflection," they usually judge it not as personal expression but as a manifestation of critical thought, something they can evaluate. Typically, they want students to voice opinions or record experiences but also to relate these to the ideas brought out in class readings or discussion and provide support for ideas. If a student has issues with understanding spoken English or with reading highly academic writing, talking to a tutor can substitute for class discussion, and working with a tutor to understand a class reading could make a great deal of difference in meeting the expectations of such an assignment.

International students may also need orientation to typical American academic genres such as literature reviews, critical essays, and research papers, especially argumentative ones. Tutors can play a valuable role in helping students analyze assignments and explore the rhetorical strategies and organization required in various genres. If, for example, a student has been asked to reflect on a reading, the tutor may begin by examining the prompt or interviewing the student about what is meant by *reflection*. It may very well be that the student must get clarification from an instructor, and the tutor can also play a role in reassuring international students that doing so is perfectly appropriate.

Students who come from cultures with large power distance and low individualism might feel reluctant not only to clarify instructor expectations but also to express beliefs that might seem to disagree with the majority view or with the instructor's view. As Fox explains, they may "fear that an honest expression of their religious or political beliefs, if different from those of their professors, will result in a poor grade" (Fox 2003, 131). Students may need explicit reassurance that disagreement is welcome, but tutors should explain how to express that disagreement in a scholarly tone, through argument and with evidence. If the tutor can determine the student does come from such a cultural background, helping the student find a more middle ground or use more conciliatory argument techniques (such as Rogerian argument, which seeks to start from common ground) might be the best path.

To help students with rhetorical strategies, spend time looking at sample writing. For graduate students, dissertations or research articles are easy enough to find online. When undergraduates can supply a model, or when they can find a sample paper, such as a research paper in a handbook, this technique can work well for them, too. The analysis should be geared to helping the writer see the moves that are typical in academic and critical writing.

- What is the author's stance and relationship to the audience?
- What verbs describe how the author evaluates other ideas or research?
- How are citations worked into the text?
- Does the author use first-person pronouns (especially if it is a coauthored work)?
- How are opinions and facts expressed?
- What kinds of evidence support the thesis (if there is one)?
- What is the thread of the argument and how is it presented to the reader?
- Can the writer look at something from multiple perspectives? Can they accurately describe other viewpoints?

The goal of this exercise is to expose tacit assumptions about the conventions of critical thinking.

It all comes back to what a student needs, of course. Ming typically had difficulty deciding on the level of detail to add to a paper; too much, she feared, would insult her professor's intelligence, and sometimes she was unsure how much to elaborate on quotes or reluctant to add transitions. These are all problems Fox attributes to the Chinese writing style, in which it would be inappropriate to tell a reader something they already are presumed to know and to make implied connections between ideas so obvious you insult the reader's intelligence (Fox 2003, 78–83). Tracing the thread of the argument and thinking about the author's stance and relationship to the audience would probably help her far more than focusing on passive voice.

INTERCULTURAL CRITICAL THINKING

In 2009–2010, our writing center worked through training to improve tutors' attitudes toward and understanding of diversity. A tutor I interviewed in 2010, herself an international student, felt that tutor attitudes toward international students specifically had improved at our center since she began work in 2004. She claimed to hear less frustration voiced over accents, or how to teach sentence structure or articles, and much less stereotyping. Her observation shows a lessening of tension. At our center, we've managed to get over the attitude that international students only need or want help with English proficiency. But sometimes our tutors still need help in seeing them as dedicated and serious writers who, in a collaborative process, enrich the tutors' understanding of literacy as much as they need the tutors' help in conforming to US English and rhetoric. Vishnal, one of the international graduate students I interviewed, politely explained that a few tutors, when he needed review of very basic concepts, had an almost arrogant attitude about English, which he interpreted as frustration. He explained, "They may not recognize that I am from another part of the world and that I don't know the conventions here, and they are arrogant about the right way."

The point some tutors are missing is that they are not helping Vishnal learn the right way but the dominant way in US higher education. As helpful as they are in guiding him into US forms of thinking and discourse, they should also be aware that there are other ways to make a point, other ways to argue or put forth ideas. This is not something that should surprise us, although too many US academics are unaware of how arguments might be made in other places. Many of our first-year composition textbooks teach Rogerian argument, based on finding common ground, in addition to the Aristotelian type that focuses more on convincing the opposition. Mary Field Belenky and her colleagues, feminist theorists, introduced us to concepts like "connected knowing," a different type of thinking from what they called the "separate knowing" we associate with Western critical thinking (Belenky et al. 1997). Connected knowing results from collaboration, from a greater awareness of the context of an issue, and from seeking to understand the views of others. Rather than measure right and wrong, good or bad, against an objective standard, a connected knower considers the situation and other viewpoints before judging.

Many ways of thinking do the same rigorous work of creating knowledge as the dominant form of critical thinking does. Frankie Condon and Bobbi Olson argue in chapter 2 that linguistic diversity should find a home in writing centers. In the same spirit, we need to create a space for diversity in ways of thinking and move away from deficient models. In writing centers, at least, we can be open to differences and learn from them ways to broaden our own rhetorical strategies and linguistic repertoires.

Questions to Consider

1. Have you experienced or heard instances of Othering in your academic setting in the classroom, the writing center, or elsewhere on campus? How did the people around you react to this situation?

2. When a writer or a speaker uses language to assert identity or membership in a group, they may purposely violate the conventions of academic
writing. How might this lead to an assumption that the writer or speaker
lacks critical-thinking skills?

3. List five attributes you think indicate critical thinking (e.g., skepticism,
questioning of authority). Can you imagine situations in which a writer
displaying these characteristics is not actually thinking critically? What
elements must be present besides these attributes before we can call
something critical thinking?

4. Find a short text (a web page, an essay, an opinion piece from a blog or
a newspaper) you think demonstrates critical thinking. Explain what
makes this text fit your definition of critical thinking.

5. Examine this quote from Charles Eliot Norton, which has been thought
to exemplify critical thinking.

> The voice of protest, of warning, of appeal is never more needed
> than when the clamor of fife and drum, echoed by the press and
> too often by the pulpit, is bidding all men fall in and keep step and
> obey in silence the tyrannous word of command. Then, more than
> ever, it is the duty of the good citizen not to be silent. (The Critical
> Thinking Community)

What elements of this view of critical thinking might be culturally
determined?

For Further Reading

Connor, Ulla. 2011. *Intercultural Rhetoric in the Writing Classroom.* Ann Arbor: University of
Michigan Press.
   The study of intercultural rhetoric asks provocative questions, like whether or not
each culture has its own rhetoric distinct from others', whether or not this rhetoric (if
it exists) can be observed in its members' speech and writing, and whether or not it is
a factor in students' learning and performance. Tutors will appreciate Ulla Connor's
clear and compelling writing, along with illustrations of text analyses and applications
of her theory to classroom teaching.
The Critical Thinking Community. http://www.criticalthinking.org//.
   This website presents a fairly comprehensive overview of the concept of critical
thinking from a Westernized academic perspective. The Library section (top menu
bar) provides the most information, including different definitions of critical thinking
and a brief history of the critical-thinking movement in education. It is notable in that
it focuses on a unitary definition and on common denominators and does not address
critical thinking as related to specific cultures, academic disciplines, or genres.
Graff, Gerald, and Cathy Birkenstein. 2014. *They Say I Say: The Moves That Matter in
Academic Writing.* 3rd ed. New York: W. W. Norton.
   Helping students with critical thinking can be advanced by helping them discover
the moves typical in academic writing. Gerald Graff and Cathy Birkenstein demystify
the process using the metaphor of a conversation. They provide short, readable chapters with examples on how to summarize, paraphrase, and quote; how to respond to
others; and how to identify and compose patterns writers use to discuss their own and
others' work.

The Higher Education Academy. http://www.heacademy.ac.uk/home.

This web page from the United Kingdom provides a review of the debate over whether critical thinking is a single concept or one that is culturally determined. Use the keyword *search* under the Resources Centre tab to discover their resources on the topic. Of special interest is the page on critical thinking and international students, which explores common myths about the lack of critical thinking in certain cultures or the inability of some cultures to engage in critical thought.

Hornberger, Nancy H., and Sandra Lee McKay. 2010. *Sociolinguistics and Language Education.* Tonawanda, NY: Multilingual Matters.

This textbook is geared to students and provides a clear exposition of language and social issues as they play out in Westernized educational systems. In the chapter entitled "English as an International Language," the authors address how the ways we talk about critical thinking have served as a means of Othering.

Moore, Tim. 2013. "Critical Thinking: Seven Definitions in Search of a Concept." *Studies in Higher Education* 38 (4): 506–22. http://dx.doi.org/10.1080/03075079.2011.586995.

Tim Moore's article provides background on how the concept of critical thinking is an ill-defined concept in spite of attempts to find a single, unified definition. His study of how academics from three seemingly similar disciplines—history, philosophy, and cultural studies—define critical thinking differently shows how the concept is a cultural one. In the end, he urges that teachers clarify their own definitions of critical thinking as part of their pedagogies.

References

Atkinson, Dwight. 1997. "A Critical Approach to Critical Thinking in TESOL." *TESOL Quarterly* 31 (1): 71–94. http://dx.doi.org/10.2307/3587975.

Belenky, Mary Field, Blythe McVicker Clinchy, Nancy Rule Goldberger, and Jill Mattuck Tarule. 1997. *Women's Ways of Knowing: The Development of Self, Voice, and Mind.* 10th anniversary ed. New York: Basic Books.

Bickford, Crystal. 2006. "Examining Writing Center Training Texts: Towards a Tutor Training Pedagogy." PhD diss., Indiana University of Pennsylvania, Indiana, PA.

Blau, Susan, and John Hall. 2002. "Guilt-free Tutoring: Rethinking How We Tutor Non-Native-English-Speaking Students." *Writing Center Journal* 23 (1): 23–44.

Cogie, Jane. 2006. "ESL Student Participation in Writing Center Sessions." *Writing Center Journal* 26 (2): 48–66.

Durkin, Kathy. 2008. "The Adaptation of East Asian Masters Students to Western Norms of Critical Thinking and Argumentation in the UK." *Intercultural Education* 19 (1): 15–27. http://dx.doi.org/10.1080/14675980701852228.

Fox, Christine M. 2003. "Writing Across Cultures: Contrastive Rhetoric and a Writing Center Study of One Student's Journey." PhD diss., University of Rhode Island, Kingston, RI.

Hofstede, Geert. 2001. *Culture's Consequences: Comparing Values, Behaviors, Institutions, and Organizations Across Nations.* 2nd ed. Thousand Oaks, CA: SAGE.

Holliday, Adrian. 1999. "Small Cultures." *Applied Linguistics* 20 (2): 237–64. http://dx.doi.org/10.1093/applin/20.2.237.

Hum, Sue. 2006. "Articulating Authentic Chineseness: The Politics of Reading Race and Ethnicity Aesthetically." In *Relations, Locations, Positions: Composition Theory for Writing Teachers*, edited by Peter Vandergorn, Sue Hum, and Jennifer Clary-Lemon, 442–46. Urbana, IL: National Council of Teachers of English.

Kaplan, Robert B. 1987. "Cultural Thought Patterns Re-Visited." In *Writing across Languages: Analysis of a Text*, edited by Ulla Connor and Robert B. Kaplan, 9–22. Reading, MA: Addison Wesley.

Kubota, Ryuko, and Al Lehner. 2004. "Toward Critical Contrastive Rhetoric." *Journal of Second Language Writing* 13 (1): 7–27. http://dx.doi.org/10.1016/j.jslw.2004.04.003.

Leki, Ilona. 1992. *Understanding ESL Writers: A Guide for Teachers.* Portsmouth, NH: Boynton/Cook.

Leki, Ilona. 2007. *Undergraduates in a Second Language: Challenges and Complexities of Academic Literacy Development.* New York: Lawrence Erlbaum.

Leki, Ilona, and Joan G. Carson. 1994. "Students' Perceptions of EAP Writing Instruction and Writing Needs Across the Disciplines." *TESOL Quarterly* 28 (1): 81–101. http://dx.doi.org/10.2307/3587199.

Lun, Vivian Miu-Chi, Ronald Fischer, and Colleen Ward. 2010. "Exploring Cultural Differences in Critical Thinking: Is It about My Thinking Style or the Language I Speak?" *Learning and Individual Differences* 20 (6): 604–16. http://dx.doi.org/10.1016/j.lindif.2010.07.001.

Matsuda, Paul Kei. 1997. "Contrastive Rhetoric in Context: A Dynamic Model of L2 Writing." *Journal of Second Language Writing* 6 (1): 45–60. http://dx.doi.org/10.1016/S1060-3743(97)90005-9.

Medhurst, Julia. 2013. "International Students, Instructors, and Audience." *Peer Centered* (blog). http://www.peercentered.org/2013/04/international-students-face-particular.html.

Myers, Sharon A. 2003. "Reassessing the 'Proofreading Trap': ESL Tutoring and Writing Instruction." *Writing Center Journal* 24 (1): 51–70.

Nakamaru, Sarah. 2010. "Lexical Issues in Writing Center Tutorials with International and US-Educated Multilingual Writers." *Journal of Second Language Writing* 19 (2): 95–113. http://dx.doi.org/10.1016/j.jslw.2010.01.001.

National Council of Teachers of English. 2001 (revised November 2009). "*CCCC Statement on Second Language Writing and Writers.*" CCCC Position Statement. http://www.ncte.org/cccc/resources/positions/secondlangwriting.

Olson, David R. 1997. "Critical Thinking: Leaning to Talk about Talk and Text." In *Handbook of Academic Learning: Construction of Knowledge,* edited by Gary D. Phye, 493–510. New York: Academic. http://dx.doi.org/10.1016/B978-012554255-5/50017-X.

Powers, Judith K. 1993. "Rethinking Writing Center Conferencing Strategies for the ESL Writer." *Writing Center Journal* 13 (2): 39–47.

Powers, Judith K. 1995. "Assisting the Graduate Thesis Writer through Faculty and Writing Center Collaboration." *Writing Lab Newsletter* 20 (2): 13–16.

Ramanathan, Vai, and Dwight Atkinson. 1999. "Individualism, Academic Writing, and ESL Writers." *Journal of Second Language Writing* 8 (1): 45–75. http://dx.doi.org/10.1016/S1060-3743(99)80112-X.

Severino, Carol. 1993. "The 'Doodles' in Context: Qualifying Claims about Contrastive Rhetoric." *Writing Center Journal* 14 (1): 44–62.

Taylor, Virginia. 2007. "The Balance of Rhetoric and Linguistics: A Study of Second Language Writing Center Tutorials." PhD diss., Purdue University, West Lafayette, IN.

Thonus, Terese. 1993. "Tutors as Teachers: Assisting ESL/EFL Students in the Writing Center." *Writing Center Journal* 13 (2): 13–26.

Winans, Amy. 2006. "Local Pedagogies and Race: Interrogating White Safety in the Rural College Classroom." In *Relations, Locations, Positions: Composition Theory for Writing Teachers,* edited by Peter Vanderhorn, Sue Hum, and Jennifer Clary-Lemon, 471–99. Urbana, IL: National Council of Teachers of English.

13

UNFAMILIAR TERRITORY
Tutors Working with Second Language Writers on Disciplinary Writing

Jennifer Craig

I barely remember the student—an engineering major from rural Maine—but I still remember his report. As I flipped through the pages, I saw thick blocks of text divided by headings and subheadings, equations, and graphics with units of measurement in an illegible font. Across the top of the report, his professor had slashed in red ink, *Get help with your writing*, the grade was low. The student was discouraged; he'd done his best, he said. He didn't understand the grade, nor did I. I looked through the draft, puzzled by technical terms, confused by the esoteric graphics, and intimidated by the equations sprinkled through the dense text. Gradually, I glimpsed one or two of the main ideas the student was trying to convey. But still I was lost in this unfamiliar genre, technical vocabulary, and terse style. The whole document was about a series of activities and a way of thinking foreign to me and—I realized—to the student.

We were in unfamiliar territory, and while he went on to become an engineer familiar with that terrain, I have continued as the perennial 'outsider' since I will never be an authentic practitioner of engineering or science or any other technical discipline. I will never participate in the activities and ways of knowing in a discipline other than writing studies nor will I be able to communicate from a perspective deeply grounded in technical knowledge. Although I may learn a great deal about how engineers or professionals in other disciplines work and think and communicate, I will always be an observer of their disciplines.

DOI: 10.7330/9781607324140.c013

WORKING WITH WRITERS IN THEIR DISCIPLINES

Oddly enough being an 'outsider' puts me in a strong position to work with students beginning to write in their disciplines. I can't be sure why this alliance—two people who are both 'outsiders' in the discipline in question—works. In fact, some students ask me directly, "If neither of us is an expert in this kind of communication, then how can you possibly help me?" There is probably more than one reason. Perhaps it is because I am not absorbed in the technical content that I can look more objectively at the organization of the writing. Or perhaps it is that I am a fresh and responsive reader—a scarce resource for a beginning disciplinary writer. Perhaps it is just precisely that I am *not* a disciplinary professor who has to give a grade that frees the writer to look critically at the text she has produced. Or perhaps it is that my responses and suggestions prompt the student writer to reflect at several levels and then to move toward revision.

Despite my confidence in what I bring to my work with a developing disciplinary writer, I am always clear about the limits of my expertise. For example, I might say, "We both know I am not an engineer (or scientist or architect or . . .), and even though I have worked with many writers in that discipline, I cannot assess your technical knowledge. So I want to emphasize that you should get feedback from your professor or teaching assistant or project advisor. What I do know about is how this kind of writing comes together, and I think that by looking at your writing together, we can make it stronger." Based on that clarity about expectations, the writer and I begin to work. What I have observed is that usually the writer emerges from that contact with a stronger assessment of the document (or presentation) under construction and then is able to engage in more productive discussions with her professors and peers. Over time, most student writers go on to become 'insiders' in their disciplines, and competent writers, too. For my part, I continue as a writing teacher who is increasingly knowledgeable (but never fully expert) about communication in another discipline.

WORKING WITH L2 WRITERS WHO ARE
WRITING IN THEIR DISCIPLINES

Much of my work with disciplinary writers has been with students learning to write and to present in their second or other language (L2), and in this chapter, I focus on some of the challenges many of them experience. The transition into disciplinary writing and communication is not easy for any student, but there are particular challenges for L2 writers.

Each L2 writer must not only manage the task of learning to write in a discipline, but she must also continue to strengthen second language skills while simultaneously encountering and negotiating new national, local, institutional, and disciplinary cultures.

In addition, just as we acknowledge the added challenges to L2 disciplinary writers, we must reflect on the heightened challenges to their tutors. *Diversity*—a buzzword in our globalized world—is usually constructed as a benign characteristic that is attractive and a bit exotic. However, in reality, those of us who work with culturally and linguistically diverse students know there are two sides to the notion of diversity. On the positive side, learning about new cultures can be rewarding. However, it is also true that at times, cultural and linguistic diversity can be correlated with awkward communication, implicit and incorrect assumptions, confusion about objectives, and some degree of discomfort in our exchanges with students. Moreover, tutors may be L2 writers themselves. Their backgrounds may contribute a welcome sensitivity to their engagement with L2 students, but L2 tutors also may feel a slight sense of uncertainty when tutoring other L2 writers. When we add disciplinary diversity to this mix, our discomfort may escalate to anxiety or even to fear.

"What is there to be afraid of?" one might ask. Often, in this situation, I think we experience a basic human aversion to looking foolish because we are not experts in that field. The fact is—we don't know. We don't even know what it is we don't know. Although as tutors we may accumulate some knowledge about that discipline over time, for the most part, in that territory, we are strangers. As such, we feel—like many strangers in an unfamiliar place—some degree of being awkward, lost, vulnerable, and out of control. One thing feels certain; as we work with the student writer, we may be on the brink of revealing our lack of knowledge in some yet undetermined but potentially embarrassing way. That suspicion doesn't feel so good.

Anxiety can lead us to some unproductive behavior with the writer. Perhaps we avoid the very issue that needs to be addressed. Perhaps we seize on grammar or punctuation errors because we feel knowledgeable in those areas. Perhaps we minimize the issues before us because that reduction helps us feel more comfortable. Or our anxiety prompts us to take control of the tutoring so what ought to be collegial and collaborative becomes autocratic and potentially misdirected.

Over the years, I have learned several ways to work with those uncomfortable feelings. First, the very awareness of the anxiety is instructive. When I feel that discomfort, I know I need to check in on several levels.

Am I expecting myself to be a disciplinary expert? What does the student expect? Do I feel out of control of this writing conference? Is this a time to remember my disciplinary boundaries? Is it a time to remind the student of the limits of my disciplinary expertise?

Second, I remember that anxiety often surfaces when the scope of the work is too broad and I am trying to address too many issues at once: language, writing, grammar, critical thinking, or structure. Is this a time to refocus the conference on shared objectives?

Also, the anxiety reminds me that I am human and that if I am feeling a bit tense, the student writer is feeling even more so. At times, just being able to say to a student, "This really is confusing to me!" or "I am not sure what to make of this section" allows the writer to take a deep breath and admit she feels somewhat the same way. Then, together, we prioritize what can be done with this piece of writing in this particular session. Always, I remind myself that—and experienced tutors will echo this insight—the next cue is there on the written page. When in doubt, I look at the writing, and in that writing, I see something about what the writer is able to accomplish with the text. That reality—however small—puts firm ground under my feet and allows me to move forward.

The remainder of this chapter focuses on L2 writers and some of the work they must do as they become disciplinary writers. (The term *L2* may seem simplistic since many L2 writers are linguistically diverse, but it is used here for efficiency. See Michelle Cox, this volume, for a full discussion.) To begin, I describe the common challenges faced by both native English-speaking writers and L2 writers. Then, after focusing more closely on L2 writers, I offer three vignettes in which I illustrate ways tutors can work effectively with L2 disciplinary writers.

HOW NATIVE SPEAKERS AND NONNATIVE SPEAKERS DEVELOP AS WRITERS

Most university students develop along a continuum as individuals, as members of their academic and professional communities, and as critical thinkers. Their writing shows their progress along that continuum (Poe, Lerner, and Craig 2010). Although their development is individual and unpredictable, we generally observe an evolution that is the result of their growing expertise in what Anne Beaufort describes as knowledge domains (Beaufort 2004). For example, competent academic writers gradually develop knowledge about subject matter (courses she has taken) and familiarity in genre knowledge (the common intellectual activities and the formats to which she has been introduced). She also gains expertise in rhetorical knowledge (how those genres can be used for the construction of knowledge and of argument in varying situations) and some competency in writing-process knowledge (how to create and refine a piece of writing). However, until she has begun to write and to present within her discipline, she probably has little discourse-community knowledge—that is to say, awareness and competency in those values, attitudes, activities, and ways of constructing knowledge often implicit and deeply situated within a discipline (Lave and Wenger 1991).

This progression through writing development is never linear. In fact, developing writers often re-learn and refine skills as they practice with new genres, areas of subject matter, and rhetorical strategies. This development is complicated by the increasingly complex content about which they write, and this is especially true as a writer enters her disciplinary community. There, she must begin again on another developmental continuum. She carries with her what she has learned about genre, about rhetoric, about specific subject-matter areas, and about the writing process, but even these domains of knowledge may have to be refined or redefined in significant ways. In a sense, she must immerse herself in a new disciplinary culture of knowledge, thought, and behavior. She must learn a great deal of complex subject matter rapidly. She is introduced to disciplinary standards for thinking about and constructing knowledge. In conversations with peers and mentors, she experiments with new genres that capture the activities of the community. She learns the conventions of her new peers, modeling the style and tone of their communications. Her membership —her 'insider' status—is assessed by her progress in negotiating these professional networks and mastering the expected forms of communication with all their subtleties. As she progresses further in her discipline, her writing abilities continue to be taxed by increasingly complex tasks, so even an advanced writer at the undergraduate level finds herself faced with new demands on those previously adequate abilities.

The developmental continuum and the apprenticeship in the discipline are similar for both native English speakers and L2 students as they manage the transition into their disciplinary communities (Stoller et al. 2005). However, linguistic diversity is a factor in this process for L2 writers. First, all but the most advanced L2 writers continue to acquire and refine their second or other language in subtle and complex ways. Second, they are also learning to write *in* that new language, a very different cognitive activity. (Harris and Silva 1993; Kroll 1990; Silva 1993; Williams 2002). These two distinctly separate processes are not in opposition. In fact, they are reciprocal. For example, the abilities to use correct syntax and extensive vocabulary are essential for advanced writing, but those abilities alone do not produce meaningful writing (Canagarajah 2002). Alternately, iteration and reflection cannot produce depth, clarity, coherence, and effective rhetorical strategies if an L2 writer does not have enough vocabulary or lacks sufficient control over grammar. An L2 writer must juggle both processes—the rule-based, additive process of language acquisition AND the iterative and reflective process of writing—if she is going to build strength in each.

Moreover, this challenge becomes more complicated when an L2 writer begins to communicate in her disciplinary community. Perhaps she has been a successful writer in L2 when essays were shorter, vocabulary more general, and rhetorical strategies less complex. But now—writing in her discipline—the complex technical material may strain her ability to read, to listen, and to comprehend in L2. Moreover, in the disciplines of science, technology, engineering, and mathematics (STEM), she must absorb and produce language not only in textual form but also through equations and technical graphics.

Acquiring and using a disciplinary vocabulary may be more difficult for her since she may lack the intuition about words and pronunciation that many native English speakers have. She must master the rhetorical habits that embody the ways in which professionals in that community think about and construct new knowledge (Johns 1990). Moreover, the L2 writer must grasp not only the larger features of a new genre but also the nuances within those features, the ways in which sources are used and cited, and the style and tone of writing (Lillis and Curry 2010).   hard!

Even as L2 writers face language challenges in their discipline, many of them encounter cultural challenges. The most obvious cultural difference is that an L2 writer often is influenced by a different ethnic or national culture that in turn has shaped the educational culture, curriculum, and pedagogy in which she has been prepared. Thus, in the new cultural context, an L2 writer may find that the language abilities that worked well in hierarchical, lecture-based classrooms may not work as well in a team-based or open-ended, problem-based course—pedagogy currently popular in US universities. Verbal abilities and listening comprehension may be taxed by the rapid and unstructured classroom interaction often common in US universities and by group work with peers (Reid and Kroll 1995; Zamel 2004).

In addition, the L2 writer now plunges into a disciplinary culture in which she needs new cognitive skills in order to advance. Her native English-speaking peers encounter this new culture, too. Yet native speakers approach these disciplinary communication tasks with deep, implicit cultural knowledge that allows them a certain intuition about how to approach tasks and negotiate their way in their new community (see Balester, this issue, for a discussion of the cultural construction of critical thinking.) Also, native speakers have a lifetime of experience in the language in which they are writing or speaking: syntax, mechanics, and an extensive general vocabulary onto which they begin to layer disciplinary language. Moreover, native speakers already may share disciplinary expectations about use of sources, rhetoric, and graphics, and they may be quicker to conform to style and tone. In addition, native speakers do not have to think critically about these tasks in another language. The L2 writer, on the other hand, may share only a few or perhaps none of these advantages, thus facing a more complex set of challenges than does a native speaker of English (Harris and Silva 1993; Matsuda 1999, 2001; Reid and Kroll 1995; Silva 1993; Zamel and Spack 2004)

The natural question then is how can a tutor is who not an expert in language acquisition or a member of a disciplinary community work with an L2 writer who presents a range of linguistic and cultural issues? As a population, their single common characteristic is heterogeneity, and thus there is nothing as simple as a one-size-fits-all approach. With each L2 writer, we find ourselves somewhere on a spectrum that ranges from sentence-level problems to the more advanced issues of organization of information (at times, information that is highly technical) and the crafting of rhetorical strategies. Perhaps our best initial strategy is to feel confident in our areas of expertise. For example, we have deep knowledge about the mechanics of language and the writing process. And we also understand language can be shaped in order to persuade, to inform, to argue, or to analyze. And second, it is wise for us to clearly communicate the boundary of that knowledge and to encourage students to seek feedback from disciplinary mentors (Mackiewicz 2004).

Experienced tutors know our work is easier when a writer comes to the conference with a specific question about the writing. Although we may think there are more important issues to address, the writer's question points to the writer's greater concern, and thus we pay attention. But often sessions begin when the writer has no specific question but only a wordless, exhausted hope that we can help. When tutoring sessions begin in that way, the disciplinary text produced by an unskilled L2 writer can seem impenetrable. Yet over the years, I have developed a list of questions, one or more of which usually helps me find a way into the text.

- Does the writer show a clear sense of audience and purpose for the writing?
- Does the writer show an understanding not only of top-level features of a genre but also of the nuances within those features?
- Is the writer using and citing sources appropriately?
- Does the writer demonstrate an ability to synthesize, analyze, and organize information?
- When appropriate, does the writer show an ability to argue for a claim, using evidence in that effort? When appropriate, does the writer demonstrate an ability to interpret data?
- When appropriate, is the writer creating and using substantive and professional graphics?

Exceptions and additions to this list apply in various disciplines, but it is safe to say that advanced (and developing) writers in all disciplines must learn to manage these tasks.

Does the Writer Show a Clear Sense of Audience and Purpose for the Writing?

Beginning disciplinary writers often struggle to understand audience and purpose for their disciplinary writing, and it is easy to see why. Most beginning writers have only read textbooks in their disciplines, yet the genres they are asked to produce are modeled more on authentic, professional activities and discourses (Stoller et al. 2005). Thus, when asked to write a report or a proposal or a memo, beginning writers often flounder because they lack a clear sense of audience and purpose, a sense that is important in developing organizational and rhetorical strategies as well as style and tone.

Students writing in L2 may have an especially hard time focusing on a sense of audience and purpose since their sense of agency with language and their perception of cultural context may vary from their native English-speaking peers. For example, L2 writers from some cultures may be reluctant to write critiques, a skill commonly expected in Western-based academic writing. Or perhaps the L2 writer comes from a reader-responsible culture rather than a Western-based, writer-responsible culture. That writer will resist making explicit interpretations of data, feeling that such an action expresses some disdain for the reader. Thus, a tutor can begin by talking with a writer about the imagined audience (other than the professor) for such a piece of writing, by clarifying the purpose of the writing assignment, and perhaps by sharing cultural information that frames the context for the L2 writer (Reid and Kroll 1995).

Does the Writer Show an Understanding Not Only of Top-Level Features
of a Genre but Also of the Nuances within Those Features?
Writers who are advancing in their disciplines are asked to write in
genres that enact the disciplinary activities in which they are engaged.
But often these genres are modeled on workplace formats unfamiliar to
a student rather than on conventional academic genres. Moreover, the
disciplinary activities reflected in the genre also are unfamiliar to the
writer. Thus, native English-speaking writers and L2 writers alike may
tend to see the top-level features of a genre as a static template they can
fill with text, and they may be unaware of the nuance required within
those top-level features. This lack of awareness is partly a consequence of
not understanding the audience and purpose for a document, but even
when the audience and purpose have been clarified, writers may not
understand the rhetorical "moves" that are second nature to an experienced writer. For example, introduction sections in many disciplinary
documents have three rhetorical moves: the writer establishes the context of the work; the writer then points to a need, a problem, a challenge
or an opportunity for improvement; and then the writer positions her
work in that gap in knowledge (Swales and Feak 2009). Without that
insight and the language that allows her to make those moves, a writer's
introduction section can become an unfocused mass of description.

When a tutor works with an L2 writer on genre features and the
rhetorical moves within those features, it can be useful if the tutor has
reviewed several exemplars in that discipline. For example, proposals or
technical reports in STEM fields may be unfamiliar, and thus knowing
something about that genre helps a tutor guide an L2 writer in noticing
not only those features but also the more subtle language within those
features. Once those elements begin to emerge in a student writer's text,
a tutor can then suggest transitional words and phrases or perhaps organizational patterns that allow a writer to move skillfully through a text.
Exemplars in particular disciplines can be collected from disciplinary
professors and kept up to date by writing center staff. Strong student
exemplars can be used effectively but should be used only with explicit
permission of the writer and should be kept at the writing center and
not distributed.

Is the Writer Using and Citing Sources Appropriately?
All advanced writers at the university level must learn how to use sources
in their work since that ability not only acknowledges the intellectual
work of others but also allows a writer to establish context, achieve

credibility, and craft powerful rhetorical strategies. Thus, writing centers, writing teachers, and tutors often are ready with a primer on citation styles. That material is relatively easy to transmit. However, it is much more difficult to teach students not only *how* to cite but *when*. In addition, tutors who do not perceive the cultural attitudes behind those citation practices have a challenging task since L2 writers' perceptions about how to use the work of others are often culturally influenced. For example, students from collectivist or communal cultures argue that using the work of others, verbatim, is only a mark of respect and not an unethical act of plagiarism (Bouman 2004). Also, L2 writers may lack the facility with language necessary to summarize, paraphrase, and critique. Thus, they use the text of others inappropriately, including chunks of text as block quotes or copying text without any attribution.

Moreover, knowing when to cite the work of others can be influenced by the discipline. For example, theoretical perspectives or broad methodological approaches usually are not cited in engineering literature reviews while peer-reviewed research is always carefully cited. An L2 writer can be caught not only between her ethnic culture and that of her current university but also between general academic culture and the culture of her discipline. And if that is not confusing enough, principles of citation practice may be upheld in theory but interpreted differently by different engineering faculty.

Does the Writer Demonstrate an Ability to Synthesize,
Analyze, and Organize information?

Students who advance in their disciplines are expected to develop higher-order critical-thinking skills, specifically analysis and synthesis. Moreover, we expect those skills will be reflected in the writing students are asked to do. While advanced L2 disciplinary writers usually can do the analysis, they often have a harder time synthesizing those ideas and explaining both analysis and synthesis in clear prose. For L2 writers, this challenge may arise if they are still thinking in L1 and then translating and trying to write in L2. Also, as they struggle with the complex ideas involved in analysis and synthesis, they may have difficulty finding accurate language to represent those ideas.

Organization of disciplinary writing is a skill closely linked to a writer's ability to analyze and synthesize information for a reader. In addition, disciplinary communication standards have specific and often implicit patterns for organization of information. Thus, if a disciplinary writer has only a slender grasp of audience and purpose and little awareness of disciplinary standards, she may struggle with clear, coherent organization. Students writing in L2 especially may fall back on non-disciplinary patterns of organization, and again, culture often influences the choices they make.

When Appropriate, Does the Writer Show an Ability to Argue for a Claim, Using Evidence in That Effort? When Appropriate, Does the Writer Demonstrate an Ability to Interpret Data?

Most disciplinary writers must learn to interpret data, often writing about it or creating graphics that explain the data. In Western contexts, a reader of disciplinary prose expects a writer to interpret that data. However, L2 writers working with data may be challenged in two ways. First, there may be cultural patterns that constrain them as they make claims about data, especially if a writer comes from a reader-responsible context in which readers are expected to draw their own conclusions. Second, a writer may not have the language to make an appropriate claim about the data. She may understand the information well enough, but qualifying that claim may be difficult for her. For example, an L2 engineering writer writing about data must learn how to modify various claims. Does the data show X? Or does the data *seem* to show X? A writer working with this challenge needs to have not only thought critically about the evidence but also to know a range of transitional phrases and have a clear command of verb tenses and modifiers.

When Appropriate, Is the Writer Creating and Using Substantive and Professional Graphics?

Informative graphics are another challenge for the L2 writer. An expected communication element in most disciplines, graphics pose both linguistic and cultural challenges. We cannot know what cultural perspectives on graphics that the L2 writer brings with her, but now she must conform to the expectations of graphics in her current disciplinary community. Almost certainly, those graphics must contain substantive information that will support the reader's cognitive task. Yet how does an L2 know the possible options unless she has seen similar graphics? And in addition to choosing the right graphic that shows the necessary information clearly, she must also create the textual language that supports and interprets that graphic. Here, a tutor will see that several challenges converge: understanding audience and purpose, creating rhetorical strategies, and using language to interpret data.

How Does a Tutor Most Effectively Approach Sentence-Level Error in Writing?

One or more of the entry points described earlier usually give a tutor a useful way to begin working with a writer. Wisely, we avoid beginning by addressing sentence-level errors. As tutors, we want to see a writer create meaningful text, and while correcting all errors may produce 'clean' text, it cannot produce substantive, meaningful writing. Yet, those errors present a distraction for a tutor. L2 writers tend to make more sentence-level errors than do native English speakers, and these errors tend to be different from the ones native-speaking writers make. Sentence-level errors can range from a few minor mechanical problems to errors so severe they disrupt the meaning of the writing. Dana Ferris (2002) terms these "local" and "global" errors. The tutor who is working on writing may feel distracted by local errors and confused by global errors. In both cases, the tutor may be puzzled about how to address those errors in a logical, timely way. Moreover, it can be more comfortable to spend time correcting the sentence-level errors and feel competent than it is to tackle the tougher issues with the text and feel confused. Generally, experienced tutors of L2 writers learn to set aside sentence-level errors and instead assess how successfully the writer is creating meaning (Matsuda and Cox 2004). Writing, after all, is about creating meaning, and we can understand a lot about a student by observing whether she is able to transform facts into knowledge and put together a coherent argument or organize information (Scardamalia and Bereiter 2006). However at some point in our work with an L2 writer, we must decide if the sentence-level errors interfere with the clarity of her disciplinary writing and, if so, how and when to address those errors.

Many L2 writers need only a cue to help them notice the error. Those errors tend to be invisible to them either because their native language doesn't have a corresponding feature or because those errors have become fossilized to the point that they seem normal. Also, L2 writers are often so taxed by trying to write and make meaning in complex disciplinary prose that they have no more cognitive space for error identification. But once they can locate the error, many L2 writers know how to correct it (Ferris 2002, 2009). In these cases, gentle guidance and the revision process help writers remove most of the errors from the prose.

However, there are L2 writers who cannot locate the error, nor do they know how to correct it. Students who have learned English by ear are usually in this category. When this occurs, the tutor may find himself delivering a mini-lesson. Scholars in both language-acquisition pedagogy and in writing studies point to the necessity for those of us who work with L2 writers to be able to respond in knowledgeable ways to both rhetorical issues and sentence-level language problems. (Ferris 2002; Johns 1986; Linville 2004; Matsuda and Cox 2004) In fact, learning the correct grammar rule in the context of meaningful writing is thought to be one of the more successful ways to help L2 students learn correct grammar (Ferris 2002).

VIGNETTE #1: PAULA

In this vignette, we see a tutor working on the rhetorical strategies in an introduction to an experimental proposal. We also see how the tutor prioritizes writing skills over language-acquisition skills while still respecting the writer's request.[1]

Paula is a third-year engineering student who has brought a draft of her engineering research proposal to Louis, a tutor at the writing center. She is knowledgeable about engineering theory, but her disciplinary writing has been limited to short answers on exams, a short collaborative lab report, and her lab notebook. This proposal is her first piece of extended writing about her engineering work.

Louis has been working at the writing center for a year. He is not an engineer, but he has worked with a number of engineering writers. Moreover, he has studied some of the exemplars collected in the writing center. As Louis meets Paula for the first time, he asks her about the assignment and about the course. He is not an engineer, he tells her, so it's important for him to understand specifically what she is trying to accomplish. Louis is wise to begin in this way. First, he puts her in the position of being the knowledgeable one, which helps her relax a bit. Second, he learns more about this assignment and discipline. Third, he can assess her verbal language and her listening comprehension.

"Where would you like to begin?" Louis asks. "What is most challenging for you?"

Paula tells Louis, "I know my English is not good." This apology about writing is not surprising; many L2 writers are accustomed to think first of sentence error rather than composition and meaning.

Louis reassures her that they will talk about correctness of language, but he redirects her attention, asking, "Where shall we start?" When Paula seems hesitant, he asks, "Can we begin with this introduction section?" As Paula has been telling him about the course and her research project, Louis has paged through the draft of the proposal. He thinks the introduction section seems underdeveloped based on some of the exemplars he has read. Also, since the section is relatively brief, he thinks they can do some focused work in the time they have. He also knows clarity and focus in that section will help her develop and organize the rest of the proposal. Thus, he decides to explore Paula's thinking about that section. "What can you say about this section?" Louis asks. "What do you want this section to do?"

As Paula explains, she produces more language than Louis sees on the page, and moreover, she gives specific details that contextualize her research plan. What she says is a little unfocused, and her language is hesitant, but Louis helps her by asking a few guiding questions. Then he comments, "What you just said was full of good details, but not much of that content is here on the page." Paula tells Louis, "I was afraid I would make mistakes."

Second language writers often produce compressed text for one or more reasons: they have too little vocabulary, so they only write what they know they can write correctly; in their efforts to write correctly, they write so slowly they run out of time to produce text; or they cannot transfer their knowledge and critical thinking from L1 to L2. Paula's skimpy introduction may be the result of those issues, but it's also possible she does not understand the material fully because her receptive skills of reading and listening may be minimal. Also, depending on the clarity of the professor's assignment, she may not fully understand the audience and the purpose for the proposal. Thus, Louis's discussion with her functions as a kind of prewriting activity.

As he talks with Paula, Louis explores her understanding of the genre she is being asked to produce. He thinks Paula has a limited understanding of the purpose of an introduction section and does not know how to move the reader through that section. He encourages her to write down some of the things she said in their discussion. Then, together they outline an expanded introduction section that better reflects her knowledge. As he does this with Paula, he points out some of the rhetorical moves common in introductions in engineering.

Louis also notices that Paula rarely chooses strong, active verbs, and often she writes in general rather than specific terms. Borrowing a strategy from English for Specific Purposes, a pedagogical focus within EFL pedagogy, Louis suggests to Paula that she add to her technical vocabulary. He guesses Paula does not have anything close to the vocabulary of a native speaker. She may acquire that over time, but what she needs right now is more technical vocabulary. He suggests that she make a list of twenty-five verbs and nouns she sees in the textbook the class uses or in journal articles she is reading or from lectures with her engineering professor. "For example," Louis says, "engineers use active verbs like *calculate, calibrate, characterize, model, simulate, quantify*. Find the common words used in your discipline. If you know the exact meaning, then you can use some of those words as you revise, and the writing becomes more precise."

Louis suggests that Paula show a revised version of the introduction section to her professor or to the teaching assistant to gauge whether or not the revision meets their standards. Although he's not an engineer, he has seen and read a number of engineering documents, and the revision fits the general pattern of organization. Still, he wants her to get confirmation from her professor.

The tutoring session is nearly over, but Paula is not ready to leave. She asks, "Can you help with my English?" She means her grammar, not her writing, and not only does she want this feedback, she also expects it (Ferris 2002). Louis has noted several kinds of sentence-level error in Paula's draft, but he has not mentioned them since he does not want to interrupt her process of making meaning about her engineering proposal. Nor does he want to undermine her confidence. However, he guesses she is unlikely to find the errors on her own—she hasn't thus far—and also she has made a direct request for his help. Louis decides to address errors he notices in the introduction section: sentence-construction problems that are producing a mix of sentence fragments and run-on sentences. He brings of few of these to her attention and asks her if she can correct them. By her quick correction and her articulation, he sees that she knows how to correct the errors. Paula says she will correct the other errors like that.

A week later, Paula returns to the writing center to see Louis. "The professor says my paper is better, but still he crossed things out." Looking at the draft, Louis sees that Paula has begun her introduction,

> In the 21st century, it is really important to find energy sources that do not pollute our environment. Many people are interested in "green" energy because it is cleaner. However, "green" energy can be very expensive. Also, not all "green" energy is effective. It is important to find solutions that are clean, economical, and also produce significant amount of energy. In the field of wind energy, air turbines can be a source of clean, economical energy but they are limited in how much energy they can produce because . . .

Louis sees that the professor has crossed out lines of the paragraph, writing *Too flowery. Get to the point.* But the professor seems to approve the rest of the more-developed introduction. "I see what you're trying to do," Louis says. "You want to create a sense of context for the research, right?" Paula agrees; it's just as they outlined the introduction in the previous session.

Louis asks Paula if she thinks the professor crossed out any important information about her research project. "He took out all my words that I put there to make it interesting," she says. "In engineering, it is more common to get right to the point," Louis says. What she wrote is not incorrect, but it is not the way most engineers write. Paula says, "So . . . write more dry . . . empty. . . and kind of short but not the way I write in my language?"

Louis tells her, "Style and tone, the way sentences are constructed, the way that writing is organized—these elements of writing shift between different disciplines and between cultures." He suggests that she pay attention to the style of engineering writing in articles she reads. "It isn't only what you say," Louis tells her. "Notice the style and tone that the engineering writers use."

Paula's dilemma is familiar to many L2 writers; "It doesn't sound like me," they say, even though they clearly have written the text. Yet the shift in style and tone and perhaps in organization make the text feel 'other' to them. All developing writers try to find a professional voice as they begin to write in their disciplines, but since they have little real-world experience, they often fall back on the strategies that have succeeded in other academic contexts. Thus, we see writers trying out literary or reflective styles or choosing the wrong register or perhaps being too enigmatic as they imagine how 'real' writers in that discipline would sound.

Writers writing in L2 also may show evidence of negative transfer—the influence of the first or primary language on the newer language. Sentences in their native language may be longer and more complex; paragraphs may be organized differently; style may be more formal or elaborate; composition habits may be influenced by inductive rather than deductive reasoning; and cultural expectations about rhetorical strategies in disciplinary prose may differ. Even when the transfer doesn't produce error, the text can still bear the markers of the first or primary language and thus sound 'wrong' to a native speaker. Alternately, even when L2 writers can conform to disciplinary expectations in style and tone, their text then sounds 'foreign' to them.

VIGNETTE #2: HAZIQ

In this vignette, we see a tutor uncertain and possibly anxious about how to approach elements of a writer's text, and we see her working with a writer's resistance.

Haziq is a fourth-year engineering student who brings part of a design report to the writing center. He is writing collaboratively with a team of students, and he is responsible for only one section of the document. Abhi is a tutor who, although she is not an engineer, has worked in a number of engineering courses for several years as communication support staff. Abhi herself is a L2 writer. Her family moved to the United States when she was twelve years old, so she is familiar with some of the challenges that face young L2 writers.

The section Haziq presents is relatively short, but the challenge for Abhi is that the subject—analysis and design of a power and propulsion system for a small satellite—is very technical. The design choice is based on calculations that are difficult for her to understand. However, because she has worked with engineering students before, Abhi understands the rhetorical purpose of this section; Haziq is writing a trade analysis of the various options for the subsystem. These options will be evaluated against a set of criteria that meet the overall system requirements.

Knowing this, Abhi looks at the writing and asks Haziq to highlight the key decisions about the power and propulsion system design options. She observes that key information is at the end of the section after minutely described analysis and not at the beginning where an experienced engineering writer would have put it. Moreover, Haziq does not clearly specify the design choices. Like many student writers, Haziq has written the section in the order of his activities and his internal thought process. Abhi tells him, "It's expected that you will tell the reader right away what your recommendation is. Then back it up with your analysis." But Haziq resists: "No, this is how we do it in my other university. We explain and then we give the decision. The reader cannot understand if you do not give all the details. I want the reader to read all this."

Abhi feels overwhelmed by the document. Not only are the final conclusions buried at the end of the section, the writing is broken by calculations and several tables filled with numbers and specifications. She studies the pages and says to Haziq, "To me, this seems confusing. All these numbers seem to distract from the point you say you want to make. Let's talk about all the numbers and tables. Why do you include so many?"

Haziq is quick to answer: "They have to be there. I want the teacher to see what I did. I did a lot of work." Abhi reminds Haziq that she is not talking about right and wrong but rather about what is expected in the conventions of engineering taught in the United States. "We could outline it a different way," suggests Abhi. "You can get some feedback from your teammates and your professor. Then you can decide." They work on a more succinct outline with straightforward organization; Abhi suggests some language to introduce the section. As they work and talk, Haziq can see the section becoming more focused. It sounds better to him, and soon he seems to be more positive about the different organizational structure. About the tables of numbers? Haziq volunteers, "I could put some of that analysis in the appendix—that would be okay, I think."

VIGNETTE #3: GUAN YANG

In this vignette, we see a tutor working with a writer who is trying to present data and argue for conclusions. We also see a tutor guiding a writer toward deeper reflection about the graphics chosen.

Guan Yang is a graduate student in bioengineering. He brings a rough draft of his thesis to the writing center, asking Abhi to read the results and discussion section. When Abhi turns to that section, she sees many small graphics that show Guan Yang's data, but the interpretation of the data seems too brief. "What do you want to say about this data?" Abhi asks. "Usually, readers expect you to interpret that data for them, to tell them what it means. They expect you to argue for your conclusions based on your experimental results."

Guan Yang looks uncomfortable. "In my country, that would be rude—to tell a reader what to think. The reader should look at the data and make up his own mind." Abhi agrees partially. "Yes, the reader will make up his mind, but a reader still expects that interpretation. Let's try to develop some language that says what you think."

Then Abhi looks at the graphics. Now that she understands Guan Yang's ideas somewhat, she can ask, "Is this the best way to show these results?" She doesn't know if the information is accurate—she relies on Guan Yang for that—but she wonders if a different type of graphic might illustrate Guan Yang's conclusions more effectively. Abhi shows Guan Yang an exemplar the writing center has collected from another engineering writer (with the writer's permission). Guan Yang and Abhi review the exemplar's results and discussion section together, noticing how the graphics show the data and the way the text supports and interprets that data. Abhi ends the session with Guan Yang by reminding Guan Yang to talk with his advisor soon in order to get the advisor's feedback on any possible change in graphics and the accompanying text.

Guan Yang is ready to leave the center, but Abhi points to a few sentences she cannot understand. She has wondered if her own L2 background prevented her from understanding clearly, but she has taken time to study the sentences and she regains her confidence. Guan Yang's spoken English is fairly fluent, so Abhi is puzzled. "How did you write this?" she asks. The sentences are free of grammatical error, the punctuation is correct, and the words are properly spelled, but somehow, the short paragraph isn't clear. This type of error can result from the difficulty a student has in transferring critical thinking from L1 to L2, or perhaps it is because the student gathers technical terms from reading and can organize them into a sentence but fails to truly understand what he is writing. Alternately, it can happen when a student puts text through an electronic translator and then tries to edit it.

Guan Yang tells Abhi he was pressed for time so he created those sentences by using an electronic translator and then editing them with a thesaurus. She explains that most web-based tools produce such flawed text, that they are not useful for more than a phrase, and that they don't work for advanced disciplinary prose. "How can I fix it?" Guan Yang asks. "You can't fix it," Abhi says. "It's better if you rewrite."

WHAT TUTORS CAN CONTRIBUTE

Earlier, we asked what a tutor who is not a disciplinary expert could contribute to an L2 writer learning to write in his/her discipline. In these vignettes, we begin to see partial answers. Because of his understanding of writing and language-acquisition processes, Louis is able to stay focused on Paula's writing task and resist the temptation to correct the sentence-level errors in her text too quickly. His accumulated knowledge about the rhetorical purposes of sections of documents cues him to look more closely at the underdeveloped introduction section of Paula's proposal. Abhi's awareness of her own discomfort helps her reflect as she reviews Haziq's daunting pages of calculations and tables full of numbers. In addition, her own experience as an L2 writer gives her some perspective on Haziq's efforts. Thus, she decides not to confront Haziq's resistance directly, guessing it may be a sign of his own anxiety about looking foolish in front of his peers and his desire to please his professor. Working with Guan Yang, Abhi's understanding of cultural difference helps her notice Guan Yang's difficulty in interpreting data. While the technical nuances of Guan Yang's thesis are a matter for him and for his thesis advisor, Abhi's ability to be present with what she sees on the page raises key points for discussion. Because of that discussion, Guan Yang leaves the writing center with more options for that section of his thesis.

Abhi and Louis also make strong contributions by acknowledging disciplinary boundaries. The authority that comes when we recognize our limits has several positive effects. First, that internal clarity usually reduces our anxiety. Second, the writer tends to have more confidence in us when she knows we speak from the depth of our own knowledge about writing and language and that we are clear about those boundaries. This awareness of ourselves as knowledgeable tutors and of the writer as a developing professional then can be the basis of a collaborative exchange as both tutor and writer work from their areas of strength. Because we respect disciplinary boundaries, a writer can begin to see herself not as a writer who is 'bad' at writing (the tutor's area of expertise) but one who is becoming knowledgeable about disciplinary communication (the writer's growing area of expertise). She begins to own those abilities, and they become integrated into her sense of professional self. As a developing disciplinary writer moves into that new territory, she is better able to identify the challenges that lie before her. The insight into those communication challenges, the support from a knowledgeable tutor, and mentoring from disciplinary faculty are a powerful combination. Together, those factors foster a sense of agency with disciplinary language. Steadily, the writer—once an 'outsider' without much insight into disciplinary language and culture—transitions into her discourse community. As for her tutors, we remain as 'outsiders.' We continue to be guides with valuable insight about language and perhaps about another discipline but rarely members of any disciplinary community other than our own.

Questions to Consider

1. What strategies have you learned for dealing with the anxiety of the L2 writer in a tutoring session? And what strategies help you deal with your own discomfort, frustration, or confusion?

2. This chapter suggests a framework for approaching an L2 writer's text. Do you already use some or all of these approaches? Do you have other approaches that work well for you?

3. Even the most advanced L2 writer may make sentence-level errors in his/her disciplinary writing as s/he struggles with a new formal or conventional style. Or perhaps the writer constructs sentences that are correct but sound 'wrong.' How do you approach sentence-level errors as you tutor? When do you take up those errors with the writer? How do you talk with writers about text that may be correct but is not phrased as a native speaker would phrase it?

Further Reading

Cox, Michelle. 2011. "WAC: Closing Doors or Opening Doors for Second Language Writers?" *Across the Disciplines* 8 (4). http://wac.colostate.edu/atd/ell/cox.cfm

In this article, the author describes the challenges L2 writers must negotiate in a communication-intensive curriculum. Tutors will also be interested in Michelle Cox's review of current work in this area. The author concludes with a list of suggestions for working with L2 writers.

Craig, Jennifer. 2014. "Teaching Writing in a Globally Networked Learning Environment (GNLE): Diverse Students at a Distance." In *WAC and Second Language Writers: Research Toward Linguistically and Culturally Inclusive Programs and Practices,* edited by Terry Zawacki and Michelle Cox, 369–86. Anderson, SC: Parlor.

As technology continues to create expanded learning environments, some tutors may be working with L2 students over distance. In this article, the author describes how teaching and tutoring must be adapted with L2 writers in virtual spaces.

Ferris, Dana. 2002. *Treatment of Error in Second Language Student Writing.* Michigan Series on Teaching Multilingual Writers. Ann Arbor: University of Michigan Press.

In this book, the author shares her strategies for addressing sentence-level error in L2 writing. All tutors will find useful strategies here, no matter what level of writers they are tutoring.

Poe, Mya, Neal Lerner, and Jennifer Craig. 2010. *Learning to Communicate in Science and Engineering: Case Studies from MIT.* Cambridge, MA: MIT Press.

This award-winning book describes how students in science and engineering develop as disciplinary writers. Case studies in three departments and six courses illustrate the authors' findings.

Zawacki, Terry Myers, and Anna Habib. 2010. "'Will Our Stories Help Teachers Understand?' Multilingual Students Talk about Identity, Academic Writing, and Expectations across Academic Communities." In *Reinventing Identities in Second Language Writing,* edited by Michelle Cox, Jay Jordan, Christina Ortmeier Hooper, and Gwen Gray Schwartz, 54–74. Urbana, IL: National Council of Teachers of English.

The voices of L2 writers in this article are compelling, and the authors raise key insights about writers' identities that all tutors should consider.

Note

1.   The vignettes here are based on work with L2 writers and tutors with whom I have worked although the names have been changed.

References

Beaufort, Anne. 2004. *College Writing and Beyond.* Logan: Utah State University Press.

Bouman, Kurt. 2004. "Raising Questions about Plagiarism." In *ESL Writers: A Guide for Writing Center Tutors,* 2nd ed., edited by Shanti Bruce and Ben Rafoth, 161–75. Portsmouth, NH: Boynton/Cook.

Canagarajah, Suresh. 2002. "Multilingual Writers and the Academic Community: Towards a Critical Relationship." *Journal of English for Academic Purposes* 1 (1): 29–44. http://dx.doi.org/10.1016/S1475-1585(02)00007-3.

Ferris, Dana R. 2002. *Treatment of Error in Second Language Student Writing.* Ann Arbor: University of Michigan Press.

Ferris, Dana R. 2009. *Teaching College Writing to Diverse Student Populations.* Ann Arbor: University of Michigan Press.

Harris, Muriel, and Tony Silva. 1993. "Tutoring ESL Students: Issues and Options." *College Composition and Communication* 44 (4): 525–37. http://dx.doi.org/10.2307/358388.

Johns, Ann. 1990. "L1 Composition Theories: Implications for Developing Theories of L2 Composition." In *Second Language Writing*, ed. B. Kroll, 24–36. Cambridge: Cambridge University Press. http://dx.doi.org/10.1017/CBO9781139524551.006.

Johns, Ann M. 1986. "The ESL Student and the Revision Process: Some Insights from Schema Theory." *Journal of Basic Writing* 5 (2): 70–80.

Kroll, Barbara. 1990. "The Rhetoric and Syntax Split: Designing a Curriculum for ESL Students." *Journal of Basic Writing* 9 (1): 40–55.

Lave, Jean, and Etiene Wenger. 1991. *Situated Learning: Legitimate Peripheral Participation.* Cambridge, UK: Cambridge University Press. http://dx.doi.org/10.1017/CBO9780 511815355.

Lillis, Theresa M., and Mary Jane Curry. 2010. *Academic Writing in a Global Context: The Politics and Practices of Publishing in English.* London: Routledge.

Linville, Cynthia. 2004. "Editing Line by Line." In *ESL Writers: A Guide for Writing Center Tutors*, 2nd ed., edited by Shanti Bruce and Ben Rafoth, 116–31. Portsmouth, NH: Boynton/Cook.

Mackiewicz, J. 2004. "The Effects of Tutor Expertise in Engineering Writing: A Linguistic Analysis of Writing Tutors' Comments." *IEEE Transactions on Professional Communication* (December). http://dx.doi.org/10.1109/TPC.2004.840485 http:// ieeexplore.ieee.org/lpdocs/epic03/wrapper.htm?arnumber=1364079.

Matsuda, Paul Kei. 1999. "Composition Studies and ESL Writing: A Disciplinary Division of Labor." *College Composition and Communication* 50 (4): 699–721. http://dx.doi.org /10.2307/358488.

Matsuda, Paul Kei. 2001. *Practicing WAC is Practicing ESL.* Fort Collins, CO: WAC Clearinghouse; http://wac.colostate.edu/aw/forums/fall2001/matsuda_opening. htm, Accessed September 14, 2015.

Matsuda, Paul Kei, and Michelle Cox. 2004. "Reading an ESL Writer's Text." In *ESL Writers: A Guide for Writing Center Tutors*, 2nd ed., edited by Shanti Bruce and Ben Rafoth, 2: 42–50. Portsmouth, NH: Boynton/Cook.

Poe, Mya, Neal Lerner, and Jennifer Craig. 2010. *Learning to Communicate in Science and Engineering: Case Studies from MIT.* Cambridge, MA: MIT Press.

Reid, Joy, and Barbara Kroll. 1995. "Designing and Assessing Effective Classroom Writing Assignments for NES and ESL Students." *Journal of Second Language Writing* 4 (1): 17–41. http://dx.doi.org/10.1016/1060-3743(95)90021-7.

Scardamalia, Marlene, and Carl Bereiter. 2006. "Knowledge Building: Theory, Pedagogy, and Technology." In *Cambridge Handbook of the Learning Sciences*, K. Sawyer, 97–118. New York: Cambridge University Press.

Silva, Tony. 1993. "Toward an Understanding of the Nature of L2 Writing : The ESL Research and Its Implications." *TESOL Quarterly* 27 (4): 657

Stoller, Fredricka, James K. Jones, Molly S. Costanza-Robinson, and Marin S. Robinson. 2005. "Demystifying Disciplinary Writing: A Case Study in the Writing of Chemistry." *Across the Disciplines.* http://wac.colostate.edu/atd/volume2.cfm/.

Swales, John, and Christine Feak. 2009. *Academic Writing for Graduate Students: Essential Tasks and Skills.* 2nd ed. Ann Arbor: University of Michigan Press.

Williams, Jessica. 2002. "Undergraduate Second Language Writers in the Writing Center." *Journal of Basic Writing* 21 (2): 73–91. http://wac.colostate.edu/jbw/v21n2/williams.pdf.

Zamel, Vivian. 2004. "Strangers in Academia." In *Crossing the Curriculum: Multilingual Learners in College Classrooms*, ed. Vivian Zamel and Ruth Spack, 3–17. Mahwah, NJ: Lawrence Erlbaum Associates.

Zamel, Vivian, and Ruth Spack, eds. 2004. *Crossing the Curriculum: Multilingual Learners in College Classrooms.* Mahwah, NJ: Lawrence Erlbaum Associates.

14

HELPING SECOND LANGUAGE WRITERS BECOME SELF-EDITORS

Pimyupa W. Praphan and Guiboke Seong

Writing in a second language is a highly complex skill that involves the knowledge of vocabulary, syntactic and discourse structures, and the sociolinguistic rules of a target language. The struggles of even highly successful L2 writers were documented in Connor and Belcher (2001). Tony Silva (1997) also attested to the difficulty of L2 writing and admitted that he was always amazed and humbled by the vast efforts of L2 writers in his classes. As both learners and now teachers of English at our universities, we can also attest to the struggles and the success of our own and students' attempts at writing in English on a daily basis. It is beyond question that second language writers bring to writing centers a written product that is a result of their educational and cultural backgrounds. The encounter between the tutor and the second language writer is as challenging as it is fascinating. This chapter deals with this encounter, focusing on the editing process, which is often the tip of the iceberg. It identifies issues the tutors face every day at work, provides tips to handle confusion, and aids tutors with some practical editing strategies based upon up-to-date empirical studies and theories.

It is hardly surprising that many students, L2 and L1 students alike, do not fully understand the philosophy of the writing center: the focus on improving the writer's skills, not the particular piece of writing s/he brings on a given day. From our experience with L2 and EFL students, especially Thai and Korean students, it is very common for the students to expect tutors or teachers to edit their writing line by line for them. Some of our students have said they would like every single mistake to be corrected. Some even express their preference for correction or written feedback in red ink. This is often the case for undergraduate students. For graduate students, we notice they are more sensitive to different styles of feedback. Many feel intimidated with written feedback in red

DOI: 10.7330/9781607324140.c014

ink, but they do expect the tutors or teachers to "correct" their writing. Their expectation of an "ideal" text resulting from this editing process makes it hard to instill the idea of self-editing. To complicate the matter, some tutors' expectations of second language students' linguistic abilities can interfere with their practice. The first author's experience as an EFL teacher in Thailand and tutor at a writing center in the United States illustrated that at times L1 tutors can overestimate L2 writers' skills while some L2 tutors can underestimate them. This mismatch between tutors' expectations and students' actual performance might sound counterintuitive, but some tutors' and teachers' practices in helping students edit their papers do reflect that mindset. Some L1 tutors might assume students have certain knowledge and understanding, thus skipping some needed explanations. Some L2 tutors might assume certain words or structures are too advanced, when in fact students can learn through various channels in this day and age. Nevertheless, this assertion about tutors' expectations needs empirical studies to support.

One thing is clear from our over ten years of experience as L2/EFL teachers: it is always challenging to gauge the students' ability to self-edit and thus to decide on the most effective ways to give feedback. Some L2 teachers in our contexts tend to provide feedback in a way that does not encourage students' self-reliance. In other words, some teachers believe it is often easier and less time consuming for the teachers to "correct" the product rather than help improve the writer in the writing process. However, it is in the best interest of the two parties that tutors or teachers resist the urge to merely correct the errors. In doing so, the tutors or teachers will move beyond being proofreaders or editors.

Although some L2 writers are still attempting to move beyond their interlanguage (Selinker 1972)—a linguistic system developed by an L2 learner who has not become fully proficient—research has shown that college-level L2 students are capable of becoming efficient editors of their own texts after proper training (Linville 2009). There lies the importance of writing center work and the roles of the tutors and tutor training. Editing students' papers is always a challenge for tutors on multiple levels. Let us first review what core issues have become the center of attention in the professional debates relevant to tutors' encounters with L2 writers.

ISSUES AND DEBATES IN EDITING L2 STUDENTS' PAPERS

A significant part of editing L2 writers' papers involves error correction or how to improve what applied linguists call *formal accuracy* in English language in their written work. One of the well-known debates on the topic is whether to treat errors or not. It would be surprising to most university writing tutors to know that the efficacy of written error correction or written feedback itself has been questioned among writing scholars. Based upon several theoretical rationales and empirical studies, John Truscott (1996) argued that error correction, for the purpose of improving "correctness," or accuracy, in students' writing is in fact not effective and thus should not be encouraged in the L2 classroom. He claimed practitioners should focus more on productive aspects in helping to improve students' writing than on editing students' writing for error correction. Although he later (Truscott 1999) admitted the possibility of certain range of potential benefits of written corrective feedback in response to other scholars' criticisms against his arguments (e.g., Ferris 1999), he still maintains (Truscott 2004; 2007) that the practice should not be recommended. Some other scholars have also raised doubts about the effectiveness of teachers' written corrections due to the possibility of the teacher's being misunderstood or being vague in addition to being too directive (Sommers 1982; Zamel 1985). However, a growing number of research studies have been providing empirical data to support the position that written corrections or editing students' writing does in fact have greater pedagogical advantages than not in terms of developing formal accuracy in their writing (Bitchener 2008; Bitchener and Knoch 2009; Ferris and Roberts 2001; Sheen 2007).

As life-long learners of English, we have valued the written corrections we have received from tutors and teachers, especially when it comes to discrete grammatical points in our writing. For example, many count versus noncount nouns (such as *point* versus *information*) are difficult to learn because they have to be memorized. When we make a mistake regarding a noncount noun (e.g., a lot of informations are needed) and our teachers point it out, then we see what is wrong and are able to learn a new form. The feedback helps us to learn and remember that *information* is a noncount noun.

Based on the existing literature and our practical experience, it is reasonable to believe written corrections are helpful. Our next concern is what types of errors to treat or edit. Are all errors made by L2 students equally important and in need of correction? What kinds of errors require the tutor's attention? Are there kinds that deserve more attention than others? This issue is related to error gravity. Error gravity refers to the degree of acceptability of errors and how it influences readers' judgments about the writer's performance in the tasks (Vann, Lorenz, and Meyer 1991).

In one of the earlier studies on error gravity in writing instruction, Vann, Meyer, and Lorenz (1984) investigated faculty's opinions regarding L2 students' written errors. In terms of sentence-level errors made by L2 writers, 164 university faculty members' responses at a US university revealed that not all errors are perceived as being equally serious. There is a hierarchy of perceived errors, and faculty perceptions on error gravity differ depending on their age and disciplines. Age-wise, the least tolerant group was the forty-five- to fifty-four-year-old group and the most tolerant group was the fifty-five-and-older one. The second most tolerant group was thirty-four and under, but they became less tolerant as they grew older. Among three groups of academic disciplines, faculty in social sciences, education, and humanities were considerably more tolerant toward some local errors, such as articles and certain spelling errors, than faculty in hard sciences, engineering, and nature sciences. All faculty groups, however, showed unified opinions about the relative gravity of the errors in the following order of increasing seriousness: spelling-1 (British or colloquial), articles, comma splices, spelling-2 (deletion or substitution), prepositions, pronoun agreement, subject-verb agreement, word choice, relative clauses, tense, *it* deletion, and word order.

Research shows that not only L1 respondents but also language learners can have different perceptions on error gravity in writing. According to Bardovi-Harlig and Dornyei (1998), learners in EFL situations perceived grammatical errors to be much more important than other kinds of errors, while those in the L2 contexts perceived pragmatic errors as more important. A pragmatic error in applied linguistics refers to the way a text "works" or what effect it has on readers. In the example below, the pragmatic error relates to the impression of herself the author conveys to readers. The author was an EFL student writing an application essay for a graduate school in the United States.

> I held a Bachelor's of Engineering with first class honors and also gained the gold medal with my outstanding academic performance. Considering my profile in terms of solid academic background and professional experiences, I am confident that my qualification would be suitable for a Ph.D. program at First Choice University, and I believe that I would be an asset to your program.

In the above excerpt, grammar is not an issue, and the writer, before meeting with the tutor, was not aware of the possible pragmatic problem in her essay. The tutor pointed out that certain words in the essay (*outstanding, solid,* and *asset*) caused her to come across as being arrogant and pompous, which actually contrasted with her demeanor. As Jenny

Thomas (1983) points out, grammatical mistakes may impede communication, but L1 speakers of the target language seem to have little difficulty accepting them. However, pragmatic failure reflects badly on the writer as a person. Based on our experience, most EFL writers are not aware of pragmatic errors and seem to be more worried about making grammatical errors.

With regard to the kinds of errors considered most serious, the goals of science, language studies, and education of the era should be considered. In the last century, when structuralism and behavioral psychology prevailed, grammatical structures and formal aspects of language held higher priority. As evidenced in audiolingualism, helping students achieve grammatical accuracy and error-free performance in language was language teachers' primary concern. However, as the notion of communicative competence and awareness of pragmatic competence emerged, and the communicative need in language teaching arose, higher-order concerns in writing (Reigstad and MacAndrew 1984), such as organization, content, focus, complexity, and coherence, came to receive more attention.

James Hendrickson (1980) argued that global errors that interfere with the overall content and organization should receive greater attention and be corrected, while local errors may not be perceived as serious. Nevertheless, scholars today are aware that the distinction between local and global errors does not always hold. A local error involving a key word or phrase may have consequences for an essay's focus or meaning at the global level. By the same token, an essay that contains no local errors can nonetheless be difficult to understand at the global level. Time and again, we get essays that do not have good organization, most often because they lack a thesis statement in the introduction. The following example is an introductory paragraph from a Thai student's argumentative essay. The writer was trying to make an argument, later in the essay, that bad sleeping habits are the most important factor in students' academic failure at his university.

> Nowadays, most students spend time to study, work, eat and do other activities. Some do not have enough sleep and often ignore the essential of sleep. Inadequate sleep can affect to brain, physical health, emotion, meditation and skin aging. There are many activities that university students often do before go to bed such as playing Facebook, watching TV, talking on the phone, playing sports, etc. All of these activities will make university students do not want to sleep anymore and create bad sleep habits. The amount of sleep each person needs depends on age. Infants need about 16 hours a day, teenagers need about 9 hours and adults need 7 to 8 hours a night for the best amount of sleep.

Although the student's essay above has some local errors, it is still intelligible. The most serious problem is that there is no argument presented at all; only some background information on the topic is provided. The writer states his argument in the last paragraph, which is rather common in Thai students' essay organization. This global error is considered far more serious than the local errors students make.

Another debated issue in editing students' writing is about specific error correction methods and the differential effects of the types of correction. Feedback options in writing are often discussed in two larger dimensions: direct or explicit and indirect or implicit approaches. The direct approach involves the teacher's explicit provision of the correct form, while the indirect options use a range of devices to help learners notice, diagnose, and correct the errors on their own (Bitchener, Young, and Cameron 2005). Studies have reported that some L2 writers prefer their teachers' direct and explicit error corrections more than implicit kinds (e.g., Ferris and Roberts 2001). In Asian cultures, it is a readily accepted myth that those teachers who "burn the night oil" giving extensive direct corrections on students' paper are the dedicated ones. While these teachers may be hard working, correcting as many errors as possible is not necessarily effective. It may even hinder more effective efforts. Recommendations for specific editing or correction methods will be described in a later section of this chapter, but it is important to note that a greater number of scholars have reported the relative advantages of implicit kinds rather than explicit and direct kinds (e.g., Hedgcock 2005). Implicit kinds of feedback include indicating the approximate, not the exact, location or the identity of the error and making general comments about the learner's core errors on a separate sheet of paper attached to the draft.

Some arguments for this approach lie in the fact that implicit kinds give learners opportunities to discover their own errors and to reformulate correct forms, which leads to longer retention and develops learners' responsibility and autonomy. The indirect approach shares a core element with the process approach in writing in that it involves multiple steps in giving corrections. It also involves a characteristic of meaningful learning in that while trying to self-correct their own errors, students activate their schemata in a meaningful and contextualized task. In addition, the process of self-correction is more challenging and fun. Thus, students are intrinsically motivated. Caveats are in order for the writing teachers who deal with learners from different cultures. In implementing indirect methods, they might experience unwillingness or resistance from students from cultures of greater power distance (Hofstede 1986) in which students are accustomed to passive roles in learning due to the mismatches in their expectations. For example, Korean and Thai are considered to be two cultures with higher scores in the power distance measure. This means that less powerful people in organizations in the society accept inequality in power distribution and consider it normal. In the classroom situation, students in such cultures expect the teacher to be the most powerful member of the group, so they believe the teacher should provide all the information directly, with authority. When the teacher, using implicit methods, asks students to identify the location and the nature of the error in their writing, some students do not feel comfortable and some may even think the teacher is not competent. Clear justifications for the technique, preparation, and well-thought-out execution of the method are needed to gradually lead students to believe in the benefits of the technique.

TUTORING STRATEGIES IN EDITING

L2 writers bring in a wide range of expectations to tutors in a writing center. Based on our knowledge of the research on error gravity, it is evident that tutors must make clear to students the hierarchy of what they can help them with. L2 students might come to the writing center with the expectation that their writing will be edited to the point that it is error free. Some tutors might not understand why these students are very insistent on such editing. An explanation we could offer lies in the tradition of English-language teaching in L2/EFL contexts in which grammatical accuracy is stressed. Although in theory communicative language teaching, which places less emphasis on grammar, is promoted in those contexts, in practice grammar still holds high priority. Students are novice writers, and they expect to learn the language through corrections on their writing to improve their confidence. When asked why they want all errors to be corrected, some of our students asked back, "Why not? We want to learn from our mistakes and who better to learn from than the tutor or teacher? If we had known the right way, we wouldn't have made the mistake in the first place!" In our contexts, teachers are usually viewed as providers, not as facilitators or trainers as they should be.

It might be feasible in some cases for tutors or teachers to correct all errors depending on the students' performance and experience, but more often than not, L2 students' texts need attention on many levels. In the context of the writing center, a forty-minute one-on-one session is not likely to be a magic encounter to improve the text and writer in all aspects. Thus, the question becomes, how can tutors help L2 students to achieve the "best" result in one tutoring session? The general procedure we suggest for a tutoring session consists of three steps—before, during, and after tutoring. We try to provide some specific examples with each step, but some strategies are illustrated in the extended example at the end of this chapter.

Before Starting the Tutoring Session

1. Tutor, Know Thyself

The first thing a writing tutor must do before helping L2 students edit their papers is self-assessment. Some L1 tutors might find it daunting to work with L2 students because it requires explicit knowledge of and the ability to explain the English language, apart from the writing conventions of the language. Some may have L2 teaching experience but still feel they lack the knowledge base needed to deal with L2 writers. It is recommended that during tutor trainings, tutors are directed to print and online resources that can help them develop this knowledge (a list to get you started is at the end of this chapter). Some tutors might have apprehension about holding a session with L2 students, and such tutors often refer students to more experienced tutors. If this is the case, tutors need to get out of their comfort zone and try working with L2 students so they will become aware of what they (the tutors) lack and need to improve on. By having real experience, they can learn about their strengths and shortcomings. Another strategy is to observe experienced tutors working with L2 students. That way, tutors can learn from them and feel more confident. From our experience, shadowing a real tutoring session is one of the best ways new tutors can learn and develop self-awareness and confidence. It is highly important to have awareness of what you know, what you do not know, what you are good at, and what your limitations are. This self-awareness and constant search for knowledge will help you become an efficient tutor.

2. Negotiate Expectations and Set Priorities

In order to meet the tutees' needs and perform the tutor's job successfully, it is important to ask the tutees what their priorities are, and after that, tell them what you can and will do based upon the self-assessment addressed above. Remember that the goal of a one-on-one tutoring session is not to spoon-feed the tutees with direct error corrections made with a colorful pen but to make them independent writers and effective self-editors in the end.

For these first two steps, Cynthia Linville's (2009) descriptions about goals for the student and the tutor can be helpful. She argues that the goals for the student are to "acknowledge the need to become a proficient self-editor, learn what his most frequent patterns of error are, learn how to recognize these errors, [and] learn how to correct these errors," and the goals for the tutor are to "teach the student how to become a proficient self-editor, learn how to diagnose frequent patterns of error, learn how to correct (and teach students to correct) six major error types, [and] learn when to refer students elsewhere for more instruction" (118). Some of these goals could be addressed at the beginning of a tutoring session to make sure the tutor and the tutee are in agreement about their needs, expectations, and the service that can be provided. Tutors can also take a quick look at the tutee's draft and prioritize tasks.

During the Tutoring Session

3. Read Generously

Based on what we learned from how to read an L2 writer's text (Matsuda and Cox 2009), the tutor should read the whole text, from start to finish, aloud or silently, based on the level of the student's writing. If there are many surface errors, reading silently might be more effective so the tutor can focus on meanings. The tutor should withhold judgment and maintain an open mind while reading the text. Since L2 writers might use a different organization in presenting their main idea, such as a thesis statement at the end instead of at the beginning, it is important to keep reading until the end.

4. Assess Organization

After reading the whole text, determine whether it meets genre expectations, which means whether the text follows an established rhetorical pattern that each type of writing requires. For example, if it is an argumentative essay, the paper has a clear point of view in the introductory paragraph, and the body paragraphs contain supporting details to convince the reader. If it is a statement of purpose to apply for graduate schools, it states early the writer's specific area of research interest and has an opening that grabs the reader's attention. Even resumé writing, the format of which we might expect to be clear, could be a challenge for some L2 students. We have had ample experience with L2 writers whose text organization does not meet the genre requirements of mainstream US rhetorical traditions. Student writers coming from a reader-responsible language have a tendency to delay the presentation of their thesis or sometimes to state their thesis only implicitly. They do so by providing different perspectives first and coming to their conclusion toward the end, or sometimes they leave it up to the reader to infer what their main idea is. It is the tutor's job to help them build awareness of the differences between the two rhetorical traditions, that is, reader-responsible versus writer-responsible language. The US tradition expects the author to elucidate their thesis and to do so early. With this in mind, the tutor will be able to determine from the very beginning that some texts might need more than editing, meaning they need major revisions. It is best to be honest with students and explain that they need to reorganize certain parts, then give them advice on how to go about doing that. We understand it is hard to say what students do not want to hear, but sometimes "bitter" is a medicine when "sweet" is poison. Since delivering bitter medicines can be hard, tutors should consider the strategies that follow (7 to 9).

5. Look for x of Errors

If the organization of the text is not an issue, the tutor should reread the text and start putting marks, circling or underlining the features or parts that need editing. There might be several error types, but remember to work with global errors first; these are errors that affect the comprehension of meaning. Some of these errors might be beyond the level of L2 students to self-edit. Thus, the tutor can, for example, help explain why a certain word choice is better. Nevertheless, some global errors such as verb tenses are treatable, meaning students can learn to self-edit because the errors are rule-based. The tutor should spend some time discussing these kinds of treatable errors with students and allow them to practice correcting them.

For specific error types, Linville (2009) addresses six kinds while Dana Ferris (2002) recommends five criteria. Linville's six major error types include the subject-verb agreement, verbtense errors, verbform errors, singular and plural errors, wordform errors, and sentence-structure errors. These are specific, treatable, rule-based errors, so by attending to these easy-to-accept and visible errors, tutors can increase learners' satisfaction and confidence in their tutors. Ferris's five criteria are genre-specific errors, stigmatizing errors, comprehensibility errors, frequent errors, and student-identified errors (those the student would like the teacher to focus on). These criteria could also be useful for tutors in deciding what to target in their editing sessions.

6. Be Flexible in How You Correct Errors

Errors can be corrected in different ways using various direct and indirect strategies. Tutors must decide which way is best for each writer and for each error. Tutors should consider the writer's proficiency, the nature of the error, and other factors as they decide which approach to use. Direct corrections can be useful when the following factors are present:

- the students' level of metalinguistic awareness in the English language and the proficiency level in general are too low to make it possible for the students to identify and self-correct their own errors;
- the tutor faces strong resistance to alternative correction methods resulting from the students' cultural background, learning styles, and other possible factors;
- the students are under a strict time limit for improving their writing for the tutor to try indirect correction methods.

However, in many cases, direct and explicit corrections can be form-oriented and directive, and if they are, they could rid learners of opportunities to reflect upon their own errors. In order to help students develop a keen sense of responsibility and confidence, it is a recommended practice to give students opportunities to self-correct in some ways. This may involve allowing some time for students to think for themselves about how to edit or correct their errors or asking a question to activate their background knowledge about the topic or elicit reformulation. A variety of methods are available, some of which will be described below. Often, a combination of feedback and correction is needed. The point is to give learners at least some chances to self-correct. Indirect methods take more time than direct ones. Thus, effective time-management skills along with patience and elicitation skills are also crucial in successful implementation of indirect editing or correction in writing. Examples of elicitation skills are asking leading questions to draw the student's attention to grammatical points in question, suggesting a strategy in rewriting the sentence, and pointing the student to specific online and print resources. Nevertheless, correcting errors, either directly or indirectly, does not prevent reoccurrences of the same errors. Tutors should not forget that their long-term goal is to help the tutees become independent editors by learning from both self-correcting practices and direct corrections by the tutor. The strategies below are ordered based on the levels of students, starting from low to advanced. Illustrations of each strategy are provided in the appendix at the end of the chapter.

- *Inform the student of the exact location and identity of the error.* The tutor lets the tutee know of the word or point where the error occurs and also explains what it is about. An example comment would be, "Look at the subject and the verb of this sentence, 'He work at a factory.' 'He work' is problematic. The subject and the verb do not go together. Can you change it to make this sentence grammatical?" In written comments, using a set of previously agreed upon error codes could be useful; for example, the code AGR stands for errors regarding subject-verb agreement, TNS is for tense-related errors, and ART is for articles. This type of error-correction method could be particularly useful for clearly definable or grammar-centered errors and in tutoring lower-level students (see Fig. 14.1 in the appendix.)

- *Indicate the exact location but not the identity of the error.* Tutors may find this method beneficial for tutees who have developed a certain amount of ability in the target language to self-correct their own errors when their locations are pointed out. This correction method is an attempt to give the tutees a feasible but still challenging task. Tutors can indicate the exact location of the error by pointing, circling, underlining, or highlighting, and the tutee is asked to identify the nature of the error there and correct it (see Fig. 14.2 in the appendix for examples). The tutor can also offer additional help here by giving hints in forms of grammatical rules, prompting questions, patterns, or examples.

- *Indicate only the approximate location or identity of the error.* At the tutoring session, a tutor can inform the tutees (by telling them or with a pen) that there is an error in a particular line or small paragraph and ask them to locate the error and correct it. This way, the tutee can be involved in a self-correction process with partial information about the location of the error. Figure 14.3 in the appendix illustrates how the approximate locations of the error(s) are check marked in the margin of the line where they occur. The tutor can also give information about the identity of the error in addition to its approximate location, depending on how the tutee reacts to the task and the tutee's proficiency level. This method, among the three types described here, requires from tutees the most advanced level of knowledge in the target language.

7. Do Not Overwhelm Students with Negative Evaluations

Like any human being, learners are sensitive to criticism. Foreign-language students can be particularly vulnerable in dealing with their L2 egos. Editing or correcting their papers in almost all cases involves some kind of criticism. In order to make it more effective without hurting the tutee's feelings, tutors can sweeten the pot by coupling the criticism with praise of some sort and/or with a suggestion for improvement. However, empty praises are not effective, nor can they make students happy (and sometimes they are harmful), so tutors should look hard to see good points as well as points to improve in students' writing.

8. Balance Softening the Criticisms and Being Clear

Dealing with students' papers in a one-on-one writing conference—facing them in person with their limited English abilities—is not an easy task. The difficulty is partially due to the nature of a writing conference in which the tutees expect corrections and partially because the students may misunderstand tutors or get confused by the given comments. Sometimes tutors need to mitigate their criticism, but there are times when they must be very clear about what needs to be changed. In order to mitigate the criticism, tutors can use the above-mentioned strategy (presenting the criticism with a praise and/or a suggestion), incorporating modal auxiliaries (e.g., *might, could, would*, etc.). We believe that in critiquing the students' writing, the most important thing is to start by showing your appreciation of the students' effort (e.g., by saying "I really like your idea about . . . " or "You've done a lot of research on . . ." or "This part is very impressive") and then drawing their attention to the parts they need to improve on. By doing so, it is clear the tutors can clearly indicate that they are aware of the hard work students put into their writing and are trying to help them improve it. We are positive that most international students who go to the writing center expect to hear advice and critique from tutors. Thus, tutors need not be overly worried about offending them by critiquing their work.

9. Ask Effective Questions

Questions can be useful for a number of purposes in a writing tutorial. Questions keep the tutee focused and alert. By asking properly formulated questions, the tutor can also give the tutee time to reflect upon the point in question and an opportunity to self-correct the error. This process can give the tutee a sense of shared power and responsibility. For example, if the student has trouble writing a clear thesis statement, the tutor might say, "It's not very clear to me what your main argument is in this paper; what is the most important message you want your readers to get?" or "Where do you stand in this debate?" Asking questions can also mitigate the tone of criticism.

After the Tutoring Session

10. Encourage Self-Study

It is important to point L2 students to resources that can help them learn to improve their writing on their own. Give examples from those resources, such as how to increase the level of formality in their writing by using nominalization, which is common in academic English. Books and dictionaries focusing on collocations are great for self-study. The tutor can tell students that studying these resources can help their text to sound natural and smooth. There are also countless online resources that can help L2 students enrich their writing skills. It might be useful to have a handout that lists all the resources, both physical and online, that tutors can give to L2 writers in particular. Some suggested resources are listed at the end of this chapter.

11. Keep Records of What You Learn

Working with L2 students at a writing center can be a very enriching experience. Once you have the chance, do not let it pass by. Keep a tutoring journal; write down what you learn from each session, whether your entries are about surprising mistakes students make, different cultural expectations, what you feel you did right or wrong, and so forth. This personal journal can potentially be a rich and practical resource for a writing center. After some time, you could put together the knowledge you have gained to share with other tutors or to be used in tutor training.

To make the process of helping L2 students edit more vivid, we provide a vignette of a tutoring session with an L2 student at a writing center in the United States. The tutor is the first author of this chapter. The relevant strategies are identified in parentheses after they are used.

On a snowy afternoon, Hala came to the writing center with a statement of purpose as a part of her application to a master's program. She asked if she could get help with proofreading her essay. The top part of her essay read:

Goal Statement of Hala Al Habia

Thank you for taking a moment to consider my application for enrollment into your graduate program. My name is Hala Al Habia. I'm an international student from . . . . I graduated from the College of Education for Girls in the second semester of 2005 with honors. I also earned Diploma of Computer during the period of one year in 2007 with excellent grades. I'm now working a lecturer at College of Education at . . . since beginning of 2010 until now.

As soon as I saw the first part, I could tell the essay needed some editing, not just proofreading, as Hala expected (Strategy 4: Assess Organization). After skimming through the essay, I said to Hala, "Your profile is impressive! Now, your essay was written in a different style from American students (Strategy 8: Balance Softening the Criticisms and Being Clear). Maybe it's done this way in your country, but in the US this type of essay is not written in a letter format. I hope it's okay with you that I give comments based on the organization as well. It should be in an essay format with an interesting introduction, then body paragraphs, and conclusion. It seems you will need to edit this quite a bit." (Strategy 2: Negotiate Expectations and Set Priorities)

Hala looked a bit tense but seemed willing to go on. I then explained that it is not effective to only repeat the information in the resumé, but it would be more interesting to state what drew her to pursue a particular program at the university she was applying to. Then, I read the whole essay aloud and found some parts that could be used at the beginning of the essay, so I pointed them out to Hala: "Although your essay has unexpected organization, it has some very well-written parts. I like this part here that says, 'I want to achieve my dream to be an artist. I like to live in the world of nature and color. . . . The brush became the most effective way to express my feelings. . . . My self-confidence increased from my professors' support and awards I received while I was studying in the university.' I think it'd be more interesting to open your essay with this." (Strategy 8: Balance Softening the Criticisms and Being Clear)

After discussing with Hala how her essay could be reorganized, I picked one paragraph in the essay to work with in terms of correcting errors. The paragraph read:

> Besides teaching, I'm in charge of student activities since 2010 [verb tense]. Which is a voluntary work free of charge [redundancy] the purpose of the implementation of programs serving the students and the community based on our area of specialization [fragment and sentence structure]. The targets of these activities first, develop the student's personality and closer the relationship between students and teachers [sentence structure]. Then, taking into account individual differences among students with develop a plan to suit their abilities [sentence structure]. After that, administration gave students the freedom right [word choice] to choose the activities that they are interested in. These are some of our targets in these student activities and I'm glad to supervise these activities [redundancy].

There are many types of errors in this paragraph, but the most serious and recurring is about sentence structure (Strategy 5: Look for Patterns of Errors). In this case, it was questionable that the student could spot her problems and self-correct. Nevertheless, I decided to work with her on that point. I told her, "I'm impressed with what you have written about here, but there are some problems with sentence structures that we have to work on. Can you pick a sentence in this paragraph that you think is problematic?" (Strategy 8: Balance Softening the Criticisms and Being Clear; Strategy 6: Try to Avoid Direct Corrections) Hala took some time and pointed hesitantly to the fragment in the paragraph ("Which is a voluntary work free of charge . . .), so I said, "Exactly, that one is not a complete sentence, right?" She nodded and said, "But I don't know how to correct it."

I then explained to Hala that it is not acceptable to start a sentence with *which* because it is used to join a noun and its modifying part. After giving an example of how to use *which* correctly, I asked her to try to join the first sentence of the paragraph with *which* in the fragment. With my help, the sentence became, "Besides teaching, I'm in charge of student activities, which are voluntary work." In this case, it was necessary for me to help her to put the words together to form a sentence because she could not do it on her own. So instead, we did it together. Then once the sentence was formed, I was able to explain its structure. I told her the rest of the sentence was ungrammatical because there was no main verb in it (". . . the purpose of the implementation of programs serving the students and the community based on our area of specialization"). I asked her, "Can you circle the most important verb in the sentence?" (Strategy 9: Asking Effective Questions). Hala circled the verb *serving* and asked why it was not grammatical. I explained to her that the *ing* form cannot be a main verb and that she had to rewrite the sentence to read, "The purpose of the implementation of the programs *is to serve* the students and the community based on our area of specialization."

The session went on, and I tried to help her by focusing on sentence structures. It was clear that her first language interfered with her English writing. Since I was not familiar with her first language (Arabic), it was quite challenging to help her edit the essay. I had to ask her constantly to explain to me what she wanted to say. One session was obviously not sufficient. After about one hour, I asked her to try revising on her own at home and to come back the following day to continue working with me.

In Hala's case, the challenge was the level of the student's writing proficiency. We have to admit that at this level, helping the student to become a self-editor might be far-fetched. However, we believe it is still worth a try. In a case such as this, some explicit feedback is needed. Also, it is a good idea to recommend that the student take a writing class specifically for L2 students before starting her graduate program. We hope the short vignette helps illustrate strategies tutors could use with L2 students.

Helping L2 writers one on one in a tutoring session is a great endeavor in which both the tutor and the student writer can learn and grow professionally. In this chapter, we have discussed issues pertaining to tutoring these students and offered some advice on how to lead a tutoring session to encourage development in both parties. Based on existing literature and our own experiences as L2/EFL writing teachers and tutors, we feel it is productive to help students learn to become self-editors by giving both oral and written feedback tailored to individual students' needs and proficiency levels. This process can be time consuming and painstaking at times, but as a good tutor knows, there is no shortcut to becoming a good writer. Assisting students to do so in their second or foreign language is a double challenge, yet a rewarding experience well worth the effort.

Questions to Consider

1. Various suggestions for tutoring strategies are introduced in the chapter. From your experience as a writing tutor, are there any strategies you used that did not go well or meet the student's expectations?

2. In the process of editing international students' writing and giving corrections, what kind of resistance have you experienced, and what do you think are the causes?

3. As discussed in the section about tutoring strategies, giving a negative evaluation is like delivering bitter medicine to the tutee. We suggest three strategies in points 7–9 (do not overwhelm students with negative evaluations, balance softening the criticism and being clear, and ask effective questions). Can you think of any other strategies? Also, do you think these strategies will work differently with individuals from different cultures? Based on your tutoring experience, discuss these questions with your partner or in a group.

4. Consider this scenario: an international student brings her work to the writing center and asks for help with grammar. You explain to her that instead of helping to correct all her grammatical mistakes, you will find the most common pattern of errors and work with her on that. She looks puzzled and insists that the writing center should do the editing job for her. How would you respond to her reactions?

Appendix

People who are related to education often discuss whether mixed gender school is **SG/PL** more beneficial for students that boys/girls-only school. Some students prefer mixed gender **SPL** **SG/PL** schools, but others prefer boys/girls-only schools in various reasons. There are some good **PREP** points and bad points about each sides. However, I believe that mixed gender schools are **SG/PL** more appropriate than the other one because of developing sociality and having chance to **ART** compete with various kinds of students.

I think students can understand differences between boy's and girl's characteristics in **ART** mixed gender schools. Nowadays, most students has a nucleus family so they did not have **AGR** **AGR** many chances to know other gender's behaviors or thoughts. They can observe each other's **ART** conduct and also exchange their thoughts through school life. Some people have trouble with other gender because they don't comprehend each other. After graduation, students have to **ART** work or live with people of other gender, so if they study in mixed schools they get along **ART** with others easily.

Next, there are obvious unique characteristics between men and women. They have different prepositions about the subjects, and behave differently. For example, men are more **VC** interested in the math and science, on the other hand women in the English. In this situation, **ART** **CONJ** **ART** they can compete with various kinds of people who have diverse characteristics. All of these **FRAG** things into accounts, I think mixed gender schools are needed to students than one gender only schools. As boys and girls associate with each other in the school, they can understand the stance of other gender and facing with various kinds of people. **ART** **VF, VC**

Figure 14.1. Inform the exact location and identity of the error.

When I was a student, I could see the teacher who always says something to us for whole class, and we just listen to him. That was my English class. At that time, I felt bored and my friends either. I think it is because of teacher-centered class. It is clear that discussion in class time is important to students in that they are motivated the class and give chance to think deeply to them.

Suppose that some teacher always say to students all the class time, students feel bored and some could fall a sleep. Students are intrinsically motivated when they participate in the class. If students can choose their topic or activities by themselves, they are interested in the class more. It makes them concentrate on the lesson and it is also one way of making students learning more effectively.

Next, when it comes to the students have chance to discuss in the class, they can think more deeply. Before discussion, they can summary their own opinions and exchange their background knowledge. Discussing their opinions together, students have to interact with their friends they can also expand their intelligence. All of these things account, it is important to make students participate in discussion in the class. It help students are intrinsically motivated and think deeply.

Figure 14.2. Indicate the exact location but not the identity of the error.

People often discuss whether children should begin their formal education at an early age or not. There are some good points and bad points about each side, but I believe that young children should spend most of their time playing because of creativity and social skill. ✓

I think that making children be free is needed in early age because it can be help ✓ them enhance their creativity. If young children focus too much on studying, they can't go through various useful experiences. As children undergo the various things around the world, ✓ they can extend their knowledge and get flexible thought. Being based on flexibility, they can ✓ think in different ways.

Next, Getting along with peers help children learn and enhance the social skills. ✓ Children are influenced by peers because they spend much time with their friends. In formal education situation, children should compete with one another. Unlike formal education, while children play with peers, they can learn the collaboration and partnership. As they share their opinion and mediate their ideas, they can know the way of cooperate one another. These ✓ kinds of activity make them learn not contesting with other people but partnership with peers. ✓

All of these things into account, I think it is required to have children be free in terms ✓ of creativity and sociality. They can cultivate their thought which is unlike others and ✓ characteristic which is mixed with their friends. ✓

Figure 14.3. Indicate only the approximate location or identity of the error.

People who are related to education often discuss whether mixed gender school is more beneficial for students that boys/girls-only school. Some students prefer mixed gender schools, but others prefer boys/girls-only schools in various reasons. There are some good points and bad points about each sides. However, I believe that mixed gender schools are more appropriate than the other one because of developing sociality and having chance to compete with various kinds of students.

I think students can understand differences between boy's and girl's characteristics in mixed gender schools. Nowadays, most students has a nucleus family so they did not have
                  AGR   TNS
many chances to know other gender's behaviors or thoughts. They can observe each other's
                        ART
conduct and also exchange their thoughts through school life. Some people have trouble with other gender because they don't comprehend each other. After graduation, students have to
  ART
work or live with people of other gender, so if they study in mixed schools they get along
                  ART
with others easily.

Next, there are obvious unique characteristics between men and women. They have different prepositions about the subjects, and behave differently. For example, men are more interested in the math and science, on the other hand women in the English. In this situation, they can compete with various kinds of people who have diverse characteristics. All of these things into accounts, I think mixed gender schools are needed to students than one gender only schools. As boys and girls associate with each other in the school, they can understand the stance of other gender and facing with various kinds of people.

Figure 14.4. All strategies.

For Further Reading

Bitchener, John, and Dana Ferris. 2012. *Written Corrective Feedback in Second Language Acquisition and Writing*. New York: Routledge.

    For tutors who may be interested in learning about the many ways researchers have investigated the topic of error correction in second language writing, including a history of this research, John Bitchener and Dana Ferris offer a well-organized and readable text. Reading this book is particularly useful for those who are wedded to a particular approach to correcting errors because the book explains why many different approaches are necessary. The book also contains practical applications for preparing teachers (and tutors) to provide corrective feedback.

Linville, Cynthia. 2009. "Editing Line by Line." In *ESL Writers: A Guide for Writing Center Tutors*. 2nd ed. Edited by Shanti Bruce and Ben Rafoth, 116–31. Portsmouth, NH: Heinemann.

Cynthia Linville offers many good suggestions for how to help students correct their grammar mistakes. At the end, she also includes a set of worksheets tutors can use in their sessions with second language writers. Each worksheet focuses on a specific problem (e.g., subject-verb agreement, verb tense, verb form, singular/plural forms and agreement, etc.) and provides a concise explanation of the rule, examples of incorrect and correct usages, and a short exercise to test the writer's understanding.

Sheen, Younghee. 2012. *Corrective Feedback, Individual Differences and Second Language Learning.* New York: Springer.

Younghee Sheen thoroughly reviews research on oral and written corrective feedback and how it contributes to second language acquisition. The author presents her own study in which she stresses the need to examine how individual factors such as anxiety and language aptitude affect the way learners can benefit from the oral and written feedback they receive. The book can help deepen the understanding of error correction strategies.

Self-Study Resources for L2/EFL Writers

Benson, Morton, Evelyn Benson, and Robert F. Ilson. 2010. *The BBI Combinatory Dictionary of English: Your Guide to Collocations and Grammar.* Philadelphia, PA: John Benjamins. http://dx.doi.org/10.1075/z.bbi.

Caplan, Nigel A. 2012. *Grammar Choices for Graduate and Professional Writers.* Ann Arbor: University of Michigan Press.

Fogarty, Mignon. 2011. *Grammar Girl Presents the Ultimate Writing Guide for Students.* New York: St. Martin's Griffin.

Indiana University of Pennsylvania. 2015. The Writing Center. http://www.iup.edu/writingcenter/default.aspx.

McCarthy, Michael, and Felicity O'Dell. 2008a. *Academic Vocabulary in Use: 50 Units of Academic Vocabulary Reference and Practice: Self-Study and Classroom Use.* Cambridge: Cambridge University Press.

McCarthy, Michael, and Felicity O'Dell. 2008b. *English Collocations in Use: Edition with Answers—Advanced.* Cambridge: Cambridge University Press.

Megginson, David. n.d. "*Hyper Grammar.*" The Writing Center, uOttawa. http://www.uottawa.ca/academic/arts/writcent/hypergrammar/.

Purdue University. 2015. "*ESL Students.*" Purdue University Online Writing Lab (OWL). http://owl.english.purdue.edu/owl/section/5/25/.

Swales, John, and Christine Feak. 2012. *Academic Writing for Graduate Students: Essential Tasks and Skills.* 3rd ed. Ann Arbor: University of Michigan Press.

Straus, Jane, Lester Kaufman, and Tom Stern. 2014. *The Blue Book of Grammar and Punctuation: An Easy-to-Use Guide with Clear Rules, Real-World Examples, and Reproducible Quizzes.* Hoboken, NJ: Wiley.

University of Chicago. n.d. "*Grammar Resources.*" University of Chicago Writing Program. http://writing-program.uchicago.edu/resources/grammar.htm.

University of Illinois at Urbana-Champagne. 2013. "*Writers Workshop: Writer Resources.*" Center for Writing Studies. http://www.cws.illinois.edu/workshop/writers/.

Resources for Tutors

Babcock, Rebecca, Kellye Manning, Travis Rogers, Courtney Goff, and Amanda McCain. 2012. *A Synthesis of Qualitative Studies of Writing Center Tutoring, 1983–2006.* New York: Peter Lang.

Bruce, Shanti, and Ben Rafoth. 2009. *ESL Writers: A Guide for Writing Center.* 2nd ed. Portsmouth, NH: Heinemann.

Celce-Murcia, Marianne, and Diane Larsen-Freeman. 1998. *The Grammar Book: An ESL/ EFL Teacher's Course.* 2nd ed. Stamford, CT: Heinle.

Indiana University of Pennsylvania. 2015. The Writing Center. http://www.iup.edu/writingcenter/default.aspx.

Rafoth, Ben. 2005. *A Tutor's Guide: Helping Writers One to One.* 2nd ed. Portsmouth, NH: Boynton/Cook Publishers.

Purdue University. 2015. "Tutoring Grammar." Purdue University Online Writing Lab. Last modified July 7, 2011. http://owl.english.purdue.edu/owl/resource/944/1/.

References

Bardovi-Harlig, Kathleen, and Zoltan Dornyei. 1998. "Do Language Learners Recognize Pragmatic Violations? Pragmatic vs. Grammatical Awareness in Instructed L2 Learning." *TESOL Quarterly* 32 (2): 233–95. http://dx.doi.org/10.2307/3587583.

Bitchener, John. 2008. "Evidence in Support of Written Corrective Feedback." *Journal of Second Language Writing* 17 (2): 102–18. http://dx.doi.org/10.1016/j.jslw.2007 .11.004.

Bitchener, John, and Ute Knoch. 2009. "The Relative Effectiveness of Different Types of Direct Written Corrective Feedback." *System* 37 (2): 322–29. http://dx.doi.org/10 .1016/j.system.2008.12.006.

Bitchener, John, Stuart Young, and Denise Cameron. 2005. "The Effect of Different Types of Corrective Feedback on ESL Student Writing." *Journal of Second Language Writing* 14 (3): 191–205. http://dx.doi.org/10.1016/j.jslw.2005.08.001.

Connor, Ulla, and Diane Belcher. 2001. *Reflections on Multiliterate Lives.* Buffalo, NY: Multilingual Matters.

Ferris, Dana. 1999. "The Case for Grammar Correction in L2 Writing Classes: A Response to Truscott (1996)." *Journal of Second Language Writing* 8 (1): 1–11. http:// dx.doi.org/10.1016/S1060-3743(99)80110-6.

Ferris, Dana. 2002. *Treatment of Error in Second Language Student Writing.* Ann Arbor: University of Michigan Press.

Ferris, Dana, and Barrie Roberts. 2001. "Error Feedback in L2 Writing Classes: How Explicit Does It Need to Be?" *Journal of Second Language Writing* 10 (3): 161–84. http://dx.doi.org/10.1016/S1060-3743(01)00039-X.

Hedgcock, John S. 2005. "Taking Stock of Research and Pedagogy in L2 Writing." In *Handbook of Research in Second Language Teaching and Learning*, edited by Eli Hinkel, 597–613. Mahwah, NJ: Lawrence Erlbaum.

Hendrickson, James. 1980. "Error Correction in Foreign Language Teaching: Recent Theory, Research, and Practice." In *Readings on English as a Second Language*, 2nd ed. Edited by Kenneth Croft, 153–73. Cambridge, MA: Winthrop.

Hofstede, Geert. 1986. "Cultural Differences in Teaching and Learning." *International Journal of Intercultural Relations* 10 (3): 301–20. http://dx.doi.org/10.1016/0147 -1767(86)90015-5.

Linville, Cynthia. 2009. "Editing Line by Line." In *ESL Writers: A Guide for Writing Center Tutors*, edited by Shanti Bruce and Ben Rafoth, 116–31. Portsmouth, NH: Boynton/ Cook.

Matsuda, Paul Kei, and Michelle Cox. 2009. "Reading an ESL Writer's Text." In *ESL Writers: A Guide for Writing Center Tutors*, edited by Shanti Bruce and Ben Rafoth, 42–50. Portsmouth, NH: Boynton/Cook.

Reigstad, Thomas J., and Donald A. MacAndrew. 1984. *Training Tutors for Writing Conferences.* Urbana, IL: National Council of Teachers of English.

Selinker, Larry. 1972. "Interlanguage." *International Review of Applied Linguistics* 10 (1–4): 209–41. http://dx.doi.org/10.1515/iral.1972.10.1-4.209.

Sheen, Younghee. 2007. "The Effect of Focused Written Corrective Feedback and Language Aptitude on ESL Learners' Acquisition of Articles." *TESOL Quarterly* 41 (2): 255–83.

Silva, Tony. 1997. "Differences in ESL and Native-English-Speaker Writing: The Research and Its Implications." In *Writing in Multicultural Settings*, edited by Carol Severino, Juan C. Guerra, and Johnnella E. Butler, 209–19. New York: Modern Language Association.

Sommers, Nany. 1982. "Responding to Student Writing." *College Composition and Communication* 33 (2): 148–56.

Thomas, Jenny. 1983. "Cross-Cultural Pragmatic Failure." *Applied Linguistics* 4 (2): 91–112. http://dx.doi.org/10.1093/applin/4.2.91.

Truscott, John. 1996. "The Case against Grammar Correction in L2 Writing Classes." *Language Learning* 46 (2): 327–69. http://dx.doi.org/10.1111/j.1467-1770.1996.tb01238.x.

Truscott, John. 1999. "'The Case for 'The Case against Grammar Correction in L2 Writing Classes': A Response to Ferris." *Journal of Second Language Writing* 8 (2): 111–22. http://dx.doi.org/10.1016/S1060-3743(99)80124-6.

Truscott, John. 2004. "Evidence and Conjecture on the Effects of Correction: A Response to Chandler." *Journal of Second Language Writing* 13 (4): 337–43. http://dx.doi.org/10.1016/j.jslw.2004.05.002.

Truscott, John. 2007. "The Effect of Error Correction on Learners' Ability to Write Accurately." *Journal of Second Language Writing* 16 (4): 255–72. http://dx.doi.org/10.1016/j.jslw.2007.06.003.

Vann, Roberta J., Daisy E. Meyer, and Frederick O. Lorenz. 1984. "Error Gravity: A Study of Faculty Opinion of ESL Errors." *TESOL Quarterly* 18 (3): 427–40. http://dx.doi.org/10.2307/3586713.

Vann, Roberta J., Frederick O. Lorenz, and Daisy E. Meyer. 1991. "Error Gravity: Faculty Response to Errors in the Written Discourse of Nonnative Speakers of English." In *Assessing Second Language Writing in Academic Contexts*, edited by Liz Hamp-Lyons, 181–95. Norwood, NJ: Ablex.

Zamel, Vivian. 1985. "Responding to Student Writing." *TESOL Quarterly* 19 (1): 79–101. http://dx.doi.org/10.2307/3586773.

ABOUT THE AUTHORS

SHANTI BRUCE is professor and chair of the Department of Writing and Communication at Nova Southeastern University in Fort Lauderdale, Florida, where she earned the Faculty Excellence in Teaching Award. She coedited *ESL Writers: A Guide for Writing Center Tutors* (Heinemann) with Ben Rafoth and *Creative Approaches to Writing Center Work* (Hampton) with Kevin Dvorak. Both books were honored by the IWCA with its Book of the Year Award. She coauthored *What Every Multilingual Student Should Know about Writing for College* (Pearson) and has been a keynote and invited speaker at conferences, leader of IWCA Summer Institutes, and co-chair of SWCA and NCPTW conferences.

BEN RAFOTH is Distinguished University Professor at Indiana University of Pennsylvania, where he directs the Jones White Writing Center. He teaches undergraduate courses in writing and graduate courses in IUP's composition and TESOL program. He served on the IWCA executive board and chaired the first joint conference of IWCA and NCPTW in 2003. He has been a Summer Institute co-chair and leader. Ben received NCPTW's Ron Maxwell Award, and he and Shanti Bruce received IWCA's Book of the Year Award for *ESL Writers*. He edited *A Tutor's Guide*. Ben's most recent book is *Multilingual Writers and Writing Centers* (Utah State University Press).

JOCELYN AMEVUVOR earned her master's degree in TESOL and applied linguistics at the Indiana University of Pennsylvania. She is also a graduate of the bachelor's degree program in Spanish at IUP. She has worked as a tutor in both the university writing center and the American Language Institute. Currently, she supervises the IUP international student tutoring program, SkillZone. She also teaches English-language classes at the American Language Institute.

REBECCA DAY BABCOCK is associate professor of English at the University of Texas of the Permian Basin, where she serves as literature and languages department chair, freshman English coordinator, and director of the university's undergraduate research program. Her research interests include writing centers, disability, folk linguistics, and meta-research. Her latest book is *Tell Me How It Reads: Tutoring Writing with Deaf and Hearing Students in the Writing Center* (Gallaudet University Press). She is also the coauthor of *Researching the Writing Center: Towards an Evidence-Based Practice* and *A Synthesis of Qualitative Studies of Writing Center Tutoring, 1983–2006* (both published by Peter Lang).

VALERIE M. BALESTER, professor of English, directs the writing center and writing-in-the-disciplines program at Texas A&M University. She authored *Cultural Divide* (Boynton/Cook); coedited, with Michelle Hall Kells, *Attending to the Margins: Writing, Researching, and Teaching on the Front Lines* (Boynton/Cook); coedited, with Hall Kells and Victor Villanueva, *Latino/a Discourses: Teaching Composition as a Social Action* (Boynton/Cook); and coauthored, with James MacDonald, "A View of Status and Working Conditions: Relations between Writing Program and Writing Center Directors" (in *WPA*). She recently contributed "How Writing Rubrics Fail: Toward a Multicultural Model" to *Race and Writing Assessment* (Peter Lang).

FRANKIE CONDON is associate professor in the Department of English Language and Literature at the University of Waterloo in Ontario, Canada. Her books include *I Hope I*

Join the Band: Narrative, Affiliation, and Antiracist Rhetoric, and she coauthored *The Everyday Writing Center: A Community of Practice* (both published by Utah State University Press). She is currently completing research for her third book, *Absolute Equality: The Radical Precedents of Post-Racial Rhetorics in the Twenty-First Century*. This work is funded by a grant from the Social Sciences and Humanities Research Council of Canada. She lives in Waterloo with her partner, children, two dogs, a cat, and a chinchilla named Sid.

MICHELLE COX, inaugural director of the English Language Support Office (ELSO) at Cornell University, is indebted to the University of New Hampshire writing center, where, as a graduate writing center tutor, she first became interested in learning more about second language writers and invested in creating more equitable and inclusive writing pedagogy and programs. Her publications on second language writing include articles, chapters, and collections on identity, graduate-student writing, writing pedagogy, and WAC program administration. Her most recent collection, edited with Terry Myers Zawacki, is *WAC and Second Language Writers: Research toward Developing Linguistically and Culturally Inclusive Programs and Practices* (WAC Clearinghouse and Parlor Press, 2014).

JENNIFER CRAIG teaches writing and oral communication at the Massachusetts Institute of Technology in the Department of Comparative Media Studies/Writing and in the Department of Aeronautics and Astronautics. She is the author of *Integrating Writing Strategies in EFL/ESL Contexts: A Writing-Across-the-Curriculum Approach* and coauthor of *Learning to Communicate in Science and Engineering: Case Studies from MIT*. Interested in the ways in which English-language learners master disciplinary communication in another language, she has taught and consulted at universities in Russia, Chile, Brazil, Mexico, Costa Rica, and Singapore.

KEVIN DVORAK is associate professor and writing center director at Nova Southeastern University. He is president of the International Writing Centers Association and a past president of the Southeastern Writing Center Association. His book *Creative Approaches to Writing Center Work* (Hampton), coedited with Shanti Bruce, won the 2009 IWCA Outstanding Scholarship Award for Best Book/Major Work. He has also published chapters in *ESL Writers: A Guide for Writing Center Tutors* (2004 and 2009), *The Writing Center Director's Resource Manual* (2005), and *The Successful High School Writing Center* (2011), as well as articles in *Praxis, Academic Exchange Quarterly*, and the *Writing Center Journal*. He chaired the 2013 and 2014 IWCA Summer Institutes and was the recipient of the 2014 SWCA Achievement Award.

PAULA GILLESPIE is associate professor of English and the director for the Center for Excellence at Florida International University in Miami. She has served as the secretary and president of the International Writing Centers Association and has served on the executive committee of the Conference on College Composition and Communication. With Neal Lerner, she coauthored *The Longman Guide to Peer Tutoring*, now in its second edition. She is coeditor of *Writing Center Research: Extending the Conversation*, which won the IWCA prize for outstanding scholarship. Her article with Brad Hughes and Harvey Kail, "What They Take with Them: Findings from the Peer Writing Tutor Alumni Research Project," winner of the IWCA Outstanding Scholarship Award for 2010, looks at the long- and short-term skills, values, and abilities tutors retain years after they graduate. She and her FIU colleagues are working to bring peer writing tutoring to some Miami-Dade public high schools.

GLENN HUTCHINSON is assistant director of the Center for Excellence in Writing at Florida International University. He has a PhD in rhetoric and composition from the University of North Carolina–Greensboro. He writes about service learning, community writing centers, and immigration. His articles have been published in *Reflections on Community-Based Writing Instruction, Names*, and *Hispanic Outlook in Higher Education*. He writes op-eds for *The*

Progressive Media Project, which have been syndicated in newspapers throughout the world. In addition, he writes poetry and plays. His poetry has been published in several journals and his own chapbook. Glenn's plays include *Limbo*, *The Pot*, and *Salsa*.

PEI-HSUN EMMA LIU is assistant professor of applied English at Kainan University, where she teaches EFL literacy and graduate courses. She received her PhD from Indiana University of Pennsylvania. She was awarded Innovative Researcher in TESOL in the Department of English Composition and TESOL. She has extensive teaching and research background working with ESL/EFL students from all over the world in the areas of world Englishes, intercultural rhetoric, and critical pedagogy. Her research interests center on second language writing and language in social contexts. Her recent publications appear in the *TESOL Journal*, the *British Journal of Educational Technology*, and the *Journal of Second Language Writing*.

BOBBI OLSON is assistant professor of English at Grand View University in Des Moines, Iowa, where she is director of the writing center. She also teaches composition and courses specifically for multilingual students. Her research considers the politics of language teaching in both writing center and classroom contexts, and her work has appeared in *Praxis: A Writing Center Journal* and *Across the Disciplines*. She has served on both the MWCA and IWCA executive boards and has presented and facilitated sessions at several regional and national writing center and composition conferences.

PIMYUPA W. PRAPHAN has been teaching English for ten years in the Department of Western Languages and Linguistics of Mahasarakham University in northeastern Thailand since finishing her doctoral study at University of Illinois at Urbana-Champaign. During her one-year sabbatical leave, she volunteered as a tutor in the writing center at Indiana University of Pennsylvania. Her research interests include ESL/EFL writing, writing centers, and the field of world Englishes. Her article titled "Think in Thai, Write in English: Thainess in Thai English Literature" was published in the *World Englishes* journal in 2005.

JOSE L. REYES MEDINA came to New York from the Dominican Republic in 2004 and started attending Bronx Community College (BCC) in 2005. He graduated from BCC in 2007 with an associate's degree in liberal arts and transferred to New York University (NYU) on a scholarship in 2008. In 2010, he graduated from NYU with a bachelor of science in applied psychology and is currently applying to graduate school to obtain a PhD in social sciences. He is an ESL instructor in the CUNY Language Immersion Program (CLIP) at BCC.

GUIBOKE SEONG is associate professor of English education at Inha University in Korea. She received her doctoral degree from University of Illinois at Urbana-Champaign. At UIUC she taught ESL at the Intensive English Institute and in the ESL service program for graduate students. She has served as director of the TESOL program at Inha University and is now directing the College English Program. Her research interests include EFL writing instruction, pedagogic discourse analysis, and "teaching English in English" in EFL contexts.

CAROL SEVERINO is professor of rhetoric at the University of Iowa. She directs the Writing Center and the Writing Fellows Program and teaches courses that explore the relationships between writing, language background, culture, and pedagogy, also the focus of her research. She teaches the two tutor preparation seminars as well as the second language writing research and theory course for the Second Language Acquisition PhD program. She also teaches travel writing every fall in the First Year Seminar Program, tutors in the Writing Center every semester, and reviews for many writing-related publications, including *The Journal of Second Language Writing*. Carol was a Collegiate Teaching Award winner in 2003 and a Fulbright Scholar in Ecuador in 2008. She has published some of her recent work on language learning and language teaching in *Writing on the Edge*. Her travel essay "Engagement Ceremony" appeared in *The Best Travel Writing 2012*. With Shih-Ni Prim, she published in the fall 2015 *Writing Center Journal* a study of Chinese students' word-choice errors based on a sample of drafts sent to online tutoring.

ELIZABETH (ADELAY) WITHERITE is an English teacher at Gyedong Elementary in Gimhae, South Korea. She earned her MA in English-TESOL in 2014 from Indiana University of Pennsylvania. Her thesis, for which she received the IUP Innovative Thesis Award, examined writing center tutors' experiences with matters of social justice in their sessions. Her research interests include international educational practices, ethics, New Literacy Studies, and critical pedagogy.

SUBJECT INDEX

AUTHOR INDEX